Graphic News

How Sensational Images Transformed
Nineteenth-Century Journalism

AMANDA FRISKEN

UNIVERSITY OF ILLINOIS PRESS
Urbana, Chicago, and Springfield

Publication of this book was supported in part
by a grant from Furthermore: a program of the
J. M. Kaplan Fund.

Furthermore:
a program of the J. M. Kaplan Fund

®

Library of Congress Cataloging-in-Publication Data
Names: Frisken, Amanda, author.
Title: Graphic news : how sensational images transformed
    nineteenth-century journalism / Amanda Frisken.
Description: Urbana : University of Illinois Press, 2020.
    | Series: The history of communication | Includes
    bibliographical references and index.
Identifiers: LCCN 2019032053 | ISBN 9780252042980 (cloth)
    | ISBN 9780252084836 (paperback) | ISBN 9780252051838
    (ebook)
Subjects: LCSH: Journalism, Pictorial—United
    States—History—19th century. | Sensationalism in
    journalism—United States—History—19th century.
Classification: LCC PN4784.P5 .F75 2020 | DDC 070.4
    /909034—dc23
LC record available at https://lccn.loc.gov/2019032053

Contents

Acknowledgments

Research is a collaborative effort, and this book would not have been possible without the many people who have supported it in ways large and small. I honor the professionalism and kind assistance of dozens of librarians and archivists who helped me along the way. Heidi Donofrio and Christa DeVirgilio in SUNY College at Old Westbury's Interlibrary Loan Department, as well as library directors Antonia Digregorio and Stephen Kirkpatrick, helped me track down countless newspapers over many years. Dr. Heather McNabb at the McCord Museum in Montreal generously shared her knowledge about glass negatives from the *Wild West* photo shoot. I appreciate the conscientious assistance of Chamisa Redmond at the Library of Congress and Shawn Purcell at the New York State Library—and many others—for their help in gathering images for publication. I thank Eli Paul, formerly of the State Historical Society of South Dakota, for his helpful advice in tracking down an elusive photograph of the Ghost Dance.

I am fortunate to belong to a department, American Studies and Media and Communications, at SUNY College at Old Westbury that is at once supportive, challenging, and productive. Over many years I have benefited from discussions with Özgür Akgün, Laura Anker, Jermaine Archer, Llana Barber, the late Ros Baxandall, Aubrey Bonnett, Laura Chipley, the late Liz Ewen, John Friedman, Karl Grossman, the late Barbara Joseph, Joe Manfredi, Andy Mattson, Jasmine Mitchell, Orquidea Morales, Lisa Payton, Carol Quirke, Naomi Rosenthal, Elaine Scott, Samara Smith, and Denton Watson. I am deeply grateful to Lois Stergiopoulos and Anna Brewer for their invaluable support. Our departmental philosophy, embracing the intersections among media, history, and social justice, and our many conversations about how that manifests itself in the curriculum and in the larger world, have indelibly shaped this project.

Financial support from our faculty union, United University Professions, in the form of Individual Development Awards, contributed to the research at several points. Old Westbury's Academic Affairs division has also supported both research and production through a series of Faculty Development Grants. The Dean of Arts and Sciences, Dr. Barbara Hillery, provided supplemental funding to obtain publication-quality images. Crucial support from Provost and Senior Vice President for Academic Affairs Patrick O'Sullivan helped defray production expenses for the design of this image-heavy work. I am grateful to the J. M. Kaplan fund for awarding the book a Furthermore grant to support University of Illinois Press's production process.

Without the encouragement and fine example of my mentor and friend Nancy Tomes—her generosity of spirit, and her creative, cross-disciplinary methodology—I would never have written this book. For lessons learned years ago at SUNY Stony Brook I remain grateful to Karl Bottigheimer, Iona Man Cheong, Gary Marker, Bill Miller, Adrienne Munich, Sally Sternglanz, and the late Bill Taylor. I am particularly thankful to Matt Jacobson, Temma Kaplan, and Barbara Weinstein for their ongoing support and inspiration. Professional colleagues who study the nexus of media and culture have deeply influenced this work. I thank Lisa Arellano and Erica Ball for many inspiring conversations. Josh Brown generously shared his wisdom and expertise at key points in this research. From Barbara Balliet, Mia Bay, Frank Couvares, Leslie Dunlap, Matthew Guterl, Helen Lefkovitz Horowitz, and Shirley Jennifer Lim, I gained insights and invaluable suggestions in and around professional meetings, which have deepened my understanding of this period and project immeasurably.

Working with the University of Illinois Press has been a delight. I am grateful to the editors of the History of Communication series, Robert W. McChesney and John C. Nerone, for taking on this project. Senior Acquisitions Editor Daniel Nasset and Associate Acquisitions Editor Marika Christofides steered the early stages of preparation of the manuscript with great tact, enthusiasm, and expedition; Outreach and Development Assistant Julie Laut was also extremely helpful. Senior Editor Tad Ringo's guidance as project manager and Julie Gay's careful copyediting have made the book stronger. The art and design departments at UIP, and especially Jim Proefrock and Jennifer Fisher, have gone out of their way to reproduce challenging and often poorly preserved images in a positive way, making it possible for readers today to see the images nearly as contemporaries did in the nineteenth century. Anonymous reviewers provided detailed and meaningful suggestions for improvement. Any flaws that remain are, of course, my own responsibility.

Over nearly two decades, this project has interwoven itself into everyday life. Good friends have inspired and sustained me over many years, and I am particularly grateful to Lisa Handler, Annulla Linders, Susanna Taipale, and

Alejandra Vassallo for their camaraderie, insights, and suggestions. I thank my parents, Frances and Bill Frisken, and my sisters, Sarah and Barb Frisken, for their confidence and encouragement. Benny, Dusa, and Oscar Heller have influenced this work as sounding boards, skeptics, and supporters: their unconventional approaches to knowledge and their irreverent humor influence everything I write. I am profoundly indebted to Jacob Heller, my favorite contrarian; apart from everything else, including extraordinary patience, his faith and interest in this book have sustained my own.

Graphic News

Introduction

Sensationalism and the Rise of Visual Journalism

SENSATIONALISM TOOK HOLD of U.S. media on the cusp of the modern period, and images became the form's defining characteristic. Between 1870 and 1900, print news publishers became adept at translating news stories about sex, crime, and violence into emotion-based pictures. Sensational images helped publishers and editors increase circulation, expand revenues, attract constituencies, and influence political culture. This study explores how a range of news producers engaged with sensational practices. While many histories of sensational news production acknowledge the presence of illustrations, few have considered their impact. As weekly and then daily editors pursued sensational themes, they used pre-photographic techniques of illustration to shape how readers saw the news—and how they felt about it. News images conveyed racial, class, and gender anxieties in dialogue with audiences and established precedents for modern media.

The prevailing origin story for sensational journalism—when "the new journalism" became "yellow journalism"—begins in early 1897. Competition for circulation between William Randolph Hearst and Joseph Pulitzer is sometimes blamed for generating war fever, leading up to the outbreak of the Spanish-American War, and for the birth of "tabloid news," generally. As the story goes, Frederic Remington, the American artist and illustrator, was covering the Cuban rebellion for Hearst's *New York Journal* when he telegraphed in early 1897 that "everything is quiet" and requested permission to return home. According to legend, Hearst replied: "Please remain. You furnish the pictures and I'll furnish the war." Despite the dubious provenance of this account and the reality that the war's origins were far more complex,[1] the story persists, perhaps because it seems to capture sensationalism's essence: the dissemination of false news to increase sales and further an agenda—in this case, war with Spain. Strident headlines, "inventive" reporting, and—most important, I argue—eye-catching illustrations embodied the most recognizable features of the sensational style.

The Remington drawing most closely tied to this legend depicted a naked Cuban woman undergoing a strip search by Spanish soldiers (fig. I.1). Captioned "Spaniards Search Women on American Steamers," the illustration conveyed one of sensationalism's most pervasive visual codes: the narrative of sexual danger for a white woman at the hands of "dishonorable" men. The drawing conformed not to the emerging standard of visual realism but to an older tradition of "interpretive illustration" of news; it was a narrative reconstruction, rather than an observed record, of the alleged event.[2] Remington actually produced the drawing *after* he had returned home, embellishing on details of an incident reported by a journalist who heard the story from women aboard ship. The *Journal's* rival, Pulitzer's *New York World*, exposed the episode as false, publishing an interview with one of the women involved, who explained that they had been searched but not stripped—and that their searchers had been women. Regardless, Hearst continued to flog the story for several days before moving on to the next sensation.[3]

Remington's strip-search illustration lays bare the intersection of sensationalism with the period's visual culture—loosely defined as the conventions, context, and metaphorical language that define a period's imagery. His drawing resembled not his famous western scenes but rather earlier sensational images—specifically, those found in crime and sporting weeklies like the *National Police Gazette*—that had made a specialty of representing pale women under sexual threat from dark men. The strip-search illustration gave ammunition to critics of "yellow journalism" who deplored such misrepresentation and found its elements of implied sexual threat and nudity particularly objectionable. The *New York Times* viewed the drawing as a "greater horror and indignity" to the young victim than the alleged strip-search itself. Anti-vice activist Anthony Comstock and other critics who had long worked to suppress imagery in the *Police Gazette* now saw sensationalism's evils infiltrating the daily news. Amid the outcry, the Young Men's Christian Association library in Brooklyn explained its decision to ban sensational dailies on the grounds that their salacious content attracted undesirable readers: "We might as well have The Police Gazette." A campaign against "yellow journalism" resulted in dozens of libraries and social organizations banning the *Journal* and the *World*, and more than eighty clerics denouncing them publicly. The campaign did not inhibit sales, however, and did little to check the most sensational newspaper publishers.[4]

Remington's illustration also demonstrates the power of visual sensationalism to communicate complex meaning in capsule form. Along with the article's headline, "Does Our Flag Protect Women?" the image blended support for Cuban independence with fears about the sullied honor of the American flag—all

FIGURE I.I: "Spaniards Search Women on American Steamers,"
New York Journal, February 12, 1897, 2. New York Public Library.

in a single visual plea for chivalric protection of white womanhood. Decades of
illustration in a range of weekly and daily newspapers had created a set of tools
and a demand for the powerful, nonverbal messaging of the strip-search illustration. By the 1890s, reinforced by pithy headlines and captions, such images
were pervasive in sensational dailies. Provocative words and images set a tone,
and steady repetition established narratives that were compelling, popular—and
lucrative. Long before the Cuban crisis, sensational narratives had attracted a
growing readership and built a new national market for graphic news.

Between 1870 and 1900 provocative line illustrations of the news gave commercial publications across the political spectrum a way to attract readers or,
perhaps more accurately, news consumers. Publishers changed the very presentation of their newspapers to make them more appealing and accessible. They
reduced the number of columns (from nine, typically, to six or seven), increased
font sizes, and expanded headline height and breadth (eventually to span more

than one column and, for major scoops, the full page, with "decked" or stacked sub-headlines below). They moved advertisements from the front page to make eye-catching headlines and "human interest" stories—particularly anything that suggested sex, crime, and violence—more visible on the newsstands.[5] By the late 1880s a proliferation of images that filled newspaper pages, in the Sunday supplements and (soon) the daily editions, eclipsed all of these changes.

Sensationalism and the Image

News images allowed publishers to convey ideological content with what Walter Lippmann calls great "economy of effort," and editors and artists became adept at reducing complex political and social events into stark visual shorthand. Visual tactics of allusion and metaphor accessed powerful emotions, which sold papers and, in turn, unlocked the advertising revenue that fueled the rapid expansion of print media.[6] Shifts in form, along with the use of anonymous sources and a tendency toward self-promotion (of the newspaper as an agent of change and the journalist as a new kind of swashbuckling hero) became intrinsic to the sensational style. But more than anything else, news *images* lay at the heart of these changes; they transcended the reorganization of text and content. Between 1870 and 1900, the formative years of commercial graphic news production, images became the central site of struggle between truth and sensation, information and entertainment, "decency" and an uncensored press. The ability to communicate emotion swiftly (and subtly, often with deniability) constituted the new genre's most compelling feature. Sensationalism and visual journalism raised questions about the media's responsibilities to the public that resonate to this day.[7]

Nineteenth-century critics anticipated current fears that sensationalism's "trivial stories and fancy pictures" tend to dumb down the news and degrade civil society. Today, critics deplore the "tabloidization" of news, a reference not to supermarket tabloids but rather the displacement of principled reporting standards by emotion-driven content. The search for profit, they suggest, encourages publishers to cut corners, build stories on questionable sourcing, and downplay hard news. In this view, image-centered "soft" news (such as dramatic events, tragedies, crime, disasters, entertainment, and celebrity) increases consumer appeal but crowds out serious, "fact-based" news. Visual reporting and "regressive" content are not neutral, some warn; instead, they foster a reactionary ethos, one that celebrates surface values, conformity, and simplistic analyses. Fewer voices in the public square, combined with declining standards of evidence, diminished complexity in reporting, a passive readership, and, above all, a surfeit of (unexamined) visual stimuli threaten democratic values and substantial political discourse.[8]

Other critics, however, find value in the sensational style. By highlighting so-called "vulgar" over "tasteful" news stories, sensational reporting loosens elite domination of political discourse and provides a voice for the less powerful. From this perspective, sensationalism makes space for alternatives to expert sources and top-down news gathering, delivery, and production. "Soft" human interest stories may in fact widen access to the public square and give voice to marginalized groups, including women, racial others, and the poor. The form's inherent disrespect for convention and authority allows popular audiences to challenge hegemonic assumptions underlying the production of what might otherwise be called "serious news." Such media analysts uphold elements of the sensational style—particularly its emphasis on storytelling, vibrant language, and appeals to readers' senses and emotions—as compatible with the scrupulous use of evidence. Sensational elements of this kind may foster social cohesion and produce valuable debate, they suggest. Missing, however, from this school of thought is the crucial role *images* play in shaping public opinion by visually framing the news.[9]

Too little attention has been paid to the power of illustrations in the formative—pre-photographic—years of visual journalism, as daily newspapers began to experiment with news images.[10] An unfortunate side effect is the relegation of early efforts at visualization and their significance in social and political discourse to the sidelines of media history. In today's image-saturated media environment it can be hard to recognize late-nineteenth-century line illustrations as sensational—let alone striking, innovative, or shocking. To be understood, however, they must be viewed "through nineteenth-century eyes."[11] This study bridges the divide between journalism history and cultural history of the pictorial press to analyze the images that fueled the rise of visual journalism in daily newspapers and established standards, practices, and expectations that photojournalism would have to meet. The migration of sensational strategies from the sporting and crime weeklies to the cheap daily newspapers was both a byproduct of Gilded Age political culture and a driver of the period's social inequalities. In their hackneyed tableaux, news illustrations gave even publishers who disclaimed an agenda a creative means to influence political, economic, and social debate. Nineteenth-century sensational news stories and illustrations, whether in crime weeklies or inexpensive daily newspapers, commercial or nonprofit publications, both influenced and reflected U.S. society and culture. This study develops our understanding of *how*.

News illustrations in this period became far more than mere adjuncts to the text; they delivered (sometimes contradictory) meanings in their own right. Crude, small, blurry, and botched as they were, the news images of the late nineteenth century seem barely capable of influencing today's practices and standards. We may be inclined to dismiss them as lacking impact—as insignificant or indecipherable. That would be a mistake. Images constitute the most condensed packaging available for the transmission of meaning.[12] News illustrations were novel media tools for their time and revealed themselves to be powerful communicators. Commercial publishers liked illustrations because they attracted consumers, but even noncommercial editors and social activists used them in their struggles for truth and justice. News images established conventions for visual journalism that persisted through the twentieth century—and beyond.

The Origins of U.S. Sensational Media

Sensational media strategies date back to the origins of print media itself. Elements can be found in sixteenth-century Europe, in gothic melodrama, and in crime tracts (some possessing illustrations): in England, where newsbooks and ballads conveyed emotionally charged content pitched toward the lower classes; and in the American colonies, where similar stories appeared in the early broadsheets and news pamphlets that preceded newspapers. By the early nineteenth century, as wood-block and lithographic technology improved to make the mass production of images possible in the United States, firms such as New York's Currier and Ives sold illustrated commercial prints depicting a range of vignettes, including crime and other kinds of "news." Political sheets, crime novels, and morality tales, made possible by technological innovation in the steam printing press, fed a growing demand among a newly literate popular readership and fueled the rapidly expanding market for accessible and exciting print material.[13]

In the 1830s, a few enterprising newspaper publishers created a new form, now known as the "penny press." They turned sensational content (primarily in text form) into a staple of urban news production in the United States. Penny newspapers succeeded by undercutting existing daily papers, compensating in volume for the loss in price per issue. To attract readers, new penny newspapers such as the *New York Sun* (founded in 1833) and the *New York Herald* (founded in 1835) pitched their content to the broad, emerging lower and middle classes of workers, artisans, and entrepreneurs. Their pages combined lurid content, hoaxes, and scandals with lively, detailed reporting of everyday news. News in the penny press became a product in itself, sometimes indistinguishable from gothic literature in its focus on crime and mayhem. Editors deflected critics by framing their stories as morality plays and cautionary tales. While nominally independent of political-party funding, the early penny dailies had Jacksonian (Democratic) political leanings. Instead of relying on subscriptions, as traditional newspapers had done, to disseminate their papers both the *Sun* and the *Herald* employed newsboys, who hawked news about crime, suicides, gossip, and entertainment to a wide (if primarily white, and male) readership.[14]

Crime news became central to the penny press's new business model. The first major crime story published in the penny press, the Robinson-Jewett murder case of 1836, introduced such novel features as the newspaper interview and extensive trial coverage (including testimony) and set a precedent of social commentary through text-based newspaper sensation. Such content proved popular; by 1840 New York's *Sun* and the *Herald* sold more copies than did the city's other nine papers combined. Illustrations proved technically more difficult, however; the *Herald* published a modest number of illustrations, rising to about forty images *per year* in the 1840s, but technical challenges of the slow flat-bed press, poor quality of paper, and the infusion of ink slowed down the printing, which made daily image publication difficult. By 1850, even the *Herald* had largely abandoned daily news images.[15]

Unlike the penny dailies, weekly illustrated sporting publications found more success with visual coverage of crime stories in the 1840s and 1850s. With a longer production schedule, slow printing methods that made illustrations prohibitive for daily papers became feasible for weeklies. Weeklies produced images on select pages within their publications, typically grisly crime scenes and sexual scandals, which (like the dailies) promoted an "anti-authoritarian" ethos pitched at the Jacksonian (white, male, working-class, and artisanal) readers. Images in the illustrated crime and sporting weeklies had a free-wheeling, carnivalesque quality that brought publishers into conflict with authorities over standards in print, particularly over what the public should *see*. As pre–Civil War sporting papers pushed the boundaries of decency and the limits of slander laws, victims of their ribald humor attempted on more than one occasion to shut down publication, anticipating later battles over free speech in the post–Civil War period. In both periods, however, sensational publishers insisted that their revelations served the public good.[16]

Other popular literary forms in the antebellum period, such as cheap fiction ("story papers" and later dime novels) and reform tracts, provided additional sources of "sensation" for a wide readership. Many of these included illustrations, though not particularly controversial in nature: typically iconic scenes and portraits. Dime novels attempted to cater to working-class readers, who drove sales and subject matter in particular directions—notably, urban crime, captivity narratives, and frontier stories. These promoted a heroic masculinity that fused melodrama, nativism, and empire in expansive nation-building—in Mexico in 1846, in the American West, and throughout the Americas more broadly. Reformers produced so-called "sentimental" tracts to humanize marginalized groups or inspire protest. Abolitionists promoted slave narratives and published revelations about the institution to raise readers' consciousness, shame slaveholders, and galvanize opposition to slavery. Moral reformers cited sensational accounts of urban "vices" to justify policing and other interventions.[17] In these various—largely text-based—forms, sensational (that is, emotion-based) literature came to dominate the antebellum print-news marketplace.

The visualization of everyday news lagged behind sensational content and headlines before the Civil War, however. The first publication to attempt regular news illustration was *Frank Leslie's Illustrated Newspaper*, a New York weekly launched in 1855 by English engraver and illustrator Henry Carter (calling himself Frank Leslie). Leslie had worked for the *Illustrated London News* but sought to distinguish his new publication by representing the news on a weekly basis, as a supplement—rather than a substitute—for the text-based dailies. In contrast to its London counterpart (which produced uncontroversial imagery of landscapes, buildings, and portraits of famous or prestigious men), *Leslie's* included images of current events, entertainment, politics, and crime; it was sometimes sensational in tone and often exhibited a strong reform agenda. In early 1857 *Leslie's* published vivid, visual coverage of the murder of a dentist named Dr. Burdell that featured images of the crime scene, portraits of the major players, and a reenactment of the murder. Purporting to be "'eye-witness' recordings" but typically based on verbal and visual "transcription" by an illustrator or engraver (or more likely a team of both) far from the scene, such composite "storytelling" images constituted a first attempt to make news *visible* to a wide public readership.[18] *Leslie's* also pioneered advocacy journalism, as in the swill milk scandal in 1858–59, using interpretive illustrations of filthy conditions in dairies to influence municipal politics and improve the quality of milk available to poor children.[19] By 1860 *Leslie's* had mastered a sophisticated "toolkit" of sensational strategies well designed to attract readers and demonstrated that they could be used to advocate for change.

With the outbreak of the Civil War, demand for illustrated publications rose dramatically, responding to hunger among civilians and soldiers for war news—and imagery. *Harper's Weekly*, founded in 1857, though less sensational, joined *Leslie's* in providing a wealth of wartime illustrations, based on photographs and sketches of battlefields, military luminaries, camp life, and the home front. Illustrators for both *Harper's* and *Leslie's* created rough sketches from near the scene, but the chaos of the battlefield meant that most of their images of the front had to be extrapolated from details found in (text) news reports and interviews—and sometimes from the artist's imagination. As illustrated weeklies fed demand for visual news, they faced new scrutiny from cultural critics who, alarmed on behalf of young men away from home and family, feared the impact of some images on morality.[20]

After the Civil War, daily newspapers began to challenge the pictorial weeklies' monopoly on visual news. As dailies capitalized on the rise in wartime readership, they furthered the commercial newspaper revolution, relying more heavily than ever on advertising for economic success, as their geographic reach expanded with the growth of the transcontinental railroad. Ever more publications began to experiment with new presentation techniques—seeking ever more arresting images, provocative headlines, and startling content—in order to win readers and influence. Advances in technology, such as the electric-powered high-speed rotary press, cheaper (wood-pulp based) white paper, and linotype typesetting machines (replacing hand-set type), encouraged commercial papers to increase pages of content and advertisements. News stories grew longer (with embellishment and "padding") and delved into human interest and crime. But the real innovation was the transformation of the front page, where publishers attracted readers with eye-catching headlines, startling news stories, and—most novel of all—illustrations.[21]

At first, daily news images worked to amplify headlines, but they quickly transcended text as a way to attract the eye and thus enhance the commercial appeal of news. Selecting events from around the world (courtesy of the telegraph), editors had great license to select those stories best suited to interpretive illustration—those narrative-based or story-telling images that allowed people to "see" events in action. As advertising revenue became the focus of news production, editors produced a breathtaking array of content, often illustrated, to draw different kinds of consumers to their advertising pages. Pushed by advertisers' growing demand, and long before it was technologically feasible for daily newspapers to mass-produce photographs, news illustrations had changed journalism. By turning events into exciting scenes and making the plausible seem real, news images became inseparable from commercial success.[22]

The Rise of Visual Journalism

The cases investigated here—obscenity litigation, anti-Chinese violence, the Ghost Dance, Jim Crow–era lynching, and domestic violence—demonstrate how efforts to capitalize on the dramatic power of the news fueled the growth of visual journalism and changed everyday reporting. Commercial editors of weekly and, later, daily publications quickly learned the form's economic benefits; marginalized groups and social activists also experimented with sensationalism to challenge negative stereotyping and mobilize their own constituencies. By the 1890s, a wide range of publications (commercial, political, activist) had come to embrace, adapt, and expand the sensational style through news illustration—albeit in different ways for different audiences. As patterns established in entertainment publications infiltrated the commercial dailies and even low-budget political news sheets, few publications could afford to resist the power of graphic news. And the more they innovated, the more they changed the very nature of the journalism.

Publishers as famous as Pulitzer and Hearst, and as obscure as John Mitchell of the *Richmond Planet*, explored sensational illustration as a way to expand circulation and to influence political culture. Even though ephemeral imagery from inexpensive sources transmitted significant meanings to a broad audience, they rarely enjoy scholarly analysis. Daily news illustrations were (at first) small, unsophisticated, and seemingly less significant than the more complex narrative illustrations in family-style weekly magazines, the visual cacophony of raunchy sporting papers, and (by the late 1890s) the photograph. But the early forays into the visualization of daily news reached far more readers than the weeklies did. They engaged the wider cultural context of racial strife, immigration, westward expansion, and changing roles for women, as well as political contests and the basic questions about what it means to have a "free" press. As publishers and editors established new visual conventions (and adapted older ones), their news images transformed America's visual culture in lasting ways.

Sensationalism's anti-authoritarian ethos could serve many masters, but it also contained its own logic and built-in biases that proved difficult to escape. As publishers imported presentation strategies from the dime novel, the anti-vice tract, and the captivity narrative, they brought along related ideas about conquest and subjugation. Sensationalism was a wily communicator: it could sell papers, corral consumers, and rally voters. It could also enable activists to forge identities, establish group consciousness, and—ultimately—empower social movements to challenge injustice. But by its nature, sensationalism could also undermine such efforts to develop counternarratives. Various social actors embraced sensational tactics and the "crusading" spirit of the new reform journalism, to mixed results.[23] In different ways, the cases explored in this book address debates over journalism standards, commercialized media, and the destabilizing impact of new media forms. They explore how illustrated media changed over time but also how elements persisted and adapted from case to case. Together, the five cases engage lingering concerns over the fragmentation, loss of legitimacy, and overall "dumbing down" of the public square.

Each chapter focuses on a different constituency, climate, and moment in the evolution of graphic news. Chapter 1 examines the struggle over sexuality discourse and definitions of obscenity in print media just after the Civil War. Illustrated sporting weeklies like *The Days' Doings* and the *National Police Gazette* pushed the boundaries of what could be represented, which put them into conflict with cultural arbiters who deemed them a threat to morality. Anti-vice activists, such as Anthony Comstock and the New York Society for the Suppression of Vice, sought control over sporting weeklies but also over newspapers produced by women's rights and free-thought activists, establishing parameters for what might be *seen*—rather than *said*—in print. Comstock's efforts to screen out images he found shocking had an unexpected result: he successfully suppressed the visualization of rape, seduction, and other indecencies, with the exception of cases where the alleged perpetrator was African American. His interventions distorted the visualization of alleged sexual crimes as primarily the racial assault on white women by men of color.

Consequences became clearer in the late 1870s and early 1880s, as weeklies like the *Police Gazette* adapted their visual stereotype of African American men as rapists to characterize Chinese laborers as sexual predators. Chapter 2 looks at how anti-Chinese agitators distorted—and invented—news stories about Chinese predators in opium dens as a new rationale for federal exclusion legislation. Although they had limited opportunities to produce alternative imagery, a few Chinese American public figures attempted to interject a more positive iconography. Journalist Wong Chin Foo described (and in one case arranged to illustrate) alternative representations of Chinese workers, hoping to reveal Chinatown's nonthreatening social spaces. Within the larger political context, however, Wong had limited power to challenge pervasive anti-Chinese narratives that merged existing stereotypes with the exclusion campaign. Positive, observational images were no match for the mystique of the Chinatown opium den; they lacked sensationalism's power to attract the eye.

A different effort to develop a counternarrative appeared in the 1890 Ghost Dance, a nonviolent ceremonial religious practice among Native Americans that seemed to dramatize resistance to colonial expansion. Chapter 3 explores how daily editors Joseph Pulitzer (in his *New York World*) and William Randolph Hearst (in his first paper, the *San Francisco Examiner*) experimented with the limits of news illustration. News images of the 1890 Ghost Dance movement among the Lakota Sioux in the Western Plains mischaracterized a minor crisis as a declaration of war and contributed to the chain of events culminating in the Massacre at Wounded Knee. Their quest for images that were both "authentic" (in other words, photograph-based) and dramatic led both papers (inaccurately) to identify existing celebrities (such as Lakota elder Sitting Bull) as instigators, mainly because photographic images were available. Their visualizations appropriated existing narratives of westward expansion and Native American savagery, including images from Buffalo Bill's *Wild West* show, in which Sitting Bull had for a short time participated. The Lakota lacked their own newspaper and thus had no direct access to public opinion, leaving them vulnerable to sensational depictions of the dance and its aftermath. After the massacre the Ghost Dance continued in other parts of the country, but only traces of its critique of colonial expansion lingered in sensational news reporting.

Activists with access to print publications had greater success in developing counternarratives. Historians have only begun to explore how African American newspapers, such as the Indianapolis *Freeman*, developed their own visual journalism in the black press. Chapter 4 shows how artists for the *Freeman* and other African American newspapers developed interpretive illustrations and reconfigured mainstream lynching imagery to critique the prevailing rape/

lynching narrative and mobilize resistance to racial violence. In the 1890s the black press (by then one of the few constituencies still primarily funded by a political party, rather than commercially through advertisements) began to develop powerful illustrations. They countered sensational lynching imagery, widely published by sporting/crime newspapers to justify racial violence, with their own anti-lynching iconography. Within the constraints of violent suppression, their efforts had only limited power to spark legislative action but nevertheless suggest sensationalism's potential as a mobilizing tool for activists with a social justice agenda.

Sensational narratives, however, carried certain meanings, as women's rights activists discovered in the mid-1890s when they attempted to use sensational dailies to promote their own agenda. Chapter 5 analyzes how women's rights activists sought to use sensational tools to raise awareness about domestic violence in the daily press. They adapted the frontier justice notion of masculine honor, chivalry, and retributive justice to demand equal protection for a woman accused of murdering her seducer. In an effort to reach a broader public, they applied the popular "crime of passion" defense to the case of Maria Barbella (known in the press as Barberi), a woman tried twice for killing a former lover because he had "violated her honor" (a euphemism for raping and refusing to marry her). Through letters, interviews, and direct interventions, feminist activists, including Susan B. Anthony and Elizabeth Cady Stanton, introduced into daily papers a complex debate about women's rights and the double standard in domestic violence prosecution. News images of Barbella shifted radically between her two trials, reflecting changing public opinion and the adaptability of interpretive illustrations to such fluctuations. In harnessing a form they had long condemned, these activists discovered that sensationalism resists neutral usage. Sensationalist tactics and imagery helped win the campaign for Barbella's acquittal, with the unintended cost of undermining women's power to challenge the "crime of passion" defense. The internal logic of the sensational style both coopted and distorted their goals.

The Epilogue revisits key events near the turn of the twentieth century as newspapers transitioned from illustrations to photographs, connecting the five case studies with the more familiar origin story for sensational or "yellow" journalism and the outbreak of the Spanish-American War. With the emphasis on images firmly established over the preceding decades, news "art" led presentation of stories and often transformed reporting of events. Between 1870 and 1900, changing practices of news illustration had established new parameters for how consumers came to *see* the news. This trend continued after photographs replaced illustrations as the preferred form of visual evidence. Interpretive illustrations faded by the end of the nineteenth century, but the conventions for graphic news they had established remained in place, a legacy we continue to live with today.

CHAPTER I

"We Simply Illustrate"

Sensationalizing Crime in
the 1870s "Sporting" News

IN THE 1870S, two New York weekly "sporting" newspapers, *The Days' Doings* and *The National Police Gazette*, set new parameters for illustrating crime, specifically sexual violence. These sporting weeklies had changed since the antebellum days; they continued to emphasize violence but had shed much of the earlier crusading spirit and began to intensify focus on leisure activities and the pursuit of pleasure. With a selection of news stories from across the nation and around the world to choose from, editors picked those with the greatest potential for vivid illustration. Their artists used a technique of "interpretive illustration" or, in other words, visual narratives that reenacted scenarios described in text. Such images made it possible for readers to "see" crimes in action, as virtual witnesses. Always fanciful and often inaccurate, sporting "news" images resembled drawings in entertainment publications, such as story papers and dime novels. Their emotionally charged framing evoked feeling; they were designed to shock, horrify, titillate, and amuse their readers.

Sporting publishers splashed crime images on their covers in a deliberate effort to attract the passersby who saw them on newsstands in city streets. This visibility of certain kinds of imagery in the sporting news generated initial opposition from across the political spectrum: social conservatives, suffragists, health advocates, and advertisers alike. Spearheaded by anti-vice activist Anthony Comstock, this opposition coalesced to limit what kinds of images editors could publish. The struggle over decency in print resulted in the unintended consequence of increased representation of racial violence and raced sexuality as other images of sexualized violence declined.

Sporting weeklies diverged from the mainstream pictorial weeklies of the 1870s, such as *Frank Leslie's Illustrated Newspaper* and *Harper's Weekly*, that were not out of place in the family home. By contrast, sporting and crime papers, delivered discreetly ("fully wrapped") to individuals or reading clubs and other organizations, catered to the interests of young, urban men for viewing outside the middle-class household. The reenactment of crimes in action had been the hallmark of the oldest crime weekly, the *National Police Gazette*, since its founding in 1845. The paper's unsigned drawings, produced by staff engravers or artists, and of dubious provenance, typically had little relationship to the wire stories and court cases they claimed to illustrate. But they were striking. While *Leslie's* and *Harper's* (and other, even more domestic, illustrated publications) used interpretive illustration at times, those typically included captions that emphasized the source of the image: a witnessed event, a sketch drawn "at the scene," a portrait based on a photograph, or other assertions of the image's legitimacy. With the exception of political cartoons, which were inherently metaphorical in nature, most "decent" family weeklies sought to distinguish between realist/source-based news images and interpretive illustration.

Images in the sporting weeklies made no such distinction between interpretation and fact. News illustrations in the *Days' Doings* and the *Police Gazette* claimed to represent reality but were stylistically indistinguishable from their editorial cartoons. Their reenactments of crime scenarios "as fact" provided different kinds of information that influenced how readers *saw* the news. Without any pretense about witnessing the original event, an image provided for a court case might re-create an interpretation of the crime that supported the prosecution's argument rather than the defense's claims—even as a trial was underway and the facts were in dispute. Further, interpretive illustration reduced real people to familiar character types so that many faces, postures, and scenes seemed indistinguishable from one issue to the next; villains and victims were interchangeable; plots and settings merged into cliché. Interpretive illustration would lose credibility in the 1880s, when not only family weeklies paid more attention to image sourcing, but emerging illustrated daily newspapers, such as Joseph Pulitzer's *New York World* and William Randolph Hearst's *San Francisco Examiner*[1] began to do so as well. By the century's end, new printing presses that allowed rapid production of news photographs further discredited interpretive illustration as a legitimate kind of news image. Until then, however, this form was an integral feature, rather than an unavoidable technical problem, of sensational news production.

Interpretive crime scene reenactments made the *Police Gazette* and *Days' Doings* the newspapers most heavily engaged in sensationalism in the 1870s; they were exemplars of the form. In this regard, they also stood apart from the period's only illustrated daily newspaper, the *New York Daily Graphic*. While technically the first illustrated daily, the *Daily Graphic* was more novelty than news sheet, and its illustrated crime stories represented a tiny fraction of its visual coverage. The time needed to create and reproduce illustrations in the

1870s made it impossible for the *Daily Graphic* to visualize events at the speed of news. Instead, it featured scenes of expansive, historic dramas and images of famous buildings, often reproduced from European illustrated weeklies. With the exception of disaster imagery, the *Daily Graphic*'s visuals offered a diversion from—rather than illustration of—the wire stories it published on text pages; a novelty on expensive paper, it provided respectable imagery for middle- and upper-class family readers.[2] Despite heavy use of illustration, the *Daily Graphic* was even less likely than *Harper's* and *Leslie's* to challenge the sporting papers' near-monopoly on crime illustration.

Sporting newspapers used sensational imagery to cater to a variety of consumer interests for white, working men: sports, athleticism, gambling, nightlife, urban vice, city life, and—especially—sexualized bodies. But while pitched for a barroom and barbershop clientele, the papers' imagery was also visible to a wider audience. Journalist Ida Tarbell recalled her fascination as a teen with the *Police Gazette*, contrasting it with more respectable publications like *Harper's Weekly* and *Harper's Monthly*.

> On the sly I was devouring a sheet forbidden to the household—the *Police Gazette*—the property of the men around the house, for we had men around the house, men of various degrees of acceptability to my mother, but all necessary to my father's enterprises. . . . [My mother] would not have swearing, drinking, rough manners, and certainly she would not have had the *Police Gazette* in the house. But the men had it, and now and then when my brother and I played about the bunkhouse it was easy for me to pick up a copy and slip it away where my dearest girl friend and I looked unashamed and entirely unknowing on its rough and brutal pictures. If they were obscene we certainly never knew it. There was a wanton gaiety about the women, a violent rakishness about the men—wicked, we supposed, but not the less interesting for that.

She associated the paper with the saloon in town, adjacent to her family's farm, whose patrons she could hear carousing on summer nights.[3] It was precisely this potential to bring the rough public world into the home that was so alarming to critics and social reformers.

Provocative and suggestive images in sporting weeklies generated opposition from a variety of constituencies who worried about their negative influence on crime rates, on women, on youth, on the social order. Publishers defended their papers on the grounds that they offered cautionary tales that deterred, rather than modeled, criminal behavior. Reformers across the political spectrum, however, remained unconvinced and sought ways to shut the papers down or at least suppress their display in public spaces. Middle-class women's rights activists and like-minded reformers saw sporting images as covert means to intimidate women by making public spaces uncomfortable and hostile. Conservative activists blamed the sporting weeklies for glorifying vice, corrupting young minds, and providing detailed "lessons in crime." The most famous was self-appointed anti-vice activist Anthony Comstock.

On the Suppression of "Vile" Publications

Until 1872, Comstock was a little-known dry-goods clerk when he took upon himself the mantle of guardian of the nation's morality. As his influence in the debate over decency in print grew, it generated some enduring—and largely unintended—consequences. For one thing, Comstock, the man who came to define modern American censorship, also goaded into existence the radical free speech opposition movement, which came to reject any restrictions on what could be published. Comstock's pursuit of educational and sexual hygiene reformers, as if they were peddlers in obscene tracts, forced some libertarians to embrace a free press position, despite their disgust with "vicious literature" and the sporting press. More significant for the evolution of sensational content in American newspapers, Comstock's manipulations of 1870s visual culture, particularly in selectively prohibiting the representation of certain kinds of sexual violence, left in its wake heightened racial stereotyping in crime imagery. His activities led publishers of illustrated sporting weeklies to suppress the visualization of white sexual crime (Comstock's target), while allowing depictions of interracial rape of white women by men of color, a trend in representation that would persist into the next century.

Comstock achieved national fame in November 1872, when he arranged the arrest of activist and presidential candidate Victoria Woodhull on obscenity charges after she published a story in her newspaper accusing the popular Brooklyn pastor, Henry Ward Beecher, of adultery. Publication of this story launched the nineteenth century's most notorious sex scandal, and the ensuing Beecher-Tilton trial became a byword for sexual hypocrisy in the Protestant Church. Comstock was outraged by Woodhull's attack on Beecher but professed to be even more concerned about the scandal's influence on public morality. Early in 1873, Comstock used his influence over local authorities to target the *Days' Doings*, where Woodhull and her sister, Tennessee Claflin, had been regularly featured for years. The paper covered the opening of their brokerage firm in 1870 (fig. 1.1), showing them in bold stances of "fast women," with ankles visible and gazing directly into the eyes of their male clientele. Through their political campaigns (in 1872, Woodhull was the first woman to run for president), their support of "free love," and their arrest for "obscenity" for the Beecher exposure, the sisters were popular and disreputable celebrities in the *Days' Doings*.

In depicting their indictment in late 1872 (fig. 1.2), the paper represented them with the hard faces and shameless aspects more typically used to depict

THE FEMALE BROKERS OF THE PERIOD.—THE TELEGRAPHIC APPARATUS AT THE ESTABLISHMENT OF WOODHULL, CLAFLIN & CO., 44 BROAD STREET, NEW YORK.—SEE PAGE 194.

FIGURE 1.1: "The Female Brokers of the Period," *The Days' Doings*, February 26, 1870. New York Public Library.

female criminals and prostitutes.[4] The paper's coverage of the sisters over so many months suggests that they attracted news consumers, which made their disappearance, following Comstock's intervention, all the more remarkable. He sought to suppress their arguments for what they called a "single sexual standard for all," along with their open discussion of sexual matters—in any form or context.

The rapid expansion of media after the Civil War was part of what prompted Comstock's concerns about sensual imagery and the 1870s became critical years in the struggle over decency in print. The 1865 postal law under which Comstock had the New York district attorney arrest Woodhull proved inapplicable to newspapers (she was eventually acquitted), and he used the case's notoriety to push through a stronger, federal law in 1873, popularly known as the "Comstock Law." Unlike the earlier legislation, which had been designed to protect young soldiers fighting in the Civil War from erotica in books and pamphlets sent through the mail, the Comstock Law broadened the government's power to regulate printed material in general. It expanded the kinds of publications that could be deemed obscene to include newspapers, advertise-

THE MONSTER SCANDAL.—VICTORIA C. WOODHULL, AND TENNIE C. CLAFLIN APPEARING BEFORE U. S.
COMMISSIONER OSBORN AT THE U. S. COURT IN CHAMBERS STREET.—See Page 2.

FIGURE 1.2: "The Monster Scandal," *The Days' Doings*, November 20,
1872. New York Public Library.

ments, and a variety of products geared toward contraception. It also defined
obscenity in such broad terms as to include any kind of sexual information,
including basic physiological facts. The Comstock Law became, through successful prosecution, a weapon against social liberals and commercial publishers
alike. Ironically, social liberals initially shared Comstock's concerns about the
dangers of commercial eroticism and argued that their own educational publications would counteract the "invasive sensualism" of public culture. When
Comstock turned his sights on their educational tracts, however, they began to
rethink the implications of censorship itself, even for materials they, themselves,
found offensive.[5]

Comstock's anti-obscenity agitation also put the publishers of sensational sporting and crime weeklies in jeopardy. To see how, it is necessary to view nineteenth-century illustrations as their contemporaries saw them, within "the broad social context of censorship struggles." By today's standards, sporting illustrations might seem offensive on many levels, but they are hardly obscene. The 1870s debate among social liberals—freethinkers, sex radicals, anarchists, and libertarians, who were also targets of Comstock's censorship campaigns—helps illuminate the period's evolving obscenity standards for "lewd" and "vile" publications. Middle-class social activists, from moral reformers to women's suffragists, despised sporting illustrations. At first even radical libertarians denounced a wide range of publications, including dime novels and sporting newspapers, sharing Comstock's concerns about the rise of commercial, sensational media, which they believed "were undermining individual morality and the public good."[6] Comstock's penchant for legal actions against social radicals fractured this unspoken consensus and mobilized—and helped constitute—a free-press constituency.

Comstock concurrently targeted marriage reform tracts, sexual hygiene manuals, and sporting publications because he felt that all endangered the unwary reader. Indeed, he believed that their reform credentials made sex radicals like Woodhull and freethinker D. M. Bennett (a later target) worse than the sporting weeklies. Preoccupied with protecting their own educational materials from suppression, reform publishers reversed their initial sympathy for censorship but in the process lost any standing to criticize the visual content in the sporting news. Women's rights advocates, labor activists, and former abolitionists found themselves unable to object as new stereotypes of women, workers, and people of color took hold in commercial illustrations—the result of publishers' attempts to develop Comstock-proof, sensational imagery.

From the arrest of Woodhull and Claflin in 1872 to the conviction of Bennett in 1879, Comstock lumped together erotic novels, nude pictures, men's sporting newspapers, reform newspapers, and dry treatises on human physiology and marriage reform, viewing them collectively as symptoms of a wider social problem: decaying moral standards. Regardless of their intent, he believed, each kind fostered open discussion of ideas that were inappropriate for—and corrupting to—the public sphere: even factual information about the human body might encourage "wanton behavior," in his view. For Comstock, publications concerning even clinical or physiological treatment of sexuality, viewed out of context by boys and girls, might encourage sexual activity among young people.[7] Comstock's belief that government was obligated to protect the young from all manner of sexuality discourse set the stage for a lengthy struggle over the meaning of obscenity. Beyond Comstock's impact on the history of censorship, definitions of obscenity, and the role of government in social mores, his achievements profoundly changed the look of sensational imagery in the sporting papers.

It was the visibility of sensational illustrations in sporting newspapers that Comstock found particularly dangerous. As he explained a few years later, "[Satan] resolved to make the most of these vile illustrated weekly papers, by lining the news-stands and shop windows along the pathway of the children from home to school and church, so that they could not go to and from these places of instruction without giving him an opportunity to defile their pure minds by flaunting these atrocities."[8] In this he echoed concerns of middle-class reformers, many of whom were women. Comstock did not initially welcome women into his organization, the New York Society for the Suppression of Vice (NYSSV), given that his desire to curtail sporting newspapers and other salacious publications stemmed from "separate spheres" ideology, which held that the private realm (and particularly women and children) needed protection from the public realm. Some women, however, shared his perception of the immorality of sporting and crime papers. "I know of our police papers only by hearsay," veteran woman's rights activist Julia Ward Howe told the Second Women's Congress in Chicago in 1874, "but I do hear that there is much in them which can only brutalize and pollute the minds of their habitual readers." Howe abhorred the sensuality and violence of sensational print culture and saw women as well-suited to protecting children's purity from such threats: as she put it, "It becomes the guardians of society to keep a watchful eye upon the press."[9]

In a different way, women's suffrage activists objected to the way illustrated sporting newspapers demeaned women's political goals and their fight for the vote. They saw illustrated sporting news as a weapon men used to keep women disenfranchised. In 1869, one writer to *The Revolution*, for example, criticized "an obscene weekly paper" for publishing a caricature of woman suffragists in a way that she felt represented the "persistent attempt on the part of all the newspapers by personal ridicule and vilification, to choke down" the entire movement. Olive Logan, an actress and theater reformer, agreed that men disparaged or ignored suffrage coverage, while "anything . . . that is written about women, particularly if it be anything scandalous or disgraceful, is eagerly perused."[10] Demeaning images of women in sporting papers even posed a physical barrier for women in public spaces, according to Abigail Duniway, an Oregon suffrage editor and activist:

> Certain newsdealers in Portland [Oregon] from week to week exhibit to the public gaze through the medium of their shop windows obscene pictorial newspapers of the most disgusting character. No lady can enter such a place without being virtually insulted by the base caricatures of her sex.

The visibility of such images in newsstands on city streets, for Duniway, limited the freedom of "respectable" middle-class women to access certain public spaces. Sporting papers were so insulting to women, she believed, that they should be called "man's rights journals."[11] Demeaning women through sensational imagery, of course, was central to the sporting papers' business model.

Other social reformers shared concerns about sensual commercial publications. But Comstock's inclusion of physiology tracts as targets for censorship under the new 1873 postal law forced reformers to distinguish their publications from the works they abhorred. Along with readers of his journal *The Truth Seeker*, freethinker D. M. Bennett defended Woodhull's decision to publish the Beecher scandal, as well as articles on human sexuality and marriage reform, as acts for the public good; such works were educational and not obscene, he believed. As another Woodhull supporter writing to the *Truth Seeker* put it, "Obscenity is certainly a vile crime, which should not be tolerated in civilized society, and the punishment of its author should be as severe as the law can inflict, but it is incumbent upon us to well define the lines of [demarcation] between decency and indecency." Physiology writers and their supporters challenged not the existence but rather Comstock's definition of obscenity. They rejected the notion that their own works, intended to educate and protect public health, were obscene.[12]

Early prosecutions under the Comstock Law began to radicalize some of these social reformers. In 1875, Comstock had Woodhull's friend John Lant arrested for mocking the Beecher-Tilton trial and discussing the physiology of reproduction in his paper, *The Toledo Sun*. In 1876, Comstock had a reformer, E. B. Foote, arrested for advertising a birth control pamphlet in his book, *Plain Home Talk*. Bennett was appalled, calling both Lant and Foote "martyrs of a new war for liberty." Like Bennett, Foote's supporters distinguished between education and titillation:

> Laws against the sending out of *licentious and immoral books, pictures*, etc., are right, and should be rigidly enforced against the vile scoundrels, who, for a little paltry gain, are willing to debauch and ruin their victims. But to class your chaste physiological writings with these infamous publications is an utter confounding of distinctions, which even our wise legislators cannot fail to see.

In 1876 Foote and his supporters founded the National Liberal League to advocate the separation of church and state and to protest Comstock's "confounding of distinctions" between the educational and the obscene.[13]

In other words, advocates of sexual education defended publications that were intended to increase understanding of human physiology as different from those seeking to titillate or entertain. Bennett, for one, agreed with Woodhull, even before her arrest, that frank discussion of sexuality and female physiology was necessary to raising healthy children. But it was precisely this openness that so alarmed Comstock. He recognized no distinction between sex education and titillation, adhering instead to the more strict position of English (and American) common law, established in midcentury England and codified in the *The Queen v. Hicklin* decision (1868), that the intended purpose of a physiological publication was irrelevant in obscenity prosecution if it had a *"tendency* to deprave or corrupt" anyone who might come across it, regardless of the author's intent.[14] Comstock's efforts eventually made the "Hicklin test" the measure for obscenity in the United States as well.

Visualizing Sex, Crime, and Violence in the Sporting News

While reformers struggled to distinguish their publications from sensational newspapers and pornography, Comstock turned his attention to the sporting weeklies, specifically the *Days' Doings*. Never a huge seller, the paper nevertheless was a widely available source of violent and sexual imagery, published without attribution by Frank Leslie, better known for his family weekly, *Frank Leslie's Illustrated Newspaper*. By the 1870s, *Leslie's* had abandoned sensational coverage to become more family friendly; publishing the *Days' Doings* allowed Leslie to shift his more "tawdry material" out of his flagship weekly. *Leslie's* became increasingly respectable in content and curtailed its use of interpretive illustrations, moving toward sourced, "realistic" visual coverage of crime scenes and portraits of significant figures. The *Days' Doings*, by contrast, expanded its use of interpretive illustration and continued to reenact (alleged) assaults and crimes of passion. Leslie argued that publicizing the capture and punishment of perpetrators in the *Days' Doings* would deter immorality and crime,[15] a premise diametrically opposed to Comstock's commitment to suppression.

Leslie likely caught Comstock's attention early in 1873 by defending Woodhull and Claflin as they sat in jail without formal indictment following their obscenity arrest. While he condoned neither their views about free love nor their exposure of Beecher, Leslie challenged the legality of Comstock's action against the sisters, based on First Amendment arguments. Beecher should prosecute them for libel, instead of bringing federal charges against them, he argued in *Frank Leslie's Illustrated Newspaper*: "Woodhull & Co. have a right to public opinion, and public opinion depends on the press."[16] Within weeks, Comstock enlisted the New York City District Attorney's support to indict Leslie for multiple counts of obscenity in the *Days' Doings*. "At last, at last!!" Comstock wrote in his diary that day. "Thank God! At last action is commenced against this terrible curse. Now for a mighty blow for the young."[17] Apparently assuming that Comstock's real goal was to punish him for supporting Woodhull and Claflin, Leslie immediately removed their images from the *Days' Doings*, suppressing their controversial interactions with Comstock that month.[18]

Apart from suppressing Woodhull and Claflin, Leslie chose not to defend the *Days' Doings* on free press grounds, focusing instead on the obscenity charge itself. He insisted that neither the paper's advertisements nor its illustrations were inherently immoral. "Some busy, perhaps in some instances well-meaning people, for a long time past, have affected to dislike what they call the moral tone of the journal," Leslie wrote in an (unsigned) editorial on the eve of his own indictment for obscenity. Yet the patronage of "good families" testified to the paper's moral tone, he claimed; and critics needed to understand the publication's mission—namely, "to illustrate with the pencil the striking and romantic news of the day." Leslie challenged Comstock's idea that illustrations themselves made news stories obscene; he denied that pictures were more corrupting than words. "If our pencil is false to morality," Leslie argued defiantly, "then the entire news Press of the nation, which *we simply illustrate*, is a fountain of iniquity."[19]

Comstock, by contrast, believed that it was precisely sporting weeklies' *illustration* of crimes in action that made them destructive. As he later explained, "Few are aware of the fact that many of the items that are so revolting when condensed and grouped together in the illustrated papers of crime are the very same items scattered one by one each day during the week by the daily press. A cheap woodcut is added to the display type of the daily press, and we then have a thing so foul that no child can look upon it and be as pure afterward." Comstock blamed the rise of illustrated crime news on publishers' greed: "men who . . . run a muck-rake through the slums and sinks of crime, and then, for the sake of making money, do not scruple to send innocent youth headlong to ruin." Families had limited power to control exposure to these images, he believed. Because sporting newspapers "were found to be so gross, so libidinous, so monstrous, that every decent person spurned them," he wrote, they "were excluded from the home on sight." This made them more visible, however, because they were sold freely in the streets with their covers on display for all to see.[20] Comstock believed that illustration made immoral news even more destructive, in other words; Leslie disagreed.

Leslie also disputed Comstock's belief that advertisements found in the *Days' Doings* were inherently immoral. Making humorous reference to one advertisement that seemed to offer "lewd books" for sale, he noted that upon request he found that "the publications advertised were three tracts which had been issued by a Christian Association." Henceforth, he sarcastically promised, such dangerous advertising would be refused.[21] However, indictment by a grand jury on obscenity charges on January 28, 1873, changed his tone, and soon Leslie took steps to avoid a trial—and thus avoid publicly identifying himself as the editor of the *Days' Doings*, which would affect his reputation as publisher of his middle-class publications. In a sudden turnabout, he dispatched his lawyer to invite Comstock to visit his premises and promised to adhere to Comstock's definition of obscenity for images and advertisements alike. As Comstock recalled the meeting in his ledger, "Leslie gave instructions to all his men, not to receive any advertisements of doubtful characters, [and] his artists not to put in any picture of lewd character." Before prosecution could ensue, Leslie agreed to the district attorney's requests to rein in salacious material in the *Days' Doings*.[22]

Leslie's most obvious adaptation to his publishing practices following the compromise with New York's D.A. was evident on the advertising page. "Advertisements have crept into this paper which, upon very recent investigation, we find have represented such business as the proprietors of the *Days' Doings* disapprove," Leslie now explained. "We have thrown out of the present issue all equivocally-phrased advertisements. We shall receive none which are questionable hereafter, no matter how disguised whether as medical advertisements or otherwise." He referred not only to advertising relating to abortion and venereal disease but also to "divorce advertisements" and any having a "sporting character" or even slightly "tinged with a double meaning of any sort." The *Days' Doings*, Leslie promised, was and would remain a "family journal, fit for the instruction and amusement of intelligent, moral families."[23]

Leslie's capitulation reflected his position as a commercial news publisher with a reputation to defend and his desire to sustain sales and circulation in his many other publications. His compliance took immediate effect on the advertising page, where the quantity of advertisements shrank from four to two columns. Gone were promises of "Divorces legally obtained" and the more numerous mail-order cures for "certain diseases" (in other words, venereal disease). Marriage manuals (with "colored illustrations"), "rich" transparent cards, and books about French governesses likewise disappeared. Discreet propositions "to the ladies" of informative books and recipes that made "every woman her own physician" and other veiled references to abortifacients also disappeared.[24] Deprived of these sources of advertising revenue, the paper struggled for two weeks to secure replacement ads, gradually introducing a new array of products for the middle-class home. "Novelty Plaster Works Lung Protectors" and the "Wonder Camera: The Greatest Invention of Our Age" began to fill the advertising pages. By the third week, new ads designed for women appeared: dress patterns, pianos and music boxes, and that most domestic of consumer goods—a diaper.[25]

Leslie's desire to placate Comstock is also evident in his adaptation of the paper's images, upholding his second promise to prevent publication of "any picture of lewd character." His adjustments offer a rare opportunity to understand 1870s conceptions of "lewd" imagery. The most striking absence after the 1873 compromise was the line reproduction of nude paintings and statues. Partially draped with cloths and shielded by body positioning, these classically inspired nudes or semi-nudes had long been a staple in the *Days' Doings*, appearing as occasion (or lack of other news spectacles) demanded. This reproduction of a nude statue, for example (fig. 1.3), showing a woman's naked upper body in a classical pose, had the authority of a "master" behind it. Such images invoked

FIGURE 1.3: "The Aviary," *The Days' Doings*, July 2, 1871, 13. New York Public Library.

a high-art principle while mass marketing the female body to barbershop audiences. Comstock worried about the availability of "high art" nudity to "the rabble," as he described working-class readers. Comstock's intervention and his well-known aversion to nudity (he was rumored to have draped nude statues with cloth coverings to shield museum viewers) forced editors like Leslie to find new ways to meet popular demand for provocative images without violating the censor's new visual standards.[26]

To provide sensation to readers without offending Comstock, the *Days' Doings* experimented with a range of visual strategies. First, the paper further exaggerated an existing taxonomy of class and racial distinctions used to reveal, or cover, female bodies. Even before 1873, the paper had differentiated women according to categories of private and public, respectable and "fast:" some women's bodies were fair game for illustration, and some were off limits. This dichotomy in representation was shifting in the 1870s, as more "respectable" women ventured

LEAP-FROG BY THE SAD SEA WAVES.—A SCENE ON THE BEACH AT ATLANTIC CITY.—See Page 2.

FIGURE I.4: "Leap Frog by the Sad Sea Waves," *The Days' Doings*, July 27, 1872, 8. New York Public Library.

into the public realm, and thus into print. Obvious candidates for illustration were feisty, saucy, or "plucky" public women—ballet girls, circus women, and romping beachgoers (fig. 1.4). Their bodies, in revealing costumes and postures, were apparently fair game for illustration. Before Comstock, the *Days' Doings* news illustrations sometimes exposed ankles to mark "lively" women, as in cases where an artist might depict a woman inadvertently exposing herself to escape from an accident or natural disaster (fig. 1.5). An image of a "respectable" woman might reveal her ankles to indicate derision or disrespect. After Comstock's intervention in 1873, however, the paper took pains to shield middle-class ankles from view, even in cases of disaster (fig. 1.6).[27] For a time, Comstock's definition of lewdness would protect respectable middle-class women even from modest exposure in the *Days' Doings*.

To replace images of female bodies that Comstock might find "lewd," Leslie sought out other kinds of sensation. His first idea was to increase graphic depictions of violence and sexualized racial others. He made a special plea for stories from the western frontier, particularly those concerning Indians, animal attacks, or natural disasters. Immediately such stories and images filled the paper's pages, with interpretive illustrations that showed dramatic encounters with bears, wolves, and battles with "Indians," alongside fires, floods, and train wrecks. The *Days' Doings* also reconceptualized its class-based depictions of women's bodies in a new, nativist manner. One example can be found in the explicit nudity of

UNTOWARD ACCIDENT TO A CITY-BOUND "ROYAL RED" OMNIBUS NEAR THREADNEEDLE STREET.—THE LOCK GETS SMASHED, AND THE FAIR CARGO IS DISCHARGED BY THE ONLY AVAILABLE EXIT.

FIGURE 1.5: "Untoward Accident," *The Days' Doings*, January 4, 1875, 4. New York Public Library.

a news illustration titled "Episode of the Spanish Revolution." The drawing's surprisingly frank portrayal of corpses revealed several of the women's upper bodies, though kin to a "nobleman." Frontal nudity of "other" women in exotic settings, or women "dishonored" by revolutionaries, it seems, did not violate Comstock's standards for lewd pictures; his intervention shielded some white women's ankles but not even frontal nudity of poor or non-American women.[28] Through such adaptations, Leslie (and Comstock) subtly altered sexualized representation in the *Days' Doings*.

A few years later, in February 1877, Comstock more profoundly shifted sexualized news illustration in the *National Police Gazette*. At the time, the *Police Gazette* was in a period of transition, just beginning to recover from the lowest point in its publication history, with declining sales and circulation. George Matsell, a former police chief who in 1873 assumed positions of both superintendent and president of the New York City Police Commission, had recently sold the paper to his two engravers, Herbert R. Mooney and Charles A. Lederer.[29]

FIGURE 1.6: "A Con-
ductor's Gallant 'Passage
at Arms,'" *Days' Doings*,
March 1, 1873, 13. New
York Public Library.

Sales had plummeted from about twenty-eight thousand copies in 1872 to a
paltry six thousand in 1874. In September 1874, Richard Kyle Fox, a journalist
and editor from Belfast, Ireland, arrived in New York and within two months
became the *Police Gazette*'s business manager. He simultaneously worked as an
advertising salesman for the *Commercial Bulletin* and in that capacity gradually acquired partial and, by 1876, full ownership of the *Police Gazette*, in lieu of
payment for advertising debts.[30] Initially, he retained the paper's familiar look
(its folio-sized, eight-page format) and its visual focus on crime and sensation.
Within four years, however, he introduced significant changes to content and
form—partly in response to Comstock's intervention.

Incomplete archival holdings for the *Police Gazette* for the 1870s mean that we
will likely never know what caught Comstock's eye in February 1877. His notes
in this case suggest that he objected most strongly to the paper's illustration
of explicit sexual scenarios. In contrast to his approach with the *Days' Doings*
four years earlier, Comstock contacted the new publisher privately, sending
Fox a copy of the obscenity law by mail, then dispatching an anti-vice agent
to visit the *Police Gazette*'s offices. The complaint focused primarily on the paper's interpretive illustrations of compromising situations and sexual crimes,
its many "articles . . . on 'Seduction, Rapes, Brothels, [and] Assignations.'" As

Comstock's agent explained the situation to Fox, "so many cases set out with large heading and accompanied with lewd pictures and advertisements of vile matter made it exceedingly objectionable and could not be tolerated." Despite the reference to immoral text advertisements, it was the *visualization* of immoral or criminal sexual acts that angered Comstock. According to Comstock's notes, Fox agreed to do what was necessary to avert prosecution: "He said it should be changed [and] it was changed in the next issue very radically."[31] Given that no subsequent complaint over images appeared in Comstock's records, it seems that Fox honored his side of the bargain; over the next few years, Comstock pursued the *Police Gazette* only for lottery advertisements.

The available sources make it difficult to analyze the impact of this, Comstock's second intervention into 1870s sensational imagery in sporting newspapers. Without even editorial commentary from the relevant 1877 issue to shed light on Fox's thinking, the best evidence consists of the publication itself—especially its images.[32] Examination of the one available issue from December 5, 1874, when Fox occupied the position of business manager, and the only one available for 1877 (June 21) reveals how the paper adapted its sensational images following Comstock's intervention. These before-and-after snapshots indicate a dramatic curtailment of imagery of sexual crime, with a few noteworthy exceptions.

Text content, layout, and tone in the before-and-after issues (1874 and 1877) are nearly identical (figs. 1.7 and 1.8), which makes it easier to identify the *visual* adaptations necessary to appease Comstock. The 1877 edition includes more text and fewer images than the 1874 edition, partly because the number of columns on interior text pages grew from five to six, but also because the overall number of images declined. Both feature a selection of (text) stories about sexual assault, crimes, and other shocking cases of human depravity and punishment.[33] The earlier (1874) slogan, "The Only Police Journal in the United States," gave way to the more expansive "Illustrating the Sensational and Extraordinary Events of the Day" in 1877. Despite the shift in the slogan, the two issues are strikingly alike in every way but one—the nature of their illustrations.

The *Police Gazette*'s interpretive illustrations of sexual scenarios changed after the 1877 intervention, reflecting Comstock's explicit instructions and priorities. The 1874 issue included several interpretive illustrations of sexual scenarios— an elopement, a "Negro monster" appearing to attack a woman (from a news story that reported a very different event), a lecherous piano teacher, murderers disposing of a body, a betrayed woman committing suicide, and an image that claimed to show two men stopping a third from strangling a woman (which could also be viewed as three men attacking her). Such depictions of sexualized violence had long been standard fare in the *Police Gazette*—up until Comstock's intervention.

In the 1877 issue, by contrast, only two *Police Gazette* images indicated sexual misconduct or danger. The more suggestive of the two (fig. 1.9) showed a woman

FIGURE 1.8: Front page, *The National Police Gazette*, June 21, 1877. In author's possession.

FIGURE 1.9: "Selling a
Wife for Drinks," *The
National Police Gazette*,
June 21, 1877, 8. In
author's possession.

surrounded by drunken men at a bar: the image was highly ambiguous; her facial
expression indicated no alarm. It was the underlying innuendo—the caption,
"Selling a Wife for Drinks," combined with the glee of the men in general,
and the suggestive posture of the man behind her—that raised the possibility
of assault. The second merely showed a young woman chastely kissing an artist as he painted a landscape by the Hudson River. In contrast to the multiple
reenactments in 1874, neither 1877 image indicated a woman being physically
assaulted or touched against her will (though the caption of the first image
implies coercion, or worse). To fill the space that had been taken up by sensational imagery in 1874, the 1877 front page instead featured what would become
characteristic of Fox's visual style in the 1880s: bare-chested men (boxers) and a
cacophony of images that might be classed as "social" scenes—carriages at the
racetrack, a mentally ill man on the street, two women fighting in church (see
fig. 1.8). Comstock's intervention had significantly curtailed the paper's options
for sexualized news illustration.[34]

The *Police Gazette* noticeably opted not to illustrate provocative text stories in the 1877 edition, a further indication of Comstock's power to suppress some kinds of visual representation. For example, "A Villain Checkmated" tells of a New Jersey man arrested for the rape of two young women and suspected in several other assaults; "A Fiendish Crime" describes a gang rape of a young woman by three tramps near Pittsburgh; "Religion and Lust" highlights a favored theme of clergy abuse. All three wire stories, printed on text pages, would have been prime candidates for illustration in the paper's earlier years, yet none received illustration in 1877. The *Police Gazette*'s adaptations to suit Comstock, evident in such omissions, conferred no economic benefit; in fact, they likely cut into revenue by discouraging sales. Moreover, advertising on page 7 dropped to half its former column space, just as it had with the *Days' Doings*.[35] Like Leslie, Fox (who had cut his teeth selling newspaper advertising in New York City) evidently traded a significant loss in revenue to appease Comstock and avoid legal jeopardy.

Misrepresenting Sexual Knowledge

Sporting news had many readers but few defenders—no one publicly lamented Comstock's interventions into the *Police Gazette* and the *Days' Doings*. Lacking supporters—or any principle stronger than the profit motive—both Fox and Leslie capitulated. By contrast, freethinkers, libertarians, and sex radicals, who produced a variety of books and serial publications designed to challenge orthodoxy and provide basic facts of physiology, were unable to make similar accommodations after they drew Comstock's attention. Bound by conviction that their publications were beneficent, all they could do was argue about definitions. The simplicity of Comstock's position that all sexual discourse was immoral and therefore must be suppressed was difficult to counter.[36] Social reformers began by defending their work on the basis of *intent*, insisting that their publications provided necessary information, for educational purposes, meant not to corrupt but to enlighten readers.

On this basis, sex radical Ezra Heywood defended a number of reformers arrested for obscenity in the 1870s: for him, government harassment of sexual hygiene reformers revealed a "stubborn resistance to the diffusion of knowledge on subjects of the gravest importance." D. M. Bennett, arrested late in 1877 for mailing two publications Comstock deemed obscene, likewise defended them on the basis of intent. Educational works of physiology were never obscene, such writers believed: as sex radical Mattie Sawyer asked, "If it is important that physicians understand the human body and its functions why is it not equally so that *all* come in possession of the same knowledge?" Sawyer distinguished between information designed for self-knowledge from sexual titillation, discounting any non-educational uses for physiological publications. Comstock, by contrast, upheld the *Hicklin* test that it was the publication's "tendency to deprave and corrupt," rather than the intentions of its author—its interpretation by the reader rather than the author's motives—that made it obscene.[37]

Sex radicals and libertarians who saw their own work as the antidote to obscene and sporting publications, now found themselves subject to prosecution. When Comstock had Ezra Heywood arrested for selling his critique of marriage, *Cupid's Yokes*, the latter defended the publication on the grounds that it would improve morality. "My object in writing 'Cupid's Yokes' was to promote discretion and purity in love by bringing sexuality within the domain of reason and moral obligation," he wrote in January 1878. Angela Heywood was equally committed to countering commercial eroticism: she wrote, while her husband Ezra was in jail, "Gradually but surely the best minds in all schools of reform, are coming to see that our unsought conflict with invasive sensualism is theirs also." The Heywoods shared many ideas with conservative reformer Lucinda Chandler, who applauded Comstock's goal of protecting the young yet agreed that he "fails to distinguish and discriminate between helpful instruction, intended to remove low and sensual thoughts and those of the opposite character and design." Others felt that sporting weeklies and other kinds of "vile literature" were merely a symptom of social ills; education, rather than suppression, was needed to address the larger problem of immoral urban culture.[38]

Comstock's attacks on sensationalism found support, however, from women reformers who likewise sought to suppress the "invasive sensualism" of contemporary publications. "Corrupting circumstances surround the individual at every stage of growth from youth onwards," warned sanitarian and moral reformer Elizabeth Blackwell in 1878, echoing Comstock and earlier pro-censorship women. One of these circumstances, she felt, was the climate of "sensuality" in "vicious literature." As Blackwell saw it, this rampant sensuality tended "to encourage the lowest passions of human nature . . . [and] must produce hereditary as well as social effects on daughters as well as sons."[39] The women's moral reform and suffrage journal *Alpha* likewise praised Comstock for suppressing the "seeds of vice" and counteracting "the organized plans for the corruption of youth, by the circulation of indecent publications and other articles of the vilest nature among the boys and girls of this city, and of the whole country." Such women reformers saw Comstock's goal—the "suppression of vice"—as a worthy one, deserving support; freedom of expression was for them subordinate to the goal of protecting youth and communal morality.[40]

Even freethinkers shared Comstock's belief that the pernicious influence of "blood & thunder" literature, whether in dime novels or sporting newspapers, would corrupt the moral development of youth. "There is a kind of literature concerning the character and the tendency of which *all decent persons are agreed*," said liberal B. F. Underwood. "The circulation of this vile trash is, as it should be, prohibited by law." Obscenity was a crime against youth, agreed another freethinker, Francis Abbott, editor of the *Index*, sounding quite a lot like Comstock himself: "[Like libel] it is no less a crime to mail really obscene literature to school-children—a crime at once against the children, their parents, and society itself; and we therefore hold that to punish criminals of this disgusting class involves not the slightest violation of the freedom of the press." Some freethinkers abandoned their more radical counterparts, who had formed the National Defense Association (NDA) (to defend people like Ezra Heywood and Bennett from Comstockery), because the organization demanded repeal, rather than reform, of the Comstock law.[41] Yet even repealers in the NDA continued to support obscenity prosecution—for "truly vile" publishers—though they preferred this to take place through local and state statutes rather than federal postal law.

Freethinkers struggled to balance obscenity prosecution with free speech. Even with their efforts to repeal the Comstock law, in fact, only a small minority of radical libertarians fully opposed censorship. It was Ezra Heywood's conviction for obscenity that led some to embrace the free-speech position. As Heywood wrote from Dedham jail, "[The question is] whether the American people, themselves and for themselves, or Anthony Comstock, shall decide what books may be read; whether freedom of conscience, of speech, of the press, and of the mails ... are to be permanently suppressed." Increasingly, they understood Comstock's suppression campaign as part of a larger effort to introduce religion into the public sphere and proscribe scientific knowledge about human physiology. A very few reluctantly concluded that, given Comstock's inability to distinguish between reform literature and pornography, "obscenity" was too subjective a category to be enforceable. As freethinker Horace Seaver, editor of the *Boston Investigator*, put it, "better to have no laws that cannot be enforced except by the use of hypocrisy, fraud, and falsehood, for such remedy is worse than the disease it pretends to cure." Echoing Angela Heywood, he argued, "Law is of but little restraint, after all, in comparison with education and a correct public opinion."[42] Comstock's campaign to suppress sexuality discourse drove this few to embrace a radical free-speech position, despite their continued misgivings about sexualized imagery and sporting news.

Racializing Rape in Visual Journalism

As freethinkers took principled stands (and went to jail), Fox took the *Police Gazette* in a new direction. He adapted to Comstock's demands, seeking out new ways to illustrate sexual themes in ways that would attract an audience without triggering the censor. Against the backdrop of the Bennett and Heywood prosecutions, Fox did what successful media publishers often do—he innovated, dramatically altering the *Police Gazette*'s appearance and carving out a new niche for visual entertainment. A year after Comstock's intervention, Fox overhauled the paper's form and content and further skewed its visual coverage. In April 1878, in one of the last issues before the change, Fox justified the coming expansion to sixteen pages as resulting from "greatly increased demands upon our space, consequent upon an immensely extended circulation." He likely referred to his success in building readership through group subscriptions for clubs, barbershops, barrooms, and social organizations, pioneering methods to invest the reader in his paper, inviting their input, and publishing photographs sent by individuals and groups, all of which required publication space.[43] Pleasing his readers was Fox's central preoccupation in the years to follow.

On the eve of introducing his new format, Fox insisted that "accurate" crime news coverage would remain central to the *Police Gazette*. "Full and accurate reports of court proceedings and criminal intelligence generally," he promised, "written specifically for the *Gazette* by its correspondents in every section of the Union, with a variety of other news and reading matter of a lively and entertaining character, will always be found in its columns."[44] Further, Fox announced that his soon-to-be-revamped *Police Gazette* would uphold the highest journalistic standards for both reporting and illustration:

> All the striking criminal and sensational affairs of the day shall be accurately illustrated in its columns by a corps of artists of first-class talent, who will be detailed, as the occasion may demand, to sketch such events at the scene of their occurrence. Portraits, authentic only, of the principals in all such matters will also appear whenever circumstances are of sufficient interest in the general reader, to render their publication timely in a live, illustrated journal.[45]

Having artists sketch "events at the scene of their occurrence" was a respectable (and costly) goal, worthy of more expensive family weeklies and monthlies. In reality the *Police Gazette* continued to rely on interpretive illustration to sensationalize the news.

Indeed, it was impossible for Fox's artists to witness the distant news stories they illustrated, and it came as no surprise that the publisher's promise was immediately broken. While publishing "authentic" portraits (based on photographs), the *Police Gazette* continued to publish interpretive illustrations and reenactments of criminal scenarios, which were essential to the paper's business model. However, Fox introduced a new look to set the Police *Gazette* further apart from competitors: with smaller (tabloid-sized) dimensions, the more focused cover imagery and image-saturated pages seemed to make visual journalism even more central to the paper's brand. In the first issue that launched the new format, published on May 11, 1878, Fox again touted the skills of his

SHOOTING OF MOLLIE HICKEY, IN A BAGNIO, DEADWOOD, D. T.

FIGURE 1.10: "Shooting of Mollie Hickey," *The National Police Gazette*, May 18, 1878, 12. Reprinted with permission from ProQuest.

journalists—both writers and illustrators—promising that "readers may always rely upon the authenticity of its reports of events and the accuracy of its illustrations and portraits."[46]

Subsequent *Police Gazette* imagery, however, shows that accuracy was less important than artistry (and misdirection) in translating news stories into familiar and compelling visual narratives. A closer look at the relationship between news clips and their illustrations lays bare the paper's visual construction of meaning. Like the *Days' Doings*, the *Police Gazette* had always selectively revealed women's bodies according to class status, and this remained true after Comstock's intervention: women's bodies continued to be exposed, but with more exaggerated class distinctions; ankles and legs indicated women's moral standing and became recognizable visual markers in the paper's moral lexicon. For example, the exposed legs of a woman shot by a jealous lover in a house of prostitution in the Dakota Territory (fig. 1.10) signified her immorality and suggested that she may have deserved her fate. Similarly, the exposed legs of two Parisian actresses (and sisters), who allegedly committed suicide after being seduced and betrayed by the same man, conveyed a cautionary tale (fig. 1.11).[47] By contrast, the *Police Gazette* took extraordinary (sometimes ludicrous) pains

FIGURE 1.11: "A Parisian Romance," *The National Police Gazette*, May 18, 1878, 16. Reprinted with permission from ProQuest.

FIGURE 1.12: "A Tramp Horror," *The National Police Gazette*, May 18, 1878, 16. Reprinted with permission from ProQuest.

to ensure that middle-class women's bodies were shielded from view. As just one example, even the ankles and toes of a Mississippi planter's wife remained covered (in this poorly preserved image, fig. 1.12), even when fighting for her life against violent tramps.[48] The protection or exposure of women's bodies indicated their social worth; revealing images of prostitutes, foreign entertainers, and victims of racial crimes appeared in every issue, offering glimpses of female nudity otherwise off-limits in the *Police Gazette*'s postcensorship incarnation. Such class-based morality tales evaded the ban on sexual imagery.

When the *Police Gazette* illustrations did reveal "respectable" white women's bodies, they typically did so to convey a larger social message or a sense of outrage. The caption for a semi-nude drawing of a white Virginia schoolteacher identified her as the victim of a racial attack by "three Negresses" (fig. 1.13). The image implied sexual assault, even though her body was somewhat shielded from view; the caption did not explain why she was portrayed in a prone, semi-undressed, and vulnerable position. On a separate page, text reporting told a different story (based on rumors rather than trial testimony), blaming three African American women who were suspected of poisoning and robbing the woman. Later, local papers indicated that the woman had not been murdered at all; she died of natural causes.[49] The story is a good example of how the *Police Gazette*'s eagerness to insinuate sexual assault and racial violence distorted the news while providing readers with a titillating spectacle; corrections rarely appeared.

The *Police Gazette*'s most prominent sexualized illustrations, post-Comstock, were exaggerated—even mythic—representations of the black male rapist. In-

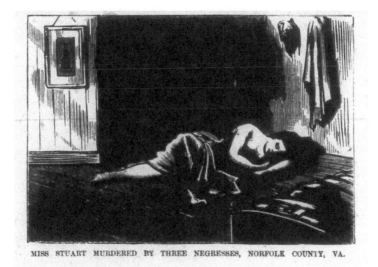

MISS STUART MURDERED BY THREE NEGRESSES, NORFOLK COUNTY, VA.

FIGURE 1.13: "Miss Stuart Murdered by Three Negresses," *The National Police Gazette*, May 18, 1878, 5. Reprinted with permission from ProQuest.

FIGURE 1.14: "The Ne-
gro Crime," *The National
Police Gazette*, May 21,
1878, 9. Reprinted with
permission from Pro-
Quest.

THE NEGRO CRIME—FIENDISH OUTRAGE OF A NEGRO RUFFIAN ON THE
WIFE OF WARREN MARTIN, NEAR BROOKLYN, IOWA.

terracial rape illustrations gave the paper a compact excuse to publish sexualized
imagery, with deniability provided by a moralizing caption or threat of extreme
punishment—the rape/lynching narrative. For example, in the May 25, 1878,
issue (shortly after the redesigned publication launched), an image captioned
"The Negro Crime" showed an alleged sexual assault and operated as justification for a subsequent lynching (fig. 1.14). The stylized image, its positioning
of the bodies, emphasized the helplessness of the young white woman in a
way that exaggerated her vulnerability and her attacker's physical power. The
image did not merely suggest physical assault but reenacted it, showing the
man grappling with his victim in a suggestive position. It was a scenario that
Comstock's intervention had all but erased from the paper when the (alleged)
attacker was white.[50]

BRUTAL OUTRAGE ON MISS CARRIE WAYNE, A RESPECTABLE YOUNG LADY OF ELLERBEE, ALA., BY WILLIS BROCK, A NEGRO PEDDLER, AND PUNISHMENT OF THE BLACK FIEND. —See Page 3.

FIGURE 1.15: "Brutal Outrage on Miss Carrie Wayne," *The National Police Gazette*, July 27, 1878, 8. Reprinted with permission from ProQuest.

It's highly unlikely that the *Police Gazette*'s interpretive rape illustrations were based on witnessed events (per Fox's promise), yet their imagery and captions nonetheless provided effective cover for the reported lynching (or other punishment) that followed. An image in the July 27, 1878, issue, "Brutal Outrage of Miss Carrie Wayne," again posed a mythic contrast between the whiteness of the young female victim and the darkness of the alleged rapist (fig. 1.15). The text described how the man was captured by the victim's brothers, tarred and feathered, and warned off from the town, but the *image* showed him tied to a tree with a bolt of lightning aimed at his lower body, a clear reference to castration. It's worth noting that this story, like the earlier one about the schoolteacher, came from a "special correspondent," but appears not to have spread more widely in the southern or national press. (In other words, it was likely based on a letter sent from an involved party rather than on a court case).[51] As in news stories about lynchings, the details of the rape in such images were typically drawn from post facto justifications for a lynching or other punishment but presented as if based on actual events.

The interracial rape images in the *Police Gazette* in the years following Comstock's intervention were all the more striking because so few other sexual scenarios remained in the paper after 1877. They were also visually arresting, presenting startling contrasts between adult black attackers and youthful white victims, which further exaggerated their mythic quality and reinforced a message of danger and brutality. Because they claimed to allow readers to *see* the crime in action, the repetition and increasing brutality of such interpretive illustrations created an indelible image of sexual assault by men of color as visible fact, all the more powerful because it was the *Police Gazette*'s primary representation of sexual assault to persist through the 1890s.[52]

By 1880, meanwhile, images of white rapists all but disappeared from the *Police Gazette*. It is not that news stories about white rapists declined; newspapers around the country continued to describe (in text) countless examples of sexual violence perpetrated by white social outcasts, such as desperadoes and tramps. Such reporting fueled the perception in courts and in popular culture that rape was an external danger, a threat to helpless women posed by invaders to the home, "ne'er-do-wells," or other strangers who took advantage of women in vulnerable situations.[53] Few such stories received illustration in the *Police Gazette*, however; in those that did, white women had little agency, appearing (as in the interracial rape images) exclusively as objects of desire or helpless victims of male lust, and increasingly as young girls. Those images that showed adult women being attacked celebrated their "plucky" resistance and the creative of methods they used to protect themselves (from frying pans to firearms) from alleged external threats.[54] As the paper's visual coverage of sexual assault declined through the 1880s, interpretive illustrations denoted rapists almost exclusively as strangers and racial others—designated by captions as "monsters," "brutes," and "fiends." They promoted a frontier justice conception of sexual assault as separate from women's social and familial relationships and requiring the administration of summary justice by men.

The *Police Gazette*'s growing reliance on this rape/lynching narrative as its central visualization of sexual violence soon crowded out even the cases of rape by "deviant" white men, a fact that becomes clearer in the stories the paper did *not* illustrate in the months following Comstock's intervention. As in other text-based newspapers, such stories were abundantly reported, but not illustrated, by the *Police Gazette*. A single (text) page in a post-redesign 1878 issue offered two scenarios that previously would have received illustration: two separate headlines, in very similar melodramatic language, announced brutal sexual assaults—rapes of two different white, "respectable women" by (white) tramps. Because these rapes were committed by "deviant" men, the *Police Gazette* condemned the acts and lamented that in both cases the perpetrators had escaped arrest. Both stories were lengthy, detailed, and vivid; neither received illustration. Prior to Comstock's intervention, striking interpretive illustrations would have accompanied such stories. Their absence confirms Fox's continued deference to the ban on the illustration of rapes by white men, leaving the *visual* impression that sexual violence was a racial (black on white) crime.[55]

One final innovation Fox introduced in 1878 may have helped reinforce the *Police Gazette*'s growing distinction in racialized illustration: the introduction of what became its signature pink newsprint. Fox had already begun to downplay racial markers for his Irish American subjects (and audience): his sports heroes, firefighters, entertainers, and everyday community members had fewer stereotypically "Irish" features than mainstream illustrated weeklies produced.[56] *Police Gazette* imagery was in fact notable because it portrayed the Irish much more respectfully than other illustrated publications did in this period.[57] Negative illustrations of the Irish were a staple in weekly newspapers and monthly magazines, which recycled earlier British iconography used to dismiss the Fenian and Land League movements. English humor magazines, such as *Punch*, typically conveyed the Irish man with brutish, ape-like facial features. Following the rise in Irish immigration to the United States in the 1850s, similar imagery, lightly softened, filtered into U.S. illustrated weeklies and monthly publications, including *Leslie's*, *Harper's*, *Puck*, and *Judge*. Perhaps the most famous is an illustration from *Harper's* (fig. 1.16) that casts working-class Irish and African American voters as equally "ignorant." The ink on the faces and their exaggerated physiognomies denoted racial difference, while other markers of clothing (lack of shoes, frayed garments) and bearing disparaged their poverty. Under Fox's editorship after 1878, the *Police Gazette* projected a more neutral Irish figure, while celebrating Irish heroes.[58] As the pink pages further diminished the racialization of Irish American subjects, the paper used darkness to convey danger and the presence of ink on the face (along with exaggerated facial features and stereotyped head shapes) to indicate racial otherness.

After Comstock's second intervention, consumers and readers of the *Police Gazette* continued to find some nudity and reenactments of sexual assaults, but in ways that reinforced class, race, and gender divisions. These images implied an honor code and celebrated white male chivalry in defense of white womanhood, confirming the summary justice ethos of popular entertainments and dime novels. Meanwhile, thanks to Comstock's regulation of social reformers, *factual* representations of bodies and physiological details about reproduction (and its regulation) disappeared from public view. While Comstock (and many reformers) sought to halt the "cheapening" or "vulgarization" of American print culture, he did not censor "lewdness" when the women's bodies were nonwhite or when rape illustrations stereotyped men of color as predators. Either such scenarios did not strike him as having a "tendency to deprave or corrupt," or they validated his other social priorities.

Post-Comstock, Fox was unapologetic about the *Police Gazette*'s imagery and deflected critics who continued to find it disreputable. First, he echoed

FIGURE 1.16: "The
Ignorant Vote: Honors
Are Easy," *Harper's
Weekly*, December 9,
1876, 985. Manuscripts
and Special Collections,
New York State Library.

Leslie's earlier defense that "we simply illustrate" the news of the day. "If there
are hideous pictures sometimes seen in our columns, it is not our fault," Fox
wrote. "The *Police Gazette* is a mirror, and we hold it up to human nature and
real life as it is to-day. If you do not like its reflections, reform yourselves and
change them. That's what's the matter."[59] Fox's bravado masked his willing-
ness to adapt further, as new cultural critics, and particularly women, gradually
joined the discussion about sensational media. In the two decades following
his relaunch of the *Police Gazette*, Fox came into conflict with activists who
used boycotts and other forms of economic pressure (rather than federal and
state laws) to suppress or at least shift the focus of the paper.[60] Over time Fox
gradually decreased crime news to focus on the "lively" illustrations that became
the paper's hallmark: coverage of sports, entertainment, and celebrity, which
attracted readers without drawing scrutiny or attacks from censors or activists.

Eventually, coverage of sports (which became the paper's signature focus) replaced most of the crime news, with theatrical reports, and specifically images of popular actresses in revealing costumes, ranking a close second. The paper thrived, thanks to what Elliot Gorn calls Fox's marketing "genius," combined with his recognition of the "public's growing appetite for amusement" and the rise of the saloons and their public, bachelor culture. As Fox became the dominant chronicler of prize fighting, he used the *Police Gazette* as a venue for news about reigning champions and emerging talent, with images of boxers increasingly infusing the paper's pages. These provided readers with a different kind of violence and delivered a new kind of scantily dressed body for public view. Images of handsome, half-naked men grappling with one another, often clinched in a tight embrace, became the *Police Gazette's* most recognizable visual feature from the 1880s through the early years of the twentieth century.[61] The paper's robust circulation and loyal following testify to the commercial wisdom of these innovations.

Capitulation combined with adaptation paid commercial dividends, while principled opposition to Comstock's strictures on free speech grounds came at a high price, as social liberals discovered. Ezra Heywood remained in prison until he received a pardon from President Hayes in 1878. D. M. Bennett was less fortunate. Again arrested in 1878, this time for selling a copy of Heywood's *Cupid's Yokes* at a free-love conference, Bennett applied for a pardon, but the political climate had shifted and his petition was denied. He served six months in jail and failed in his attempt to appeal his conviction. A year later, the U.S. Supreme Court validated Comstock's position that a marriage reform tract like *Cupid's Yokes* was just as corrupting as a pornographic book, and the ruling solidified the power of the Comstock Law to regulate public sexuality discourse. *U.S. v. Bennett* (1879) held that whether produced for educational or entertainment purposes, both kinds of publications could corrupt an audience. The decision, conforming to the *Hicklin* standard, said that any publication could be deemed obscene if any part of it, even taken out of context and regardless of the purpose for publication, had the "tendency to deprave or corrupt" any person who might come across it. In particular, it emphasized the dangers posed to the innocent, particularly children, who might encounter a publication without understanding its larger purpose.[62]

In these formative years of illustrated journalism, sporting papers embraced racialized sexual violence as one of the genre's regular features. Grotesque and mythic images of black men attacking white women became a reliable substitute for the earlier scenarios of (white) rape and seduction. In response to Comstock's attempts to control specific forms of popular representation, sporting publishers adapted their interpretive illustrations and in the process established visual conventions that went uncensored because they conformed to the period's racialized stereotypes. Sporting "news" illustrations erased (with a few exceptions) white male rape, denied white female sexuality, ignored violence against black women, and exaggerated the threat of criminal sexuality perpetrated by men of color. Even as the ideal of disinterested, scientific knowledge of sexuality lost in court and in public opinion, highly distorted representations of sexual behaviors infused public culture. Young people found access to sexual knowledge, as before, but many now learned their lessons from the racialized and class-skewed images they found in sporting news. As chapter 2 reveals, in the 1880s this kind of visualization merged with the *Notional Police Gazette*'s anti-Chinese agitation.

CHAPTER 2

"Language More Effective than Words"

Opium Den Illustrations and Anti-Chinese Violence in the 1880s

ONE *POLICE GAZETTE* NARRATIVE of sexual danger to survive Comstock's intervention[1] was the Chinese opium den. In the early to mid-1880s, the paper's interpretive illustrations of opium dens combined several popular themes— crime, of course, but also "sporting" news, theater, celebrities, urban vices, and thrill seeking—in a single, sexually charged image. Posing as a cautionary tale, opium den images bypassed the ban on sexual scenarios. They also addressed new constituencies: Irish immigrants in northeastern cities and more recent European immigrants in the Pacific and Mountain West. Political division and economic hardship fueled anti-Chinese agitation and exclusionary legislation in this period, but sensational imagery amplified the perception of crisis. The *Police Gazette* claimed that most of its anti-Chinese drawings were based on real events and court cases, yet as the 1880s progressed, they diverged from actual news stories. This was particularly true of opium den imagery, a stereotype that exaggerated a dubious story of sexual danger and, through repeated visual reenactment, made alleged sexual assaults seem real.

Confronted with exaggerated political rhetoric and negative stereotypes, Chinese American leaders responded with diplomacy, legal action, and popular culture. Notable among these was Wong Chin Foo, a journalist who launched a series of public appearances, newspaper articles, cultural interventions, and civic actions to counter anti-Chinese agitation. Wong had the right background for the task. Born in China and educated by U.S. missionaries, he had by 1880 earned a reputation as lecturer and journalist. He published articles with positive messages about Chinese history and culture in a variety of mainstream (English-language) publications. By 1877 he was sufficiently famous that *Harper's Weekly* reported on a lecture he had given, combined with a portrait, highlighting both his ethnic difference and his satirical tone (fig. 2.1). In 1882

FIGURE 2.1: "Wong Chin Foo," *Harper's Weekly*, May 26, 1877, 405.
Manuscripts and Special Collections, New York State Library.

he published a short-lived Chinese-language newspaper, *Mei Hua Xin Bao* (the *Chinese American*), New York City's first weekly serving the Chinese.[2] A gifted speaker and writer, Wong used available media tools to counter stereotypes, educate white Americans, and foster community among Chinese migrants.

Wong's positive counternarrative sought to challenge political agitation for Chinese exclusion, a cause that the *Police Gazette* wholeheartedly endorsed. Despite (or perhaps because of) its unsavory reputation, the *Police Gazette* boasted a robust circulation and claimed a readership of up to half a million.[3] As discussed in chapter 1, imagery was far more extreme than that found in the period's more genteel, family-based pictorial weeklies, such as *Frank Leslie's Illustrated Newspaper* and *Harper's Weekly*, which communicated a more muted visual message to a different audience; though steeped in stereotypes, their coverage was less sensational. *Leslie's* published some crime illustrations, but these were a small subset of news images, topical portraits, and majestic landscapes; *Harper's* consciously published imagery to inspire and enlighten its readers, making it even less inclined to illustrate sordid news stories. The *Daily Graphic*, while innovative in its daily production of illustrations, also avoided salacious news imagery. Consequently, the *Police Gazette* had a near-monopoly on illustrating sexual crime.

Visualizing the Chinese

Police Gazette images of the Chinese opium den gave cultural cover to the exclusion movement in the 1880s and a wave of violent outbreaks against Chinese workers throughout the Western states. Its interpretive illustrations of opium dens, in their very consistency and repetition, were effective propaganda; they pandered to readers' racism and nativism, using sensationalism's power to distort events for political effect. Opium den imagery erased any hint of Chinese migrants' economic and social lives as the nation expanded westward. Through a diverse range of occupations from railways to mining, along with their growing dominance in the "tertiary" employment sectors—laundry, cooking, personal service, and more—Chinese migrants played a significant role in the growing U.S. economy.[4] Needless to say, none of these positive contributions made it into the pages of the *Police Gazette*. The paper's preoccupation with opium den imagery as the dominant visual narrative of the Chinese in the mid-1880s may help explain why nativists and workers targeted the Chinese, of all immigrant groups competing for jobs, for violent expulsion. While scholars of Asian American history typically characterize such imagery as little more than background cultural noise to anti-Chinese agitation, the short-lived "opium den rapist" stereotyped Chinese migrants in a way that muted opposition to exclusion.[5]

The *Police Gazette*'s opium-den scare combined animosity for the Chinese within the Irish community in New York City with western Workingmen's Party campaign rhetoric that "the Chinese must go!" The connection between two very different local contexts helped Democrats to compete for votes in a series of elections in the 1880s. In New York, Irish and Chinese immigrants lived in close proximity to one another in the overlapping Five Points and Chinatown districts of Lower Manhattan; they also competed for similar jobs. In the Pacific and Mountain West, the Chinese competed with European migrants for mining work. Commentators blamed the Chinese for the rise in opium smoking, an ironic twist given the role of Western imperial powers (especially the British) in accelerating opium use in China. Chinese workers brought the practice of opium smoking with them to the United States, at first in small settings for their own community members. By the 1870s, wealthy and bohemian (non-Chinese) urban residents had begun to experiment with opium, visiting Chinatown to be instructed in smoking the drug. Once wealthier users established their own opium "palaces" in white neighborhoods, Irish residents began to visit the nearby Chinatown dens, which led community leaders to view the Chinese as villains.[6] The Irish in New York were also subject to negative stereotyping, of course (see fig. 1.16), but opium den iconography made it easy to scapegoat their new competitors: the Chinese.

Anti-Chinese agitation wasn't new in the early 1880s—it had mobilized voters in the Pacific and Mountain West for more than a decade. Violent outbreaks against Chinese workers had been an occasional feature of life in the west since a Los Angeles massacre in 1871, which left nineteen Chinese dead. Sporadic outbreaks of violence against the Chinese typically erupted in the context of local political organizing (for example, rioting in San Francisco in 1877; the 1880 Denver lynching of a Chinese launderer), as the Democratic and Workingmen's Parties used anti-Chinese propaganda as a strategy to compete for votes in close elections.[7] On the federal level, workers engaged in "political orientalism" in anti-Chinese campaigns that resulted in the 1875 Page Law, which prohibited most Chinese women from coming to America[8] and gave momentum to the push for a federal law for complete exclusion of the Chinese. In the 1870s a few states passed legislation that defined the Chinese as racially deviant, and municipalities enacted a host of discriminatory local ordinances.[9]

During this early phase of anti-Chinese agitation, *Police Gazette* illustrations of Chinese men emphasized *otherness*—in appearance, religious practices, and living standards—reinforcing the perception that the Chinese were not capable of assimilation.[10] Early images Orientalized the Chinese as un-Christian "heathens" with peculiar customs, vices, and outlandish behaviors. Dead cats, chickens, and other animals provided visual evidence of the "barbaric" nature of Chinese legal and cultural traditions. Some images also highlighted disease, particularly leprosy, yellow fever, and other exotic maladies.[11] Many emphasized the "queue"—the long, braided ponytail that symbolized Chinese men's loyalty to the Emperor—as an easily recognizable marker of difference. One typical image showed a group of Irish laundrywomen, direct competitors of the Chinese launderers in many cities, in the process of stringing up a Chinese man in a tree by his queue, a kind of mock-lynching. The cumulative message in these early visual narratives echoed the more sophisticated lithographs of the monthly San Francisco satirical paper, *The Wasp*, and other comparable anti-Chinese propaganda; they portrayed an alien, immoral, at times subhuman, but not physically threatening, Chinese man.[12]

By 1880, *Police Gazette* imagery of the Chinese had evolved from using dehumanizing stereotypes to emphasizing a theme of sexual encroachment. The paper began by producing a number of recurring stereotypes, such as the seductive "agreeable servant" or "favorite doctor," which played on (and to some extent ridiculed) fears of sexual competition, and challenged white male viewers to defend the domestic sphere from Chinese seducers. Echoing claims of anti-Chinese activists like Denis Kearney and his California Workingmen's Party, these images emphasized Chinese servants' sexual access to upper-class white women in the home. *Police Gazette* editor Richard K. Fox was no supporter of Kearney's, whom he derided as a "communist";[13] nor did he champion the

FIGURE 2.2: "The Chinese Must Go," *The National Police Gazette*, January 18, 1879, 1. Library of Congress.

rights of miners or laborers to a fair wage or workplace safety. Nonetheless, Fox's images amplified Kearney's exclusionary rhetoric and style. They were allies of convenience when it came to the Chinese.

"The Chinese Must Go," a Workingmen's Party slogan, captioned an image on the cover of the January 18, 1879, issue of the *Police Gazette*. The image depicted a husband observing his wife being dressed by her "overly attentive" male Chinese servant (fig. 2.2). Although an editorial cartoon, the drawing was indistinguishable from the paper's news illustrations. An editorial (on another page) warned of the sexual danger posed by Chinese men:

Custom has taught [white women] to look upon the docile, stolid, apparently stupid Oriental as a harmless, sexless creature, altogether different from other male human beings, and they become entirely unconscious of the neglect of the proprieties in the functions thus assigned them. The husband or father, however, is apt to regard the matter in another view altogether. He is inclined to see the "Heathen" a man, much beneath the Caucasian, to be sure, but still a man with a man's failings, and to consider his employment in such a capacity by his wife or daughters as a very reprehensive laxity.[14]

Text and image aligned to urge the paper's white, male readers to reassert their authority over the domestic sphere, where Chinese men were encroaching. The image was equivocal; though the insert showed the husband forcibly evicting the Chinese servant, the woman's face registered pleasure rather than disgust, suggesting her vulnerability to seduction.

News illustrations in the *Police Gazette* in this early phase reinforced a similar anti-Chinese theme, exhorting viewers to discourage and denounce consensual, loving intimacy and other kinds of associations between races. "They Must Go," insisted a caption for an 1880 image depicting an interracial couple courting on a front stoop in New York. The image accompanied a "news" story about how the embrace of a Chinese man and a young Irish woman was interrupted by buckets of water poured upon the couple by her parents (fig. 2.3). Such scenes of voluntary relationships between white women and Chinese men seemed to exhort anti-Chinese action as paternal duty. Image and text exaggerated the Chinese man's racial and linguistic difference, while the shower of cold water discouraged interracial social mixing.[15] The image made no reference to the local context of Irish and Chinese immigrants competing for jobs and housing in New York, or emerging narratives of urban vice. Instead, it asserted a more generic prohibition on interracial relationships.

Editorial cartoons and news illustrations in the *Police Gazette* both acknowledged and derided cross-racial desire while instructing readers on the proper, "manly" response. News illustrations of other kinds of white women's relationships with Chinese men—whether as patients of Chinese doctors, as teachers, or as missionaries—conveyed similar messages and typically bore little resemblance to the "news" they claimed to illustrate. One composite image (fig. 2.4) recycled the warning that wealthier women with Chinese doctors and servants might be vulnerable to seduction. The image embellished details from text on another page that recounted an entirely different news story about the "shrewdness" of Chinese servants who left messages for one another in Chinese characters on kitchen cupboards and sinks—to warn against cruel employers or to deter replacement workers. For good measure, the image did include a few sample messages (in Chinese characters) but otherwise radiated sexual innuendo, as

A MOON-EYED HEATHEN WHILE COURTING AN "ILISH GLAL," ON THE
FRONT STOOP HAS HIS ARDOR DAMPENED BY THE "OULD FOLKS";
NEW YORK.—SEE PAGE 7.

FIGURE 2.3: "A Moon-Eyed Heathen," *The National Police Gazette*, November 6, 1880, 8. Library of Congress.

wealthy white women succumbed to the attentions of Chinese servants and doctors. Only the young Irish woman in the upper left-hand image achieved a "victory" by (again) pouring water over the Chinese "masher." Starkly racialized features mocked and stereotyped the Chinese: the caption, in pidgin English, hinted that he had forgotten his place. This and other news images of debauching Chinese diplomats or a young woman who paid off her laundry bill in kisses to the Chinese laundryman conceded the reality of interracial interactions but left the women's roles unclear. Editorial commentary was typically more straightforward, urging (male) readers to take active steps to discourage Chinese sexual competition.[16] The new focus of such images added a psychosexual impetus to earlier anti-Chinese stereotypes, which (not coincidentally) echoed similar visual stereotypes used against African American men.

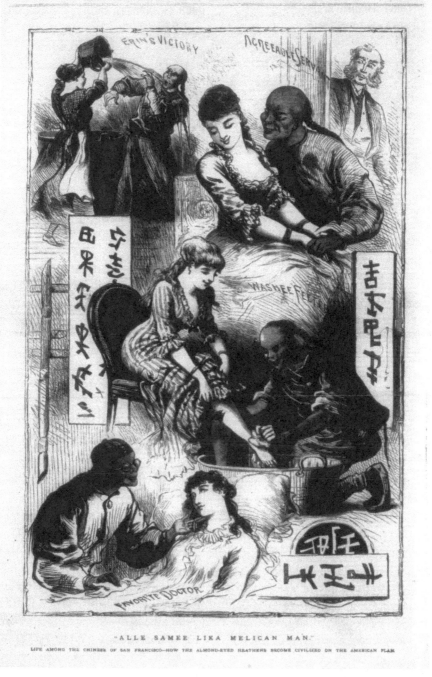

FIGURE 2.4: "Alla Samee Lika Melican Man," *The National Police Gazette*, June 4, 1881, 16. Library of Congress.

"Nameless Crimes"—Representing the Chinese Man as Sexual Predator

Emerging in the early 1880s, the *Police Gazette*'s opium den imagery encapsulated a number of interrelated social anxieties about opium use and the Chinese. One was a longstanding narrative of urban vice and danger for hapless youths that dated back to the growth of cities in the antebellum period. A second was a growing concern over opium addiction, as doctors began to understand and warn of the drug's debilitating effects and users' inability to get free of it. Women were thought to be particularly susceptible to addiction due to their perceived "weakness" as well as the availability of many quasi-medical nostrums and "tonics" for women that were derived from opium. Few blamed American apothecaries or physicians for the abuse of such "medicines." Other concerns related to women's newfound ability in urban settings to associate with men without supervision. In the American West, fears about opium use built upon on the larger issue of Chinese competition for dwindling jobs in the railroad and mining sectors and long-standing animosities toward nonwhite men. Although few Chinese lived on the East Coast, what made the opium den scenario so potent was its concise equation of urban Chinatown with sexual danger, alongside its denial of white women's agency in seeking out Chinese men.[17]

By 1880 the prevalence of opium smoking (or perhaps the fashion of slumming in opium dens) in northern cities provided the context for the *Police Gazette* to present the opium den as a sensational urban threat. At first, such representations emphasized moral rather than sexual danger, just one more vice in sporting news coverage of urban life. In 1880, for example, the paper

GABE FOSTER'S OPIUM DEN—THE PLACE WHERE THE LOVERS OF THE DEADLY DRUG—"HIT THE PIPE"—THE VICES OF SAN FRANCISCO TRANSPLANTED TO THE FERTILE SOIL OF CHICAGO—INTERIOR OF THE DEN AS IT APPEARS DURING A GOOD TRADE.—[SKETCHED BY SPECIAL GAZETTE ARTISTS.—SEE PAGE 7.

FIGURE 2.5: "Gabe Foster's Opium Den," *The National Police Gazette*, April 3, 1880, 7. Library of Congress.

FIGURE 2.6: "Slaves to a Deadly Infatuation," *The National Police Gazette*, August 20, 1881, 16. Library of Congress.

described Gabe Foster's den in Chicago as a "den of infamy [that] is the refuge for all thieves and bunko steerers" and a place "where the worst class of men and women mingle" (fig. 2.5). Racial mixing did not figure in the image. The postures of the women (identified as actresses) and their male companion indicated the influence of opium, but the women were not portrayed as being in sexual danger. The only Chinese man present appeared to be a deferential servant, a facilitator of vice, but not a predator. Similarly, in 1881, another opium den image depicted bodies of drugged "actresses" (again) near—but in a separate frame from—an adjacent image of two Chinese smokers at the "Opium Palace" (fig. 2.6).[18] Such images linked the Chinese opium den to bohemianism, drug addiction, and the moral degradation of white patrons (including women) but did not implicate the Chinese as sexually dangerous.

More respectable pictorial weeklies in this period barely discussed domestic opium use, perhaps seeing the phenomenon as unsuitable for the middle-class home or audience. *Harper's Weekly*, for example, visualized opium use as a foreign curiosity in pieces that promised to edify Americans about exotic practices. One such image, "Opium Smoking in China," represented the opium den as a sordid but foreign space. It claimed to be "a faithful representation of one of those horrible dens where the Asiatic bewilders his intellect, and eventually destroys both body and mind, by the practice of smoking opium." Another, while closer to home, used travelogue style imagery for an opium den in New York's Chinatown (fig. 2.7). The central image focused on a number of unconscious men on flat wooden bunks, while satellite images revealed the establishment's front rooms, with decorative embellishments of poppy flowers and seed pods that seemed to make light of the threat of addiction. In what was perhaps a dual message for "sporting" male readers, however, the text also provided detailed instructions about the equipment and technique required for opium smoking.[19] Neither *Harper's* article emphasized the presence of women as opium smokers.

Prior to 1883, newspapers in the Pacific and Mountain West were unlikely to comment on opium use by white women. They highlighted instead what they called Chinatown's "loathsome" qualities (vice, disease) and the negative impact of opium use on "American" men (which effectively meant "white" men—as many were in fact European noncitizens). Only a few text reports noted that "our people" were visiting the opium dens, which had the power to degrade visitors. One journalist in Red Bluff, California, noted that the Chinese were engaging in the "buying and selling of women" as (the story explained) they had done in China, but the report hastened to reassure readers that the women were Chinese and not American. In 1881, a California paper referenced an assault on a fifteen-year old girl in New York City who alleged that she had been lured into an opium den and was expected to die as a result. Such stories were extremely rare before 1883. Instead, western papers tended to mock the "worthies"—white

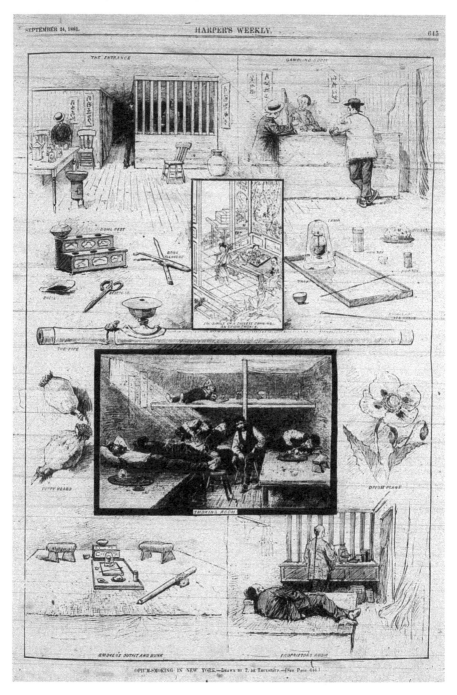

FIGURE 2.7: "Opium Smoking in New York," *Harper's Weekly*, September 24, 1881, 645. Manuscripts and Special Collections, New York State Library.

men who visited the dens and smoked opium with the Chinese—as deviant and destined for jail. Some hinted at, but did not make explicit, fears that the homoerotic environment in the dens posed a danger to young men. None of these stories included illustration, and with these few exceptions allusions to rape were virtually nonexistent.[20]

Such negative depictions of Chinese men, combined with accusations that they were stealing white men's jobs and fostering diseases, supported passage of the Exclusion Act of 1882, which stipulated that no Chinese laborers could enter the United States for ten years. Legislative victory did not appease anti-Chinese agitators, however; if anything, after the bill's passage anti-Chinese agitation increased. In fact, the law's passage emboldened efforts to push aggressively, and ever more violently, for complete Chinese exclusion.[21] In response, the Chinese used the court system to fight back against local ordinances and federal statutes, with some success.[22] Their resistance to exclusion and restriction perhaps helps explain the *Police Gazette*'s eager adoption of a more salacious (and questionable) anti-Chinese image.

Headlines—and later images—about a court case unfolding in New York in May 1883 introduced the new stereotype of the Chinese rapist, which resonated both locally and nationally. Daily papers, not yet illustrated, resorted to headlines and inflammatory phrasing to hawk the story. The most sensational daily at that time was James Gordon Bennett Jr.'s *New York Herald*. On May 10 the *Herald* ran "Horrors of the Opium Dens" on its first news page (page three of the paper, following two pages of advertisements). Reporting the trial news almost verbatim, the story quoted extensively from Father James Barry of the Young Men's Association of Mott Street's Catholic Church, who accused the Chinese of using opium candy to entice young girls to their (sexual) "ruin." The unsubstantiated claims, widely denounced in mainstream newspapers, had already resulted in violence as neighboring Irish Americans retaliated by smashing the windows of Chinese laundries. While other publications debunked the story as false or exaggerated, the *Herald* doubled down the next day, featuring the story on its main news page under the heading "The Opium Infamy," and ran a less prominent third story a day later under the headline "Rooting Out the Evil."[23] A would-be competitor in the field of sensational daily news, the *New York World*, also ran a story headlined "In the Opium Dens" on page 1, the day before Joseph Pulitzer took over as owner and editor; once under his control, the paper downplayed the story.[24] Less sensational dailies reported on the outcry and blamed it on politics or ethnic tensions; the *New York Times*, for example, no friend to the Irish Catholic residents near Mott Street, accused them of inventing the "monstrous charges" against the Chinese. "There is," wrote a *Times* editorial, "... an evident desire on the part of certain enemies of the Chinese to seize the present opportunity to provoke an Irish crusade" against their Chinese neighbors.[25]

Family-based illustrated publications struggled to find suitable visual language for the opium den story. The *Daily Graphic* discounted the opium candy story as a complete fabrication. This was not because the paper was entirely sympathetic to Chinese migrants; in fact, just a week before the story broke, the paper had published a composite cartoon drawing of a Chinese policeman drinking in uniform, abusing workers, and taking bribes at a gambling den—albeit with an opium parlor sketched in the back room (fig. 2.8).[26] But the *Daily Graphic* saw no truth in (and did *not* illustrate) the opium seduction story, writing in an editorial, "Looks as if the outcry against the Chinese had been gotten up to gratify a prejudice." On another page in the same issue, a reporter ventured into Chinatown and summarized an interview with Wong Chin Foo at his offices of the *Chinese-American*: "He said the sweeping charges made by Father Barry's literary society were not only unjust but atrocious, for the reason that one and all of his countrymen were placed under the same ban. There are some 8,000 or 10,000 Chinamen in this city, but let Father Barry take a trip to our charitable institutions or go to the Police Courts and find out how many more of his own race he will encounter there than Chinamen."[27] In this, the *Daily Graphic* did what few other papers did: it gave a community spokesman the opportunity to comment, and it highlighted the opium use of white patrons. It did not sensationalize the opium candy story and provided no visual commentary to accompany either news or editorial.

Frank Leslie's Illustrated Newspaper tried to have it both ways, illustrating the news story while expressing skepticism at the same time. Its first attempt to visualize the story clearly implied sexual danger for young women in an opium den, but the accompanying text to some extent discounted that visual message. The cover image (fig. 2.9), widely visible on newsstands, showed the inside of an opium den, with young women smoking opium, splayed out and incapacitated on bunks in a dark room, and a Chinese man carrying a tray. The caption read "A Growing Metropolitan Evil—Scene in an Opium Den, in Pell Street, Frequented by Working Girls." On a separate page, the artist recounted a local police officer's opinion that many local girls were now visiting these dens (the "richly-dressed" ladies of a few years back "do their [opium] smoking up-town nowadays"). Taken by the officer to see an actual "den," the artist claimed that his drawing was based on sketches he made at the site.[28]

A week later, *Leslie's* published a less ambiguous image, a detailed composite that was part news illustration and part editorial cartoon. It combined older travelogue-style visualizations of opium paraphernalia with sinister portrayals of the neighborhood in question that showed sneaky men keeping watch for the authorities, using Chinese characters to convey secrets in plain sight. The central image of a young (white) woman in the grip of two Chinese men (fig. 2.10) provided an unambiguous tableau; the men's faces were unsympathetic,

FIGURE 2.8: "Our Chinamen," *Daily Graphic*, May 3, 1883, 1. New York State Library.

FRANK LESLIE'S ILLUSTRATED NEWSPAPER

No. 1,442.—Vol. LVI.]   NEW YORK—FOR THE WEEK ENDING MAY 12, 1883.   [Price, 10 Cents.

A GROWING METROPOLITAN EVIL.—SCENE IN AN OPIUM DEN, IN PELL STREET, FREQUENTED BY WORKING-GIRLS.
From Sketches by C. Upham.—See Page 195.

FIGURE 2.9: "A Growing Metropolitan Evil," *Frank Leslie's Illustrated Newspaper*, May 12, 1883, 181. Manuscripts and Special Collections, New York State Library.

NEW YORK CITY.—THE OPIUM DENS IN PELL AND MOTT STREETS—HOW THE OPIUM HABIT IS DEVELOPED.
FROM SKETCHES BY FRANK YEAGER.—SEE PAGE 206.

FIGURE 2.10: "New York City—The Opium Dens," *Frank Leslie's Illustrated Newspaper*, May 19, 1883, 204. Manuscripts and Special Collections, New York State Library.

even hard, while she appeared to struggle in their grasp. Although the text suggested that she was merely "crazed by opium," a characterization that might identify the men as "helpers," visually the postures suggested an intent to assault. This time *Leslie's* text page was unequivocal: "These revelations have awakened a feeling of indignation which will not be appeased until the authorities have completely suppressed these dens of infamy. Our illustration presents some of the scenes that attend this most demoralizing traffic."[29]

Predictably, the *Police Gazette* was the least scrupulous about illustrating the opium den allegations as fact. It, too, provided a full-page composite drawing that combined seemingly realistic portraits of the alleged culprits with interpretive illustration (fig. 2.11) to visualize allegations that the Chinese were giving out opium candy to entice young children to "ruin" into the dens. In a series of frames, the *Police Gazette's* image reenacted the accusations; they showed Chinese men and women luring the children into a dark, underground den; a central image showed a drugged girl prone on a bed, vulnerable to sexual attack. The *Police Gazette's* editorial text, on another page, referred to a recent crackdown on opium joints that unearthed "many young and pretty working girls." The portrait images of the alleged perpetrators, with names, lent a sense of realism to the interpretive illustrations on the same page. By portraying the (white) women as innocent children and exaggerating the racial otherness of the alleged den keepers, the *Police Gazette* represented the opium den as a new locus of racialized crime.[30]

This representation of opium dens as sites of sexual danger contradicted descriptions found in less sensational newspapers. In one New York case, described in the *New York Times*, opium den proprietors were simply described as a Chinese man and his white (Welsh) wife; their patrons were three white women (possibly prostitutes), six white men, and six Chinese men, mostly "laundrymen." There was no indication of sexual coercion by the Chinese. The *Times* also noted the presence of dens for white patrons (run by white operators) in wealthy neighborhoods. For example, in one lavish Philadelphia opium palace for wealthy women, men were excluded, and the proprietor (a white American woman of "genteel" appearance) had established an opulent refuge for smokers, some of whom were famous actresses who wished to indulge their habit in a social yet private setting.[31] The reality that opium use had become a widespread phenomenon, in other words, transcending any single neighborhood or kind of user, did not figure in the pages of the *Police Gazette*.

The *Police Gazette's* opium dens blurred distinctions between editorial cartoons and news illustration in a way that provided emotional grounds to critique reformers, particularly women, thought to be soft on Chinese exclusion. An 1884 cover editorial cartoon seemed to illustrate a "news" story of kidnapping and enslavement to opium (fig. 2.12). The caption warned that "fair victims are

THE MONGOLIAN CURSE.

BLIGHTING EFFECTS OF THE INTRODUCTION OF A DEBASING CELESTIAL HABIT AMONG THE YOUNG GIRLS OF NEW YORK—SCENES IN AND AROUND THE CHINESE OPIUM JOINTS IN MOTT STREET.

FIGURE 2.11: "The Mongolian Curse," *The National Police Gazette*, June 6, 1883, 9. Library of Congress.

FIGURE 2.12: "In the Grip of Fiends," *The National Police Gazette*, August 9, 1884, 1. Library of Congress.

lured and dragged into the Chinese opium dens of New York, to dream away their lives and wreck both health and honor in the hands of barbarian wretched [*sic*]." Editorial text painted a grim picture of the opium den scene:

> While busybodies are moving heaven and earth to prevent even the legitimate traffic in rum, they seem to have passed by with only a cursory glance the greater evil of opium.... [In the opium dens are found] young women—rich young women, of good society, too—laid out on shelves under the influence of the insidious pipe—merchants, brokers, artists, writers, men of worth and brain, all deep in the stupor of the drug, and all mingled in utter disregard of modesty or social barriers. Over this scene presides a bestial Chinaman, who makes a rich income from the vice of these young women and men, who should be an honor to their land, but who are doomed to dream away their useless lives in rosy visions that speedily end in the embrace of the grim skeleton, Death. *Nameless crimes are quoted against the heathen keepers of these opium dens, including the ruin of young women in scores.*[32]

The first line's dig at anti-saloon activists hints at the political nature of opium den hysteria (and its appeal to a barroom readership). More important, the presentation—as if they were facts—of claims that the Chinese were sexual predators, determined to rape and ruin young white women, encouraged anti-Chinese political agitation and violence.

This new, sensationalized version of the opium den narrative filtered from the East Coast cities to the Pacific and Mountain West in two ways. First, the *Police Gazette* itself was a favorite barroom and barbershop paper, distributed by railroad, throughout the nation. Second, western papers circulated wire service briefs covering opium den stories from eastern cities, sometimes with additional editorial commentary. After the New York story came out, for example, the *Sacramento Daily Record-Union* began to publish editorials and articles describing such cases throughout the country. One suggested that the Chinese in New York City were "much bolder in their vices than those of the race in California" who had a "wholesome fear of consequences." Other papers published wire squibs that emphasized the presence of women in opium dens in Boston, Chicago, Philadelphia, and Baltimore in the months following the Mott Street scare. "In all these eastern cities," said the *Los Angeles Daily Herald*, "there is the same story to learn. Young girls learning to smoke opium in these dens of diabolical heathen vice; young men 'hitting the pipe' and lured to the fascinating pastime of fan-tan [a form of gambling], and other appurtenances of Oriental civilization." East Coast opium den stories even figured in the San Francisco Board of Supervisors' 1885 report highlighting the debilitating effects of opium use on Chinese men, who then corrupted white women.[33] In this way eastern "news" about opium abuse and urban vice combined with the western anti-Chinese movement—with the opium den as the central rationale for complete exclusion.

Sensationalism and Anti-Chinese Violence

In the months following the Mott Street incident, Wong Chin Foo took steps to counter sensational accusations against Chinese men. Wong recognized the opium den's power as anti-Chinese propaganda; as he saw it, the opium den rape accusation was "a thing too serious, too cruel, too relentless to be endured without being met by some action by those who are innocent." His first approach to the accusation was to tackle actual vice within Chinatown. Risking his own safety, he and other Chinese American community activists and the police sought to shut down opium dens and gambling halls. Dressed as "ordinary workmen," missionary Huie Kin in New York and his associates, for example, worked with Anthony Comstock's anti-vice organization, infiltrating gambling houses and then using the information to generate police raids. When they found only a single opium den, however, whose owner was not even Chinese, Wong began to suspect that sensational newspapers had invented the opium den to inflame Irish passions against the Chinese.[34]

Wong began a campaign of educational and cultural initiatives to improve perceptions and empower Chinese migrants. For example, Wong held a meeting for fifty naturalized Chinese men in the area and undertook a series of public activities designed to improve understanding of China and its people: a Chinese theater group, a Chinese language school, a legal apprenticeship (leading to his assisting in several trials), and dozens of articles in the daily and weekly press. Wong also recognized, however, the dilemma the Chinese faced: like African Americans, they were vilified by Democrats—in fact, demonizing both groups was a mobilizing tool for the Democratic Party in the 1880s—but were practically invisible to Republicans because they lacked voting power. Both parties supported some form of Chinese exclusion. Wong's response in political and cultural activism stood in contrast to China's minister to the United States, Zheng Zaoru, who admonished the Chinese to stay out of trouble and remain invisible: "Don't smoke opium, don't quarrel, don't litigate, and don't go into politics," he said. Wong clearly decided to disregard Zheng's advice.[35]

By summer 1885, Wong's campaign took on new urgency with sensational associations of the opium den with Chinese men. For example, the *Police Gazette*'s editor used the opium den trope in a news story and illustrations, depicting white women missionaries dancing with Chinese workers at an annual picnic in New York as "disgusting and abominable:"

This petting of lustful, leprous, opium-smoking, child-seducing, air-polluting, blood-poisoning Canton and Hong-Kong coolies by American women must be ended fiercely and sharply by American men. Otherwise, to the cynical and ribald gaze of Europe and Asia we shall have to meekly expose ourselves as the one other race of men in this wide world who are willing to share with the dastard and despicable Sandwich Islander this hideous reproach: *That the vile and ineffably abominable lepers of China covet our women, and that we stand by and smile complacently on their loathsome familiarities.* DO WE?[36]

It was a short step from such rhetoric to advocacy of violence against the Chinese. Just a few weeks later, the paper made this explicit in a drawing of a Chinese "masher" accosting a "white" working girl on a city street (fig 2.13). "What We Have Come To," quipped the caption below the picture; "The Chinese Coolie Thinks He Is the Brooklyn White Girl's Equal and Tries to Mash Her." Once again, this interpretive illustration blurred the line between news image and editorial cartoon, while editorial text overtly linked the alleged "mashing" to the mythic opium den rapist: "There is hardly a Chinese laundry in town which is not, at one time or another, the scene of an outrage on American white girlhood committed by a yellow and leprous Chinee [sic]," the editor wrote. An adjacent image (fig. 2.14) showing five African American men with nooses around their necks, just before they were lynched by a mob, offered a visual cue that extreme violence was a legitimate response to the Chinese "problem."[37]

The *Police Gazette*'s suggestion of violence was prescient, as two months later violence erupted in the Rock Springs massacre, in which white miners murdered many of the town's Chinese and expelled the rest, touching off violent reverberations throughout the Mountain and Pacific West. Severe economic hardship was widespread in mining regions in the mid-1880s, a fact that perhaps explains some of the anti-Chinese feeling at Rock Springs.[38] An economic depression, beginning in 1882, and related financial crises in 1883 and 1884 heightened tensions among workers. Overproduction had resulted in layoffs and rising unemployment, particularly in the railroad and mining sectors, creating fierce competition among workers for scarce jobs and stranding jobless men in remote communities with few prospects for other work. American and European (white) workers accused mining companies of deliberately hiring Chinese laborers as strikebreakers and, in some cases (including Rock Springs, Wyoming), as primary labor force, to break the unions. During the winter of 1884–85, Wyoming miners had successfully organized trade assemblies to counter pay cuts, winning a victory in wages over the Union Pacific mining company.[39] Their demand that the company fire "all Finlanders and Chinese," however, was set aside (the Finns, like the Chinese, Italians, and Mormons, were reputed to break strikes and to resist unionization). Throughout, the min-

FIGURE 2.13: "A Wholesale Lynching," *The National Police Gazette*, July 4, 1885, 4. Library of Congress.

FIGURE 2.14: "What We Have Come To," *The National Police Gazette*, July 4, 1885, 5. Library of Congress.

ers blamed management for hiring the Chinese workers in order to suppress the unions. By late summer 1885, anti-Chinese sentiment was widespread and increasingly virulent.[40]

Contemporaries attempted to dismiss the Rock Springs massacre as a spontaneous outburst arising from local tensions among miners, but there is evidence that anti-Chinese propaganda and advance planning played a role. Early on September 2, 1885, American and European (white)[41] miners, angry that a desirable work space at Rock Springs had been assigned to Chinese miners, attacked and killed two Chinese workers with picks. As news spread, disgruntled white workers gathered in the town's bars until bartenders, fearing trouble, closed them down. By afternoon a mob of 100 to 150 white men (along with a few women) advanced on the local Chinatown, ordering all Chinese to leave within one hour. Though the Chinese quickly packed their belongings, the impatient mob chased down the fleeing miners, shot some in the back as they ran, and burned alive others who had hidden in their homes. When it was over, twenty-eight Chinese miners were dead, Chinatown lay in smoldering ruins, and hundreds of surviving Chinese miners hid in the cold mountainside outside of town. Economic reasons alone cannot explain the extreme violence against the Chinese, or the *absence* of violence against other groups—Finns, Mormons, Italians—who were also acting as strikebreakers and competing for mining jobs.[42] The primary difference appears to be the demonization of Chinese miners in a way that seemed to make them legitimate targets for violence.

Hints about sexual danger posed by Chinese men also contributed to anti-Chinese feeling in Rock Springs. One largely forgotten, if spurious, justification for the attack at Rock Springs was the claim that Chinese men posed a sexual threat to white women. This was based on a single accusation by a resident white woman who claimed that a Chinese man had exposed himself to her during the previous winter (she also stated that she had easily run away). The charge seems out of place among the economic complaints that supported the "spontaneous outburst" theory—that Chinese miners received preferential treatment in wages, lower costs for supplies, and more productive work spaces—and was omitted from most contemporary published accounts of the massacre. The charge does, however, support the likelihood that the riot was not the spontaneous outgrowth of a simple workroom dispute but rather was fueled by simmering grievances, combined with intense anti-Chinese agitation in the preceding weeks and months. Leading up to the massacre, local newspapers drummed up "sensational and inflammatory" interpretations of the Chinese "menace." It is likely that the claim of sexual danger added to the intensity of violence at Rock Springs, which, in light of the refusal of the larger community to identify specific perpetrators, more closely resembled a lynching (or a pogrom) than a "riot."[43]

The *Police Gazette*'s visual coverage of the Rock Springs massacre reinforced contemporary views that it was a spontaneous, insignificant event. Its sole image, "Hackling the Heathen" (fig. 2.15), was buried on an interior page, in stark contrast to the many front-page inflammatory editorial cartoons of the previous summer and their repeated visual narrative of Chinese men as sexual threats. Instead, the paper compressed its visual coverage of Rock Springs into a single small frame showing a scuffle that centered on a white miner pulling a Chinese man's queue.[44] By contrast, *Harper's Weekly*'s sympathetic full-page news illustration, "The Massacre of the Chinese at Rock Springs, Wyoming," made clear that the Chinese were victims of a mob (fig. 2.16). As drawn by artist Thure de Thurlstrup, allegedly based on a photograph, the *Harper's* image centered on the faces of the Chinese miners, registering fear; their postures indicated their haste to flee from the indecipherable mob in the background. The image showed a few men in the throes of death or dying, struck by bullets from behind: one threw his arms up in a classic image of the battlefield; others fell back or

HACKLING THE HEATHEN.
THE MINERS OF WYOMING TERRITORY OBJECT TO CHEAP AND LEPROUS LABOR.

FIGURE 2.15: "Hackling
the Heathen," *The
National Police Gazette*,
September 19, 1885, 9.
Library of Congress.

stumbled forward with the impact of the bullets. Behind, the sky blazed with
light from their burning homes; smoke poured from windows and chimneys.[45]
Although clearly an interpretive illustration, collapsing time to capture many
different things in a single frame, *Harper's* depiction of devastation stood in
stark opposition to the *Police Gazette's* visual diminishment of the massacre.

The *Police Gazette* characterized all subsequent incidents involving the Chi-
nese through the lens of sexual predation, making its propaganda goal clear.
For example, the paper published a full-page image in early December 1885,
"A Crime against American Womanhood," ostensibly expressing outrage at a
Chinese foreman supervising female cigar rollers in San Francisco (showing
common cause with West Coast workers). The caption referred to "leprous
Chinamen as 'drivers' of freeborn white girls," further reinforcing the editor's
message:

THE MASSACRE OF THE CHINESE AT ROCK SPRINGS, WYOMING.

FIGURE 2.16: "The Massacre of the Chinese at Rock Springs, Wyoming," *Harper's Weekly*, September 26, 1885, 637. Manuscripts and Special Collections, New York State Library.

On our back page this week we illustrate a scene which *ought to make the blood of every honest and manly American boil with righteous anger.* It vividly represents the degradation to which American women in search of honest employment in San Francisco, are reduced by the hideous despotism of greed.

Our picture shows a "gang" of white girls, underpaid, half-starved, with all the decency and modesty of their sex crushed and trampled under foot, cowering under the bestial tyranny of a Chinese "foreman" or "driver."

... Does it need any letter press to emphasize the horrible lesson? Isn't every line in it a cruel presentation of a monstrous and intolerable wrong perpetrated upon the sisters and daughters of white Americans for no other offense than that they seek a chance to honestly labor[?][46]

In the wake of the massacre at Rock Springs, such graphic "news" coverage was hardly likely to check further anti-Chinese violence.

More vividly, later in 1885, the paper published its most comprehensive anti-Chinese visual narrative in a centerfold titled "The Chinese Pestilence" (fig. 2.17). The two-page editorial cartoon merged sexual, health, and moral fears about Chinese workers; only a small frame in the upper-left corner, showing Chinese cigar rollers at work beneath a sign reading (ironically) "No White

FIGURE 2.17: "The Chinese Pestilence," *The National Police Gazette*, December 19, 1885, 8–9. Library of Congress.

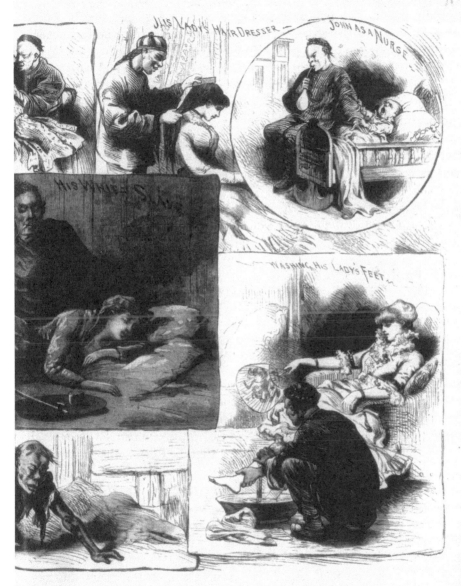

HIS LADY'S HAIRDRESSER

JOHN AS A NURSE

HIS FAMILY SLAVE

WASHING HIS LADY'S FEET

PESTILENCE.
SPREADING HIMSELF OVER THE FACE OF FREE BUT SOMNOLENT AMERICA.

Men Need Apply," referenced economic competition. Stereotypes (the leper, the seductive servant) encircled the central image of a prone and sexually vulnerable white woman flanked by Chinese men in a darkened opium den. Occupying more than ten times the physical space as the paper's Rock Springs massacre illustration—and again, published absent any actual event, news story, or court case—this image further hyped the opium den hysteria it had nurtured over many months. "In our double page picture this week," explained the editorial, "the hideous and revolting story of Chinese usurpation of the white man's place is set forth in *language more effective than words.*"[47]

Through the winter of 1885–86, *Police Gazette* news illustrations and editorial cartoons equated the sexual "usurpation" by Chinese men in opium dens to similar claims about African American men—and began to advocate lynching as a proper response. In January 1886, the *Police Gazette* published an editorial based on sensational stories from Baltimore papers alleging that "six or seven hundred sleek and vicious coolies ... are sating their lusts and filling their pocket-books at the expense of the white working girls of the city." Unfazed (or perhaps inspired) by the violence at Rock Springs, the editorial now *explicitly* advocated violence as a proper and necessary response to the Chinese "problem":

> It is a pretty comment on our boasted equity and justice that the scoundrels can, under cover of the law, and with the protection, reluctantly given, of the police, commit crimes against budding womanhood for which, if they were negroes, they would first be tortured and then hung amid a shower of bullets.[48]

Building on a single, discredited story of a New York opium den in 1883, the *Police Gazette* had developed an effective national propaganda campaign against the Chinese.

The *Police Gazette*'s opium den propaganda merged western anti-Chinese agitation with anti-vice campaigns in eastern cities in a way that seemed to justify and even incite mob violence. And violence continued. Five Chinese men were lynched in Pierce City, Idaho, days after the Rock Springs massacre. In Tacoma, Washington, that November, weeks of sensational news stories preceded the forcible eviction of Chinese workers; no indictments were issued for the twenty-seven whites accused of leading the mob. Merchants in Truckee, California, came up with a freeze-out method as a "civilized" alternative to riots that avoided bloodshed by boycotting and publicly shaming employers who hired Chinese workers, until they effectively cleared out Chinatown; the so-called "Truckee method" inspired similar purges across the west. In Seattle over the winter, newspapers published extreme anti-Chinese views and justified the expulsion of more than three hundred Chinese from the city. Five Chinese children were killed in a suspicious fire in Yreka, California, in 1886. The worst violence took place in the Snake River massacre, in Oregon, where thirty-one

Chinese miners were murdered by a group of "cowboys" who, though known to authorities, were never convicted or punished. Few voices opposed the violence. The Chinese government demanded (and eventually won) reparations for property losses for the survivors of Rock Springs; no compensation was made for lost lives, and almost no one advocated for the Chinese to remain in the United States.[49]

Wong Chin Foo's Counternarratives

Journalist Wong Chin Foo was a vocal exception, who determined that political and cultural action were necessary to prevent further demonization of Chinese men. It was a war of perception, he believed, a battle in the court of public opinion. The effectiveness of anti-Chinese propaganda and its spread through popular culture were clear to him. One strategy of his counternarrative was to question Christian values in the wake of the Rock Springs massacre. Though raised by Christian missionaries, he had lectured on Confucianism and Buddhism since the 1870s (and for a time called himself a Confucian missionary to America). In 1887 he published a controversial article, "Why Am I a Heathen?," contrasting so-called "heathen" religious practices with the violence perpetrated by Christians at Rock Springs. In a bid to force good Christians to disown mob violence, he wrote of the Chinese:

> Though we may differ from the Christian in appearance, manners, and general ideas of civilization, we do not organize into cowardly mobs under the guise of social or political reform, to plunder and murder with impunity; and we are so far advanced in our heathenism as to no longer tolerate popular feeling or religious prejudice to defeat justice or cause injustice.

Wong's anti-Christian views prompted a response piece in the same magazine by Yan Phou Lee, also a Chinese-born man, a converted Christian brought to America by missionaries. Lee rejected Wong's critique of Christian hypocrisy, instead citing the mob's violence as proof that they were not true Christians. Wong also challenged those who feared Chinese labor competition, engaging in public debate with his old nemesis, Denis Kearney, of the California Workingman's Party.[50] Such public encounters gave Wong a forum to put his case against Chinese Exclusion and restriction laws into the historical record.

In June 1888 Wong tried a new strategy, publishing a *visual* counternarrative in an article in an illustrated monthly literary magazine called *The Cosmopolitan* (a distant ancestor of today's fashion magazine). Wong likely hoped to influence debate over the Scott Bill, then under consideration in Congress, which would prevent Chinese men who left the country from returning to the United States. He styled his article, "The Chinese in New York," after the popular travelogue genre, complete with an illustrated tour of Chinatown. The piece offered an intervention in cultural politics, an effort to demystify the Chinese and remove the negative stigma. Using a non-sensational, realistic approach, the article and its images attempted to dislodge opium den hysteria with a more realistic portrait of the Chinese. Eight illustrations accompanied the piece, of which perhaps the most significant was its version of an opium den. Depicting a scene in a barbershop, the image (fig. 2.18) showed Chinese workers in a spare, tidy setting, giving and receiving a haircut, smoking an opium pipe, or dozing on a plain wooden bunk. It was a peaceful scene, Wong pointed out in the article's text, noting the contrast with neighboring Irish bars. In text and illustration, his article evoked a series of homely, nonthreatening (if Orientalized) spaces, contrary to the kind of images circulating in the *Police Gazette*.[51]

The more realistic images published with Wong Chin Foo's article, "The Chinese in New York," testify to his belief that visual culture mattered in the debate over Chinese exclusion. However, they were no match for the *Police Gazette*'s more sensational imagery. As a literary magazine with a modest circulation (roughly twenty-five thousand copies per issue, typical of an upscale, illustrated monthly magazine), the *Cosmopolitan* was unlikely to reach, let alone convert, anti-Chinese activists. Its picaresque style, intended to dispel readers' ignorance and misconceptions about Chinese culture, also hewed to many of the period's assumptions about irreconcilable differences between East and West. "Chinatown is the most interesting corner of the 'Melican man's' metropolis," Wong wrote in his satirical style, "the little world composed of every variety of Christians, heathen, Irishmen and other savages." This was, he said, particularly true of New York's "Little Hong Kong": "partly because it is only a recent institution, and largely because the Chinese are the exact antipodes of this continent, in customs and ideas as well as geographically."[52] Like narrators of other travelogues, Wong offered himself in the dual role of tour guide and interlocutor, making an alien world intelligible to curious readers. Through a combined emphasis on exoticism and familiarity, he made the Chinese visible but also exaggerated Chinatown's cultural Otherness.

Yet Wong's Chinatown also transcended the travelogue narrative with sympathetic portrayals of an unusually complex cast of characters typically invisible to a white audience. He began with the most familiar—the laundryman—describing in detail the process by which Chinese launderers established themselves, working for others until able to obtain the capital necessary to set up shop, sometimes borrowing from an earlier, more established resident, and sometimes from a syndicate created by would-be borrowers and lenders at astronomical interest rates. He carefully detailed less-familiar spaces within Chinatown, such as grocery stores and restaurants (at that time largely inaccessible to non-Chinese people). Chinese grocery stores might seem, to uninformed passersby,

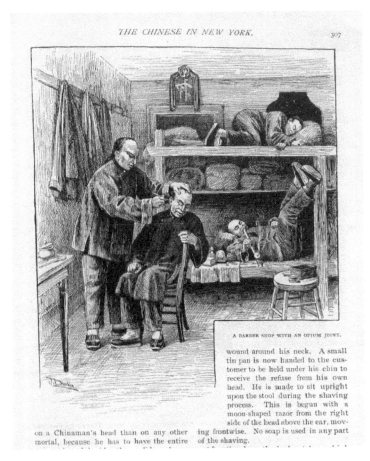

FIGURE 2.18: "A Barber Shop with an Opium Joint," *The Cosmopolitan*, June 1888, 307. New York State Library.

as "dingy dens of poverty," he explained, but in fact they were significant institutions that provided both capital to newcomers and a point of connection to China; Chinese grocers provided "not only their country stores, clubs, and general newspaper stations, but their only post-offices." He translated the names and explained the uses of several imported foods and extolled the virtues of the Chinese restaurant, from the healthfulness of its cuisine to the cleanliness of its kitchen to its communal dining practices. He explained the proverbs displayed on the walls of restaurants and emphasized distinctive practices of hospitality and the social significance of the restauranteur (fig. 2.19). Part Orientalism and part demystification, the article undertook the complicated work of introducing (white) Americans to the real and specific features of New York's Chinatown.[53]

The store of Yuet Sing, at 10 Chatham Square, shown in the illustration, is a fair sample. This firm does an annual business of over one hundred and fifty thousand dollars among the eight hundred Sing Ning laundries. A brief outline of materials

How Shi. Dried oysters.

IN A RESTAURANT.

FIGURE 2.19: "In a Restaurant," *The*, June 1888, 302. New York State Library.

Wong particularly sought to demystify the two central practices used by anti-Chinese activists to justify exclusion: gambling and opium use. He explained the fascination of the fan-tan (gambling) table: its code of honor, its economic role in the Chinatown economy. As he put it, "a Mott Street merchant would rather trust a gambler than a man of any other calling." But Wong also debunked the myths and attempted to reshape the narrative of the opium den. In the text, he detailed the mechanics of the practice of opium smoking and then attempted to allay recent fears about opium addiction. Perhaps most challenging to the dominant anti-Chinese narrative was Wong's point that opium was far less socially disruptive than alcohol as a source of addiction. He did not downplay the real damage addiction inflicted on users. He merely explained that, due to their limited financial means, the typical Chinese users in New York used opium merely as a "mild sedative."

Wong's central assertion was that the biggest opium users were American rather than Chinese. As he pointed out, the cost of opium (about $3 per day, nearly three times the daily pay for an unskilled laborer) put the debilitating habit out of reach for all but the most affluent users.

> The "opium fiends" (men incorrigibly addicted to the habit) generally become victims by abandoning themselves to the drug because of business reverses, as whisky is used by the Christians to drown their troubles. But it is much more difficult and rare to get into the opium habit than the "whisky habit," because a much longer time and much more money must be spent upon opium to fasten the craving for it.

He explained, "The opium habit can only be afforded, because of the time and means required, by the indolent and rich." Turning the tables on readers, he sounded the alarm about the growing number of *American* (in other words, white) "opium fiends" and cautioned against the drug's relaxing effect on inhibitions: echoing reformers, he called it "an insidious social evil." Only by curbing the American appetite for opium would the problem abate. Finally, he downplayed the more controversial issue of racial mixing in opium dens. He mentioned in passing the relative absence of Chinese women in New York's Chinatown (which he numbered at four) but cited the intermarriage of Chinese men and working-class, immigrant women in nearby neighborhoods as evidence that Chinese men made better husbands.[54]

In a powerful visual counternarrative to the *Police Gazette*'s opium den, the eight large illustrations (along with a photograph and two small drawings) complemented Wong's evidence-based tone. They aspired to "realism," an attempt to visually document a scene, and may in fact have been drawn from photographs. A street scene (fig. 2.20) showing "Chinatown, New York" focused on laborers going about their daily work; cultural difference was apparent in clothing styles, but, compared to the sensational imagery in the *Police Gazette*, the images were respectful. The artist was a young man named John Durkin (1868–1903), a staff illustrator for *Harper's Weekly* barely out of his teens. In a quiet, observational visual tone, Durkin's illustrations depicted the Chinatown street, the message board, the store, the restaurant, and the kitchen in a way that revealed a range of activities and social classes; they emphasized but did not denigrate cultural differences for this "city within a city."[55] Women were conspicuously absent, thus removing any hint of sexual threat. In showcasing the details of Chinatown's public and private spaces, Wong's narrative and Durkin's illustrations both reinforced the exoticism readers expected and rendered the Chinese intelligible, knowable, and familiar.

The non-sensational tenor of Wong's article and Durkin's accompanying illustrations had limited power to supplant the dominant view of New York's Chinatown. A few months after Wong's article appeared, the Scott Act passed unanimously in the House, met little resistance in the Senate, and was signed into law on October 1, 1888. The *Police Gazette*'s opium den hysteria helped to

THE CHINESE IN NEW YORK.

CHINATOWN, NEW YORK.

one
the
aliv
ans
a fr
me
to t
pre
and
m o
eate
th a
can.
porl
vori
etal
are
use
are
eno
but
ily
gre
are
in 1
eve
the
Chi
ies
at
sep.
to
tha
un-
lin
make it religious
But they all possess
able love for old hats
Chinese laundrymar
same hat for ninety
it can be kept toge
and he would even
three years' mournin
So long as a Chin
a heathen he is ge

FIGURE 2.20: "China-town, New York," *The Cosmopolitan*, June 1888, 299. New York State Library.

justify these developments. As one of its vocal supporters put it, the bill would deter the "vices . . . demoralization and ruin caused by the opium joints." Miscegenation fears formed a subtext for Chinese exclusion, as expressed by Alabama senator (and former Confederate general) John Tyler Morgan: "I do not want them to come here, because I do not want them to marry our women. I do not want them to incorporate their blood into the Anglo-American veins. I have the same objection to that that I have to miscegenation between negroes and white people. I do not want to increase or encourage the immigration into this country of the lower classes or races of the earth, the yellow and the dark men."[56]

By insisting on the victimization of white women by "barbarians," opium den hysteria sidestepped the question of white women's agency, instead exhorting "chivalrous," white-identifying men to engage in anti-Chinese violence. Opium den scenarios inserted the Chinese man, himself a victim of mob violence, into the established role of racially distinct sexual predator. *Police Gazette* editor Fox understood that opium den images were efficient propaganda, and the explosion of interpretive illustrations of the opium den in his paper coincided with the peak in anti-Chinese violence. By invoking "nameless crimes," through exaggeration, innuendo, and invention, sensational imagery escalated what had been an economic struggle into a gendered moral crusade. The concurrence of this imagery with outbreaks of violence suggests the role that sensational, visual narratives play in political culture. Opium den narratives also help explain why the Chinese were targeted for mass violence when the Finns, the Mormons, and the Italians were not. As the *Police Gazette*'s interpretive illustrations of the opium den became more uniform and less ambiguous—more like political propaganda, even when they masqueraded as news illustration—they were far "more effective than words" in providing a cultural pretext for forcible expulsion of the Chinese.

"Our crusade against these moral lepers has borne fruit," Fox exulted in an 1892 *Police Gazette* editorial, after the Geary Act, which expanded and solidified Chinese exclusion, became law. The Geary Act mandated identity cards exclusively for the Chinese and passed despite objections that it violated the Chinese migrants' rights, threatened the treaty with China, and endangered American missionaries abroad. The law's supporters, including Senator Charles Felton of California, warned his colleagues of the "rapine" habits of Chinese invaders throughout history. As he put it, "we would not permit the purity or sweetness of our national waters to be contaminated or polluted by the mingling of its pure streams with the impure from any source whatsoever." Opponents like the Chinese Civil Rights League (which Wong helped to found) and the Six Companies (an organization of Chinese merchants) encouraged Chinese migrants to flout the law. When Chinese activists were unsuccessful in testing the law's constitutionality in 1893, however, Chinese migrants had little choice but to comply with compulsory registration.[57]

Even with the advent of photography and the allegedly more "realistic" style of visual journalism, the opium den as a locus of vice (drug use, gambling, sexual danger) remained an enduring stereotype for Chinese migrants. It is hardly a coincidence that of the two images of Chinese immigrants in Jacob Riis's 1890 *How the Other Half Lives*, one was a photograph-based illustration of a man lying prone and semi-conscious on a bunk in an opium den. (The second image was a photograph of a man walking on a city street, but he was merely a prop in an image that actually focused on chalked Chinese characters on a telegraph pole indicating gambling news—the second stereotype). Neither showed any of the everyday (if Orientalized) scenes that Wong's illustrated article had provided. In the text, Riis blamed the Chinese for the ruin of young women, who, he claimed, were then doomed to die and be buried in Potter's Field, but provided no photograph to document such a scene. An *interpretive* illustration would have undercut the book's evidence-based credibility, but it was also superfluous: the opium den as a site of "ruin" for young women was by then fixed as one of the period's most influential and allegedly "realistic" representations of Chinatown.[58]

Opium den hysteria brought Fox and the *Police Gazette* commercial success in the mid-1880s, the paper's peak years of circulation and influence. Meanwhile, innovators in illustrated daily news began to challenge the paper's monopoly on the production of sensational news imagery. Chapter 3 explores how Joseph Pulitzer's *New York World* and William Randolph Hearst's *San Francisco Examiner* began to compete with illustrated weeklies—and each other. They experimented with visual journalism, first in their Sunday supplements but soon in their daily pages. They sought to attract readers who appreciated the drama of the *Police Gazette*'s interpretive drawings but also wanted "authentic" and "realistic" images: if not photographs (which could not be easily published before 1897), then illustrations with established sourcing. In covering the Ghost Dance crisis of 1890, such illustrated dailies learned to transform photograph-based images into persuasive, graphic news.

CHAPTER 3

"A First-Class Attraction on Any Stage"

Dramatizing the Ghost Dance and the Massacre at Wounded Knee

"[THE] GHOST DANCE threatened no one. The dancers meant violence to no one." With these words, in fall 1890, Sitting Bull tried to dispel reports that the Ghost Dance was a harbinger of a new Indian War.[1] Sitting Bull (*Tatanka Iyotake*) was a holy man and tribal elder among the Hunkpapa, of the Lakota Sioux, who lived on the Grand River on Standing Rock Reservation (in what is today South Dakota). He was not a passionate advocate of the Ghost Dance, but he was a national celebrity, known for his history of resistance to white colonization of the Plains West, the reservation system, and "allotment"—the division of tribal lands for private settlement. Unfortunately for Sitting Bull, the nature of sensational news made his factual statements almost irrelevant. Worse, illustrated newspapers, competing for readers, used his image—his fame—to conjure up a familiar narrative of hostility and conflict, thus making the dance more dramatic. Just a few weeks after he said these words, Indian police, sent by the Indian Affairs agent at Standing Rock Reservation, killed Sitting Bull in a botched attempt to arrest him for refusing to denounce the dancing. By the end of the month, hundreds of men, women, and children—refugees who had fled Standing Rock after Sitting Bull's killing, along with dancers from nearby Cheyenne River Reservation (led by his half-brother, known as Big Foot)—were gunned down by soldiers in the massacre at Wounded Knee.

Historians have long recognized that inflammatory headlines and misleading reporting helped create an atmosphere of crisis in fall 1890, and that provocative images in the pictorial weeklies contributed,[2] but the role played by daily news illustrations in accelerating the controversy deserves greater scrutiny. Emerging illustrated daily newspapers, seeking commercial success or political advantage, characterized the Ghost Dance as an act of war. They turned imagery from the entertainment marketplace into tools of visual journalism, connecting the dance with well-known figures from past conflicts—Indian warriors, entertainment personalities, and military leaders. Sensational imagery in the daily newspapers reinforced popular ideas about Manifest Destiny and the inevitability of colonial conquest, based on an underlying rationale that preemptive violence was necessary to protect settlers against Indian "savagery."

In 1890, daily newspaper editors used the Ghost Dance "crisis" to establish these themes as essential components of the "new journalism's" sensational toolkit. To visualize the Ghost Dance in real time, four the period's most successful illustrated daily newspapers (the *New York Herald* and *New York World*, the *Chicago Tribune*, and the *San Francisco Examiner*) began to publish images that were available and familiar, rather than accurate. They recycled material from a reservoir of popular histories and entertainment imagery, which evoked spaces, characters, and plotlines embedded in national lore. Depictions of unrelated war dances, images of the defeat of General George Custer at the Battle of Little Bighorn in 1876, and portraits of Sitting Bull and others held responsible in popular culture for Custer's "murder" helped publishers arouse emotions and attract readers. In the process, such imagery elevated a dance that the same newspapers had previously dismissed as mass delusion[3]—a "Messiah craze"—into something far more ominous.

In reality, the Ghost Dance was not a war dance, nor was it warlike. Ghost Dancers typically followed the peaceful teachings of a visionary named Wovoka, a Paiute holy man living in western Nevada. In 1887, Wovoka had revived a version of a traditional Paiute Round Dance[4] prevalent in regions decimated by California's genocidal policies toward indigenous peoples. He further refined the dance after experiencing a vision on New Year's Day, 1889, during an eclipse of the sun, when he saw a world in which a natural disaster removed white settlers, dead ancestors returned, and the land reverted to its pre-settler bounty. As word of Wovoka's vision spread, emissaries came from throughout the Mountain and Plains West to meet him at Walker Lake Reservation, in Nevada, to learn the dance. He emphasized its peaceful qualities: "I want no more fighting," he told Short Bull (a Brulé Sioux who would lead the dance among the Lakota) and other emissaries. One, a Northern Cheyenne man named Porcupine, shared the story widely, highlighting the dance's Christian, millennial connotations, calling it the coming of a "Messiah." Porcupine, like Wovoka, described the Ghost Dance vision as the opposite of warlike. Put another way, "Wovoka taught peace."[5]

The dance had already proved itself to be an effective form of intertribal communication, but it became *news* primarily due to the number of bands and tribes that embraced it. Otherwise, the practice, which was typically nonconfrontational and calm, made for boring journalism. A contemplative dance, it was performed not by warriors alone but by all members of the community, regardless of age, gender, or status. Participants gathered in a circle with joined hands and moved in slow side-steps to the left, chanting invocations to their ancestors and past ways of life. Sometimes, after several hours, the dancers would accelerate or issue louder cries, but in general it was a sedate practice. According to one local (white) trader, writing during the height of the scare in South Dakota, the dance "was nothing but a quiet religious ceremony." As it spread over the spring and summer of 1890, federal Indian Affairs agents began to blame the dance on what they called "non-progressive," "traditionalist," or "irreconcilable" Indians—or, simply, "hostiles"—disregarding the participation of a wide range of dancers, including converted Christians, those educated in mission schools, and active farmers. Agents warned officials in Washington that participants had abandoned farms and schools to join the dancers.[6] Sensational daily newspapers soon amplified these mischaracterizations.

The dance came to the Sioux reservations after the "starving winter" of 1889–90, and at a critical juncture in Lakota history. The Sioux Act of 1889, just taking effect in 1890, reduced the size of the Great Sioux Reservation by creating six small reservations on roughly half the earlier territory (fig. 3.1), opening the remaining land to settlers.[7] With the new boundaries, the Lakota lost homes, farmland, favored campsites, and hunting grounds. Indian Affairs

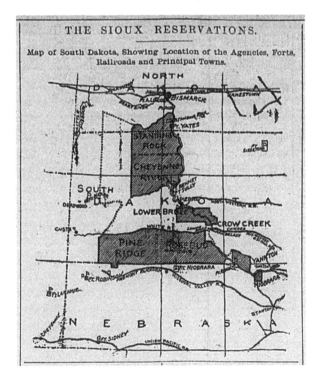

FIGURE 3.1: "The Sioux Reservations," *New York Herald*, November 24, 1890. Library of Congress.

agents expected them to adapt to a sedentary, agricultural existence, closely supervised, and to send children to reservation schools. Those who accepted private allotments of land would receive ownership rights, but these lots were typically poorly suited to farming; those remaining on reservations would receive treaty-dictated government rations. During the lead-up to the Sioux Act, as the U.S. Army and the Sioux Commission applied pressure to obtain the required signatures from tribal leaders, divisions among the Lakota emerged. Critics warned that the rations were vulnerable to cuts; this proved to be the case in 1890, when a special census at Pine Ridge and Rosebud Reservations severely undercounted the population. In this difficult moment, Kicking Bear, a Miniconjou Sioux leader, along with his brother-in-law Short Bull, returned from their pilgrimage to Wovoka at Walker Lake, and began to teach the Ghost Dance. As white settlers moved into the former Sioux lands over the summer and fall of 1890, many Lakota turned to the dance to channel dissatisfaction, restore hope, or achieve spiritual renewal.[8] Indian Affairs agents, who believed the dance signaled pan-Indian mobilization, began to forbid the practice. But the dance continued to spread.

"Attract the Eye"—Visual Journalism in Daily Newspapers in 1890

As Kicking Bear and Short Bull taught the dance at the Lower Sioux reservations (Pine Ridge, Rosebud, and Cheyenne River [see fig. 3.1]), editors of illustrated daily newspapers began to find ways to visualize the practice. The gold standard for visual journalism in 1890 was a line illustration based on a photograph (which could not yet be economically mass-produced in daily newspapers). Such images were considered distinct from—and preferable to—interpretive illustrations found in sensational weeklies, such as the *National Police Gazette*. Viewing photographs as the most "objective" form of visual evidence, dailies that used these drawings sometimes included captions that attested to sourcing in order to establish their legitimacy. Daily newspaper artists typically showed great fidelity to photographic sources, even when the images had little relevance to the story. When photographic images were unavailable or lacking in drama, however, editors continued to publish more interpretive reconstructions, produced by artists from available sources or from their own imaginations.[9] Because the Lakota discouraged white witnesses and photographers, "authentic" visual evidence of the Ghost Dance proved challenging to find. The dance was a private ceremony rather than a public performance, Lakota leaders insisted, and they took steps to keep visitors away; this encouraged considerable creative license for news illustration.

In their quest to dramatize the Ghost Dance, dailies often bypassed existing photographs, regardless of lip service paid to authentic sourcing. Yet a few avail-

FIGURE 3.2: "The Ghost Dance," Photograph by J. E. Meddaugh, 1891. Beinecke Rare Book and Manuscript Library, Yale University.

able photographs of the Ghost Dance practiced among the Lakota in fall 1890 can be found in archives today. One, by photographer James E. Meddaugh, was taken in September 1890, likely at a camp to the north of Pine Ridge Agency (fig. 3.2). Another, better-known photograph (fig. 3.3) was taken by Associated Press journalist Sam Clover, who got close enough to the dance near Sitting Bull's camp on the Grand River in Standing Rock Reservation to take a picture secretly, from under his coat, using a newly invented "portable" Kodak One camera. Clover's photograph was later converted into a souvenir cabinet card, making it more available in archives today. Both photographers captured the panoramic setting, calm figures, and relative slowness of the Ghost Dance. Though distant and hard to see clearly, these dancers displayed neither frenetic motion nor wild gestures. Both images support descriptions from Porcupine and other witnesses of a circular, group dance, undertaken in daylight, practiced by fully-clothed people of all ages and genders.[10] This is not to say that such a photograph was inherently representative (or unbiased), that it captured all phases of the dance, or that it was was more reliable as evidence than a sketch by an illustrator drawn at the scene. But it is worth noting that these two authenticated photographs of the Ghost Dance correspond well with descriptions from participants and observers, as well as with later photographs of the dance taken among other tribes in the 1890s and early twentieth century.

In fact, the only accurate news illustration of the Ghost Dance that fall appeared in a weekly pictorial newspaper: *Harper's Weekly*. *Harper's* had a clear

FIGURE 3.3: "Sitting Bull's Ghost Dance," George W. Scott (studio reprint; originally photographed by Sam Clover), fall 1890. Minnesota Historical Society Library, negative 36841.

advantage over the competition in having an illustrator at Pine Ridge that fall—the celebrated artist of western imagery, Frederic Remington. Although Remington departed before troops arrived at Pine Ridge, scholars agree that his drawing (fig. 3.4) of the Ghost Dance is the most faithful to photographic evidence and eye-witness accounts. The illustration bears a strong resemblance in composition, tone, and content to the Meddaugh photograph (fig. 3.2) taken at Pine Ridge several weeks earlier. The drawing also corresponds well to a photograph taken among the Arapaho in the southwest by James Mooney a year or two later. Remington's drawing reveals the dance's signature features: both men and women participate; the figures in the circle seem calm; and they stand close together with joined hands (precluding the possibility for holding weapons aloft or other kinds of warlike gestures). The caption claimed that Remington's image was based on a sketch he had taken on site. (It is unclear how he managed to witness the dance and sketch the scene—it is possible that he viewed it from afar and used a photograph for reference.) With its accuracy and its lack of drama, Remington's illustration proved to be the exception rather than the rule in Ghost Dance illustration.[11] It was suitable for the educational tone of the family-oriented pictorial *Harper's Weekly* but did not serve the sensational dailies' purpose to dramatize the news.

FIGURE 3.4: Frederic Remington, "The Ghost Dance by the Ogallala Sioux at Pine Ridge Agency," *Harper's Weekly*, December 6, 1890, 960–61. Manuscripts and Special Collections, New York State Library.

Images of the dance in illustrated *daily* newspapers bore no resemblance to Remington's drawing or the two photographs, in part because the motivation for publishing "news" images in this period discouraged accuracy. Adapting photographs into line illustration for mass circulation was difficult, due to time, distance, and technical printing constraints. This encouraged the use of existing images and especially portraits, which were easier to publish and for which popular narratives filled in the context. As a contemporary wrote about daily-news illustrators,

> when one considers the limitations under which they work, the productions of the better class of newspaper artists are surprisingly good. Everything must, in the first place, be drawn in a hurry. Rapid work is the prerequisite in the modern newspaper office. Then the sketches must be open. If they are closely drawn, the lines will fill and the picture will smudge, owing to the spongy paper, poor ink, and rapid press-work used in producing our newspapers. For these reasons, newspaper illustrating has come to be a separate branch of art.[12]

Portraits gave the dailies a way to transcend these artistic and technical challenges, because they were easier to draw in an "open" fashion than complex drawings showing actions or multiple participants.

To meet the daily deadlines, illustrators also had an incentive to base their drawings on existing material: photographs, if available, as well as other kinds of news "art" gathered in prior reporting, or even (if circumstances allowed) from the burgeoning advertising and entertainment industries. Because of time pressures, serial reporting proved invaluable. Flogging even a dull story over time increased interest (and had the potential to invest the reader in the outcome). Serial stories also created a sense of escalating tension, as the form demanded new heights in each installment.[13] In fall 1890, examples of serial stories in daily newspapers included the Jack the Ripper cases unfolding in England, vigilante work of Whitecaps in the rural United States, and quasi-theatrical novelties like "Succi the Faster" (a man who stopped eating as a publicity stunt). Such stories made the work of visual journalism easier. More important, repeating characters were also simpler to illustrate because their images already existed. Recurring, familiar, and controversial images added drama to news reporting, which translated into sales and circulation for the daily papers.

The most innovative daily editors were figuring out how best to combine realistic, photograph-based images and interpretative illustration to draw in news consumers. Pictures were effective "bait," explained Joseph Pulitzer in 1884, defending his introduction of images into the *New York World*, "something that would arouse curiosity and *make people want to buy the paper*." Pulitzer's investment in image production (specifically artists and faster presses) paid dividends: "there is always an extra demand for the *World* when it is illuminated, so to speak," he explained. "A great many people in the world require to be educated through the eye."[14] A few years later, William Randolph Hearst embraced the same doctrine when he convinced his father to let him take over the *San Francisco Examiner*. Hearst, a failed college student in his early twenties, justified the investment to his father in 1887:

> Illustrations embellish a page; illustrations *attract the eye* and stimulate the imagination of the lower classes and materially aid the comprehension of an unaccustomed reader and thus are of particular importance to that class of people which the *Examiner* claims to address.

The motivation was clear—as Hearst said (echoing Pulitzer), pictures helped *"to get people to look at the paper."*[15]

By 1890 the *San Francisco Examiner*, the *New York World*, the *New York Herald*, and the *Chicago Tribune* fought for supremacy in circulation and advertising revenue through the art of news illustration.[16] As these newspapers advanced the craft of visual journalism, they competed with more established pictorial weeklies. Until Pulitzer's *World* introduced images in the mid-1880s, the weeklies (and monthlies) had enjoyed a virtual monopoly on news illustrations, offering their papers as visual supplements to the daily news. Weeklies had many advantages, such as experienced artists, suitable presses, and better paper, but also enjoyed a longer time frame to produce their work. By 1885, however, the dailies began to overcome their disadvantages, turning the front page into "a billboard . . . to attract attention on the news stand."[17] Dailies also enjoyed an advantage in situations where news changed rapidly. Despite having greater resources than the dailies, the most popular family weeklies, *Harper's Weekly*, *Frank Leslie's Illustrated Newspaper*, and the *Illustrated American*, faced challenges in bringing the so-called "Indian Troubles" into family living rooms in a timely way. In a pinch, they too resorted to celebrity images to visualize the crisis. Dailies were not unique in distorting news illustrations, in other words; they simply found a way to produce graphic news more quickly.

"A First-Class Attraction"—
The Ghost Dance as Spectacle

To transform the Ghost Dance into a compelling narrative, sensational daily news editors supplemented interpretive illustration with available "realistic" images, based (if possible) on photographs or sketches taken at the scene, or from stock images if needed. A desire to bolster their dramatic images with claims about authenticity or provenance influenced their choices in visualizing the Ghost Dance. This can be seen in Hearst's *San Francisco Examiner*, the first to publish an image of ritual Indian dancing in fall 1890, as the Ghost Dance was taking hold in the Sioux reservations.[18] The *Examiner* had tracked news of the Ghost Dance for months, interspersed with wire stories of warlike activities among Native Americans throughout the Plains and Mountain West, effectively blending horror stories of Indian "savagery" with the so-called "Messiah craze."[19] It was in this context that the *Examiner* illustrated a story headlined "A Weird Incantation," which described an entirely different dance, the Navajo Fire Dance, accompanied by an image of bare-chested warriors, dancing around a fire in warlike postures. This image was not associated with any current news story but, rather, had been extracted from an ethnographic report published a few months earlier. Within the context of the spreading Ghost Dance, however, the image (fig. 3.5) was effective news "bait"—designed not so much to inform as to attract news readers. Crediting the report's author (an ethnographer) as an expert witness, the text described the Fire Dance as "extremely theatrical," one that "would make *a first-class attraction on any stage.*"[20]

Daily news coverage of the Ghost Dance became more dramatic in the days leading up to the midterm congressional election that November. On October

FIGURE 3.5: "The Navajo Fire Dance," *San Francisco Examiner*,
October 5, 1890, 13. Reprinted with permission from ProQuest.

28, 1890, the Republican-leaning *Chicago Tribune*[21] escalated its coverage of the
Ghost Dance with a story under the headline "To Wipe Out All the Whites,"
identifying the Ghost Dance as a sign of a coming Indian war. The story was
based on a leaked memorandum written by Standing Rock Indian Affairs agent
James McLaughlin to the secretary of the interior. McLaughlin reported that
Sitting Bull, though confined to Standing Rock Reservation and forbidden
from witnessing the dance at Cheyenne River Reservation, had invited Kicking
Bear to demonstrate the dance at his own camp at Standing Rock. Sitting Bull
was attempting, McLaughlin asserted, to inflame the passions of the Lakota
against incoming settlers.

For a Republican newspaper like the *Chicago Tribune*, reporting on Sitting
Bull made it possible to claim that the federal government would be justified
in providing military protection for the new settlers in the Dakotas. Within
two days of this news report, President Harrison expressed his concern about
McLaughlin's allegations, referring to the "delusion as to the coming of an
Indian messiah and the return of the dead Indian warriors for a crusade upon
the whites." He ordered the commanding officer at Fort Yates (North Dakota),
Brigadier General Thomas H. Ruger, to investigate the situation at Standing
Rock and Cheyenne River Reservations.[22] The Republican Party's political goals
influenced the *Chicago Tribune*'s headline coverage of the dance—and vice versa.

A few days later, on November 2, 1890, the Democratic-leaning *New York
World* reacted to the leaked McLaughlin memorandum with its own report,

including two images that called to mind popular history and the *Wild West* entertainment industry: Sitting Bull and Buffalo Bill Cody. Viewing these images as contemporaries did is essential to understanding their meaning and importance. Under the headline "The Red Ghost Dance," the caption identified the two men in the portrait only as "The Big Chief and Agent" (fig. 3.6). The drawing was rather large for a portrait and was signed by a New York-based illustrator, William Hofacker, who had been illustrating the news for the *World* since 1889. Despite its appearance of authenticity, the dual portrait was likely a fabrication Hofacker created through the illustrator's device of substituting familiar faces into an existing stock image. A second, and larger, landscape drawing of "A Great Camp of the Sioux" established a panoramic, *Wild West*-like setting (fig. 3.7).[23] Together, the two drawings evoked popular entertainment in a way that was likely to attract the eye. At the same time, the display appeared to mock the Harrison administration's assertions about the seriousness of the Ghost Dance.

The *World*'s portrait of Sitting Bull and Buffalo Bill committed a visual sleight of hand; the caption implied uncertainty about their identities, but the image relied on the men's fame to make them recognizable. The image of the "big chief"—though shorn of his braids and wearing civilian clothing—closely matched photographs of Sitting Bull in this period and would have been recognizable to most adult Americans. The surrounding text quoted extensively from McLaughlin's memorandum blaming Sitting Bull for bringing the Ghost Dance to Standing Rock. The article warned that Sitting Bull was bragging of

THE BIG CHIEF AND AGENT.

FIGURE 3.6: "The Big Chief and Agent," *New York World*, November 2, 1890, 27. New York State Library.

FIGURE 3.7: "A Great Camp of the Sioux," *New York World*, November 2, 1890, 27.
New York State Library.

his exploits at Little Bighorn, "where Custer and his troops were exterminated."
He was a representative of the "irreconcilables" who rejected reservation life,
McLaughlin alleged, was "ferociously [determined on a] war against the 'pale
faces'" and was in the process of building a band of "avengers" whose goal was
"to exterminate the whites."[24] The report mischaracterized Sitting Bull's influence and failed to acknowledge that he was in fact skeptical about the dance
and neither participated nor led the dance at Standing Rock. The *World*'s motivation in publishing this inflammatory account was not political—unlike the
Chicago Tribune, it was not likely to bolster the Harrison administration's Indian
policy in the Dakotas. Its goal was commercial. Sitting Bull was an exciting
and recognizable figure, and easy to visualize: his image turned a remote story
in the American West into graphic *news*.

Even unnamed, the second figure in the *World*'s portrait would have been immediately recognizable to most Americans in 1890. Significantly, the image did
not depict the "agent" that the text described—Standing Rock agent McLaughlin (who kept his white hair short and typically wore a bowler hat). Rather, the
image referenced the famous showman Buffalo Bill Cody, with his trademark
flowing hair and characteristic broad-brimmed felt hat. Even without naming
Buffalo Bill and Sitting Bull, the *World*'s pairing of the two men called to mind
Cody's nationally renowned *Wild West* show. Both men were famous celebrities
connected to the Custer legend—Sitting Bull as villain (sometimes called, to his
disgust, the "murderer of Custer") and Buffalo Bill as the man who claimed he
had taken "the first scalp for Custer" after the Battle at Little Bighorn. Sitting
Bull had toured with Cody's *Wild West* for four months in 1885, rescuing the

show from financial distress. At the same time, evoking the popular spectacle undercut the seriousness of McLaughlin's memo; calling Cody an "Agent" and Sitting Bull a generic "Big Chief" reinforced the theatrical tone. Even for those who did not try to read the text, the familiar faces of Sitting Bull and Buffalo Bill placed the Ghost Dance within a dramatic narrative of Indian warfare then at its peak within the entertainment marketplace. Like the *Examiner*'s earlier Fire Dance image, the *World*'s two illustrations operated as news "bait" rather than illustration of news. A "steady drumfire of scare stories" soon followed.[25]

By visualizing the Ghost Dance with this portrait of Sitting Bull and Buffalo Bill, the *World*'s images also obscured the dance's spiritual qualities. It bypassed Wovoka's teachings, Porcupine's interpretations, and the leadership of Lakota dance leaders Kicking Bear and Short Bull; further, it confused the story with an actual Ghost Dance prophet and religious teacher, also named Sitting Bull, who was a member of the Arapaho tribe to the southwest. Instead, the *World*'s images conflated the dancers with a more familiar narrative of militant resistance to colonization. For more than a decade, newspapers had portrayed Sitting Bull as the man responsible for the "murder" of Custer, a label he rejected by pointing out that it had been a battle in "open day." The press had variously lamented (or lampooned) his long resistance to the reservation system and the policy of allotment.[26] Popular histories of Custer's "murder"—with Sitting Bull either as stock villain or noble savage—had gone through multiple printings during the 1880s.[27] Dime novels and story papers that valorized Buffalo Bill as legendary scout, Indian fighter, and (by his own telling) "Custer's avenger" had appeared in various versions through the same decade.[28]

In other words, Sitting Bull's portrait was no neutral image. He was one of the most recognizable Native Americans in the nation's history and a potent symbol of Native American resistance to colonization.[29] Because illustrated dailies did not have existing images of Kicking Bear or Short Bull in early November 1890, they used stock photographs and drawings of Sitting Bull instead. If the Lakota hoped the Ghost Dance would allow them to disrupt the hackneyed narrative of conquest and settlement, sensational news images locked them firmly within existing popular lore.

The Democratic-leaning *New York World* and *San Francisco Examiner* soon led the way in visualizing the Ghost Dance, but politics soon motivated other publications to distort the dance and exaggerate Sitting Bull's presence. In mid-November 1890 the weekly *Frank Leslie's Illustrated Newspaper* published a story, and image, highlighting (Lakota) Sitting Bull as a "so-called high priest of the Indian Messiah Craze." The drawing (fig. 3.8), produced without an artist at the scene, showed a standing Sitting Bull addressing warriors around a fire, designating him the central player in the Ghost Dance drama. *Leslie's* new editor, Russell B. Harrison (the president's son) had since May 1889 turned the

THE INDIAN CRAZE OVER THE "NEW MESSIAH."—SITTING BULL SEEKS TO FOMENT DISAFFECTION AMONG THE SIOUX BUCKS

FIGURE 3.8: "The Indian Craze," *Frank Leslie's Illustrated Newspaper*, November 22, 1890, 280. Manuscripts and Special Collections, New York State Library.

paper into an unapologetic mouthpiece for the Republican administration. The weekly had pushed settlement in the Dakotas following the Sioux Act, in part to establish Republican control over the newly developed states (North and South Dakota) and thus maintain control over the U.S. Senate.[30] Sitting Bull provided an effective symbol to further that goal.

Beyond Sitting Bull, daily papers found other images to make the Ghost Dance seem threatening to settlement and indicative of Indian aggression, particularly once the military mobilization began. In mid-November, President Harrison decided to send troops to stop the dancing, ignoring preliminary reports from Brigadier General Ruger that the situation was manageable. Harrison was responding to pleas for support from federal Indian Affairs agents at the Sioux reservations (Pine Ridge, Rosebud, and Cheyenne River) but also to political pressure brought on by the McLaughlin leak and overblown predictions of pan-Indian warfare. Two dozen journalists followed the soldiers and camped out at Pine Ridge Agency, looking for dramatic stories—and images—to send back to their editors.[31] By this point, the emerging illustrated dailies had begun to compete fiercely with pictorial weeklies to produce news images; their higher (daily) circulations amplified their dramatic vision to a wider audience.

Headlines were the first tools dailies used to sensationalize the conflict and boost sales, and these became increasingly shrill in tone after troops arrived at Pine Ridge, fueling the nation's war fever. The *Chicago Tribune* led the way. "Red Men Are Restless," declared the *Tribune*'s November 16 headline; "An Outbreak Expected" appeared the next day. Indian warfare was always good for the newspaper business, and Democratic-leaning papers soon followed suit. "If the Redskins Rise They'll Be Put Down," said the *Herald* on November 17, while the *World*'s headline the next day warned of "An Indian War in the Near Future." The *Examiner* told alarming stories of "Sioux Indians Stark Mad" and "Sioux Indians in War Paint" who were "Moving North from the Sioux Reservation Fully Armed." The dailies celebrated the arrival of troops at Pine Ridge and circulated reports of dubious authenticity, which described "insolent" Indians and "terrified" settlers, largely based on rumor. Catherine Weldon, of the National Indian Defense Association (NIDA), who had left Standing Rock after failing to convince Sitting Bull to denounce the dancing, read these headlines in Kansas City with alarm. She wrote to Sitting Bull, warning that newspapers were "full about the Indians, and that they may make war upon the white people." Images soon amplified the impact of these sensational news stories and headlines.[32]

Theater of War

The illustrated dailies marked the arrival of troops at Pine Ridge Agency with ever-greater theatrical coverage: playbill-style images of characters and settings that delivered dramatic punch. On November 20, 1890, under the headline "Redskins' Bloody Work," the *Chicago Tribune* published eight separate reports, covering half of a front page with multiple images (fig. 3.9). One illustration claimed to show "The Ghost Dance" itself, depicting it (inaccurately) as a war dance, performed by a group of semi-naked men raising their arms in wild gestures (fig. 3.10). The interpretive drawing embellished rather than illustrated; none of the news stories on the page even attempted to describe the Ghost Dance itself. In fact, the image more closely resembled the banned Fire Dance than the practice described by Ghost Dancers and observers. Further, the caption made no attempt to establish the source of the image, which was likely drawn by a *Tribune* artist without access to the scene. It was, however, effective news "bait."[33]

FIGURE 3.9: "Redskins Bloody Work," *Chicago Daily Tribune*, November 20, 1890, 1. Library of Congress.

FIGURE 3.10: "The 'Ghost Dance,'"
Chicago Daily Tribune, November
20, 1890, 1. Library of Congress.

Beyond its distorted interpretive illustration of the Ghost Dance, the *Chicago Tribune's* visual coverage also included familiar faces from older narratives of Indian conflict. Included were images based on photographs taken in the 1870s: Chief Gall (a leader of Indian forces at the Battle of Little Bighorn), Hump, and John Grass. All were Lakota leaders known in the past for their warfare and more recently for their roles in either resisting or accommodating the Sioux Act. Most familiar, and fearsome, was the illustration of Sitting Bull, drawn from a famous photograph showing him wearing a hat with a monarch butterfly on the hatband, an image that had just been reissued by a photographer, over an etched caption "Sitting Bull of the Custer Massacre" (figs. 3.11 and 3.12).[34] As in the other portraits, Sitting Bull's visage conveyed conflicting meanings: it played down the perception of his "savagery" (for one thing, he wore western clothing), but it also resembled the iconography of outlaw photographs. A map of the Sioux reservations (similar to one in the *Herald*) and a drawing of a generic "medicine man"—without context or explanation—rounded out the visual coverage. Nowhere to be found among these images were the actual leaders of the Ghost Dance: prophets Kicking Bear and Short Bull, or fervent advocates Little Wound and Big Road of Pine Ridge Reservation, let alone Wovoka himself. Two days later, the *Tribune* did publish a dubious report about Short Bull with text of an alleged sermon in which he styled himself as the Messiah and predicted the elimination of the whites.[35] Lacking readily available images of Short Bull from past encounters, however, the *Tribune* made no attempt to illustrate the story.

SITTING BULL.

ₗ /45 0. Sitting Bull of the Custer Massacre

FIGURE 3.11: "Sitting Bull," *Chicago Daily Tribune*, November 20, 1890, 1. Library of Congress.

FIGURE 3.12: "Sitting Bull of the Custer Massacre," 1890, photograph (reprint; Northwestern Photographic Company). The Denver Public Library, Western History Collection [X-31384].

Accusations that the Indian Affairs bureau had bungled allotment after the Sioux Act allowed Democratic-leaning illustrated dailies to score points against the Republican administration while tantalizing readers with exciting tales of Indian war. "Ghost Dancers Plot to Kill Troops," announced the *New York Herald*'s November 24 headline for a full-page spread of reporting and images (fig. 3.13). The largest portrait depicted General Nelson A. Miles, the man who famously had defeated the Sioux after Little Bighorn, captured Sitting Bull, and driven him to exile in 1877. The *Herald* also included the same portrait of Sitting Bull (again, in the famous hat), among other portraits. A group image showing Agent McLaughlin "with prominent citizens," a distant view of Standing Rock Reservation, and a map of the Sioux reservations further sketched characters and scene. Unlike other papers that focused solely on male warriors of past conflict, the *Herald* was unusual in including a portrait of a woman: "Scarlet Woman, 'Mother of Christ'" (based on her photograph), who was a Lakota woman named *Waluta Winyan* who had recently been arrested for

FIGURE 3.13: "Ghost Dancers Plot to Kill Troops," *New York Herald*, November 24, 1890, 3. Library of Congress.

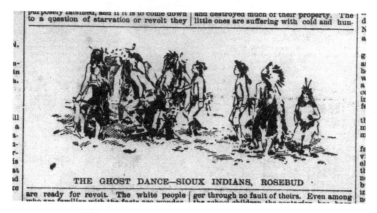

FIGURE 3.14: "The Ghost Dance—Sioux Indians, Rosebud," *San Francisco Examiner*, November 24, 1890, 2. Reprinted with permission from ProQuest.

claiming to be the mother of the (Christian) Messiah. Coming from a variety of settings and periods, none of these images attempted to depict the Ghost Dance itself. Despite their photographic sources, such images likewise distorted public understanding of the Ghost Dance and reinforced the perception that it belonged within a familiar story of conquest and war.[36]

On the West Coast, the *San Francisco Examiner* was at a disadvantage, being less able to obtain such imagery in these early days of the Ghost Dance crisis, but its "news" illustrations told a similar tale of warfare. On November 24, 1890, under the headline "Crazed by Fanaticism" and a subheading that promised descriptions of the ghost dancers' "wild orgies," the paper published two images: one showed "the scene" (in this case, neighboring Rosebud Agency, rather than Standing Rock); the other purported to show the Ghost Dance itself (fig. 3.14). Although drawn by a different artist than the one who produced the *Chicago Tribune*'s misrepresentation of the dance a few days earlier, the image in the *Examiner* distorted the dance in a similar way: it showed dancers as exclusively male, many shirtless, and some with elaborate headdresses.[37] Like the exaggerated numbers of dancers, such interpretive illustrations did more to obscure than illuminate the actual meanings and purpose of the Ghost Dance.[38]

Distorted coverage of the Ghost Dance and the focus on major figures like Sitting Bull linked the dance to stories of Indian "treachery" and Custer's "martyrdom." Perhaps this inspired General Miles in late November to ask his old friend, Buffalo Bill Cody, to make a direct appeal to Sitting Bull, authorizing him as an emissary to visit Standing Rock and negotiate the terms of Sitting Bull's arrest. For publicity purposes, Cody called himself an old "friend" of Sitting Bull's, from their days in the *Wild West* show in 1885, but he too subscribed to the prevailing belief that his friend was "dangerous." Confident that he could convince Sitting Bull to give up the Ghost Dance, Cody arrived in late November at Fort Yates to make the journey to Sitting Bull's camp on the Grand River. Standing Rock agent McLaughlin (or his allies) led Cody astray before he could make contact, however, and on November 29, President Harrison rescinded Cody's mission.[39] Though unsuccessful, Cody's attempt to capture Sitting Bull further reinforced the connection between the Ghost Dance and *Wild West* lore.[40]

By the end of November, illustrated dailies were united in identifying Sitting Bull as "behind the trouble" (often quoting Buffalo Bill Cody as their authority). They also predicted that his arrest might precipitate an "uprising": both perspectives added drama to a volatile situation and helped sell papers. Lakota men encountering these predictions in papers brought to the depot at Rushville, Nebraska (where journalists went to telegraph their copy and buy papers), at first found such accusations humorous, then alarming. The *Omaha Bee* quoted Little Wound and No Water as vehemently objecting to newspaper distortions of the dance and to assertions that the Sioux were "bad" people. Both the *New York Times* and the *Washington Post* reported at the end of November that Big Road and Little Wound were disclaiming any connection to the Ghost Dance and focusing instead on the very real grievances of lost land and declining treaty-mandated rations.[41]

Democratic-leaning sensational dailies sympathized with the Lakota when commercial or political need dictated, but they also enthusiastically endorsed the takeover of Sioux lands by settlers. Hearst's *Examiner*, a Democratic stalwart, found a new way to dramatize the crisis in early December, developing a jingoist story line from a home-front perspective. Even as other dailies reduced visual coverage, the *Examiner* now dramatized *local* implications of the largest military mobilization since the Civil War. Predicting editorially the likelihood of "serious bloodshed"—a result of "fighting and bloody fighting too"—the *Examiner* published images of soldiers in formation, embracing loved ones, and traveling by boat and rail toward the Dakotas (fig. 3.15).[42] These images mimicked familiar iconography from the Civil War years. Foreshadowing his jingoism in the lead-up to the Spanish-American war, Hearst disregarded the fact that the Ghost Dance was not a war dance. His *Examiner* made no reference to the innovations the Lakota introduced to the dance (specifically the Ghost Shirt that—allegedly—deflected bullets) due to their fears of being attacked by government troops. Unlike the *World*, which moved the story to its Sunday pages, treating it as what we might call infotainment rather than news, the *Examiner* continued to whip up the story in dramatic (and highly popular) coverage of military valor, heroes, and sacrifice.[43]

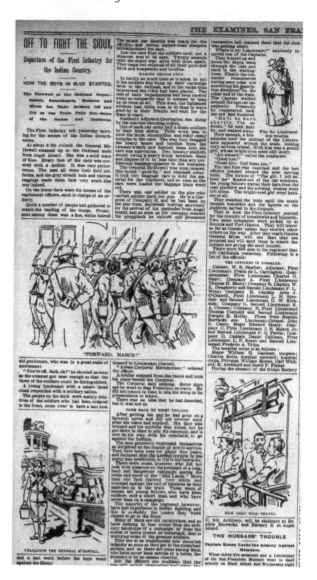

FIGURE 3.15: "Off to
Fight the Sioux," *San
Francisco Examiner*,
December 5, 1890, 3.
Reprinted with permis-
sion from ProQuest.

The Politics of Crisis

By December 1890 the now-sensational "Sioux Outbreak" had become something of a political football that spurred internecine efforts to assign blame
among different government agencies. The secretary of the interior blamed
Congress for reducing funding for rations but also demanded control over the
army's interventions. General Miles likewise blamed Congress for reducing ra-

tion funding and particularly for the recent census at Pine Ridge and Rosebud that undercounted the population, but he also insisted that only the military could properly deal with the crisis. More generally, escalating tensions provided new fodder for an effective overall attack on the Harrison administration.[44] On December 4, 1890, a *World* cartoon, captioned "A Ghastly Ghost Dance," mocked the GOP's recent election-day losses (where the party went from a majority to a one-third minority in the House). When the lame-duck Congress reconvened in early December, Democrats had public opinion behind them to pressure the Republican administration. In blaming Harrison and the Bureau of Indian Affairs for the Ghost Dance, in news stories and cartoons, dailies sensationalized the dance for political gain, under the guise of concern for the very real suffering on the Sioux reservations.[45]

With the exception of Remington's early Ghost Dance illustration (see fig. 3.4), images in pictorial weeklies, though larger and visually more sophisticated than those in the dailies, were equally distorted. For example, the *Illustrated American* supported its own ethnographer at Pine Ridge, and yet its "news illustration" was the same "Fire Dance" image the *Examiner* had used in early October—an "authentic" image, to be sure, but of a completely different dance. Ethnographer Warren K. Moorehead had brought with him several loaded cameras but decided to use the wrong illustration because the Ghost Dance was "less picturesque than the fire dance." *Leslie's* published a similarly distorted image of the dance. Captioned "The Recent Indian Excitement in the Northwest," this image depicted menacing, warlike dancers, who did not clasp hands but rather held their arms and weapons aloft (fig. 3.16). In the same issue, adjacent images showed scenes of turmoil and a long line of settlers fleeing their homesteads. Such scare stories conformed to a long history of captivity narratives and the *Wild West* show itself, in which the "Attack on a Settler's Cabin" was the longest-running feature. Like the earlier interpretive illustrations in the sensational dailies, these news images provided emotional justification for military action.[46]

Republican-leaning papers particularly exaggerated the connection between the Ghost Dance and the Custer story; emphasizing the warlike nature of the Sioux deflected blame from federal authorities overseeing the reservations. The *Chicago Tribune* kept the Custer story front and center by publishing an article submitted by a former Pine Ridge schoolteacher named Emma Sickels, titled "How Custer Died," which included a pair of pictographs (fig. 3.17), "drawn by an Indian." The captions—"Indian Picture of the Custer Fight"—suggested that the two drawings showed the Custer battle from differing perspectives. Whatever Sickels's intentions in writing the article, the headline, images, and captions invoked war, linking the current "crisis" with Custer's defeat. (In fact, the text of Sickels's article identified the second image as a drawing of an—unrelated—intra-Indian fight; the caption was incorrect.)[47] With such warlike

FIGURE 3.16: "The Recent Indian Excitement in the Northwest," *Frank Leslie's Illustrated Newspaper*, December 13, 1890, 354. Manuscripts and Special Collections, New York State Library.

images, and their misleading captions, the *Tribune* tapped into public feeling about to "How Custer Died" and tied the present situation to a past humiliation that had yet to be avenged.

A few journalists, and the Lakota themselves, recognized the poisonous effect of the dailies' scramble for dramatic news, but they were powerless to correct the record. The *Omaha World-Herald's* journalists Thomas Tibbles and his wife Bright Eyes (a mixed-race woman of the Omaha tribe, also known as Suzette LaFlesch) were probably the most vocal critics at the time. Tibbles wrote on December 13, 1890, that the accounts being spread by the "war reporters" had "not a word of truth in them. . . . The dispatches are highly colored and sensational in the extreme." Years later Tibbles described the pressure they were under for "exciting news from the front": "Our newspapers [the *Omaha World-Herald* and the *Chicago Express*] had grown indignant with us for not turning in anything interesting about this 'great Indian war,'" he wrote. Newspapers that eschewed publishing "jingoistic journalism" faced consequences in lost advertising sales and circulation—the twin pillars of commercial media.[48]

Once sensationalized, dramatic coverage of the Ghost Dance only intensified, ironically even as diplomatic efforts began to bear fruit. Democratic dailies played up the idea of Indian savagery in their Sunday pages, reinforcing the

HOW GEN. CUSTER DIED.

THE STORY TOLD THIS TIME BY THE PENCIL OF LITTLE BIG MAN.

He Would Not Put Into Words the Details of That Bloody Day on the Little Big Horn, but He Drew Them Artlessly for His Friend—Stories About Famous Indians of This and Other Days.

Two Nicks lived on the Pine Ridge Indian Reservation—father and son. They were both active members of society. Many said of the elder that they "could not deny"

As his name would imply.

But my memory of him is of a social traveling companion on a long ride through the Bad Lands country on the edge of the Bad Lands, among the washouts and buttes, "like the lay of the land where the Custer fight was," he said.

"Folks blame me for putting Red Cloud up to things. I've been with him so much. He talks to me and many times has told me what he aims to do, and many times I've helped him, but he is a very set kind of man. He don't stand out for nobody, 'cept, perhaps, his squaw. She makes it lively for him sometimes. She won't 'low no other squaw in his house. One come once, but she didn't stay. I've been with him off 'nd on most of the time for twenty years, when the tribe has been movin' from place to place, first on the Platte River, then over

and Little Big Man was bound over to keep the peace. I fear he would not have had any qualms of conscience about following his ideas of retribution if the peace were once broken. He fortunately was not tested. Those who had incurred his displeasure and lived in dread need fear him no more. He died two years ago, and was buried with military honors by his tribe. He had been a power among his people—not loyal and progressive like Young man Afraid of His Horses (the young man of whose horses the enemy is afraid is the Indian significance of his name) and Little Wound, nor wily, suave, and treacherous like Red Cloud, who has little respect from the Indians and but small following except through his agents, many of whom are squaw men and whites who live on the "profits" of disturbance and strife.

Tanka Cical Wacasa (Little Big Man) was called Little on account of his size—he measured five feet four. The appellation Big was given on account of his valor. Whenever he made his appearance among a group of young bucks they immediately recognized his authority by rising and standing until he was seated. One day he showed me a document that was given him by the President setting forth his good qualities and allowing him especial privileges. I asked him to tell me about Crazy Horse and the "time the great white chief was killed." He did not seem to understand me, so I said, "If you cannot tell me anything about it will you make a picture showing your idea of it?" He promised to do so. He provided him with pencils and paper. A few weeks after he brought me two sketches, one representing the Custer fight, the other a personal encounter he had had with the hereditary enemies of his tribe—the Crows. I asked

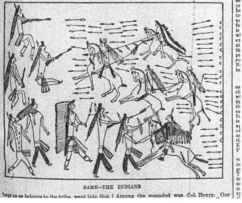

INDIAN PICTURE OF THE CUSTER FIGHT—THE CAVALRYMEN.

to the Missouri, then back again to the White, near the Bad Lands, where we be now. I was with them up in Montana, where Custer got killed. It was in a place something like that." He pointed to a kind of ravine that had been the bed of a creek. The country is full of abrupt gulches or "washouts," some overgrown with grass, others immense masses of alkali clay, deeply seamed by the inroads of wind and water. Frequently the trail follows the bed of the "dry creek," winding for miles between banks so high that they shut out the prospect of the country on both sides and vividly suggest the stories of ambush and the possibilities of invisible foes lurking on either hand or concealed among the many ragged recesses that lie along the way.

"The Sioux was camped in one of the loops of the creek where there was grass and trees and water. It was in so deep you couldn't see 'em til you got there. The creek turned so sudden and the banks was so high you had to go along the creek if you started that way. Custer's scouts hadn't seen nor known of our bein' there. He come along down the path of the creek, slap onto 'em, before he knew anythin' 'bout it. They seen him comin' and closed together 'cross the openin' of the loop, so he couldn't get back. He couldn't get out, 'cause the washouts was too high. It was all done so quick the soldiers didn't have time to shoot. Nobody got away. No white man,

him where he was; he pointed to the solitary brave wearing two horns.

"Where are the other Indians?"

"Back there. Then arrows come."

Making due allowance for their inordinate love of praise that prompts them to draw on their imagination to supply what deficiency opportunity has failed to provide it is probable that the idea of the sketch is much exaggerated and that he rushed into the fight wherever the "fray was thickest."

These views of the encounter were supplemented by Mr. Mears—a gentleman who has been on the frontier for about twenty-five years—acting as Mayor of Chadron when that town was first organized. I had been greatly interested in his reminiscences, and believe many of his experiences too good to be lost, as few are better informed as to frontier life and Indian warfare than he, and the rapid settlement of the country and the civilization of the Indian may soon relegate such experience to the past. He wrote: "I will cheerfully give you any information I can. Gen. Custer was killed June 25, 1876, on the Little Big Horn. Twelve miles above the junction with the Big Horn, where Fort Custer now stands. Col. Reno, Capt. Benteen, Lieut. De Rudio, are some of the officers that escaped. The Little and Big Horn Rivers are in the Department of Dakota, which at the time was commanded by Gen. Terry. I was with Gen. Crook in the Department of the Platte. We fought the same Indians that killed Custer eight days before his fight, on the 17th day of June. We had ten or twelve men killed and as many more wounded.

SAME—THE INDIANS

'cept us as belongs to the tribe, went into that   Among the wounded was Col. Henry. Our story's entertainment angle. On December 14 the *Examiner* came up with an illustrated special on scalping techniques under the headline "Some Real Hair Raisers." With soldiers in the field, this both mocked and established the Lakota as a savage enemy.[49] Readers were probably unaware that, despite this war imagery, U.S. Army leadership had secured agreements with most (though not all) of the Ghost Dancers to cease dancing and return to the reservations. By early December, dancers' numbers had shrunk from roughly five thousand before the troops arrived to fewer than thirteen hundred divided among three camps. One was Sitting Bull's camp on the Grand River at Standing Rock Reservation; another was Big Foot's camp at Cheyenne River. Only the third group, largely Brulés from Rosebud Reservation, led by Kicking Bear and Short Bull, had retreated to a hard-to-access plateau in the Bad Lands, to the northwest of Pine Ridge, dubbed by the press as the "Stronghold." Sensational reporting and press hysteria about "marauders" and "war paint" cultivated an atmosphere of fear, while the military buildup made the remaining dancers wary of returning to the agencies.[50]

War hysteria likely explains why General Miles insisted that Sitting Bull be arrested, a decision that began a chain of events resulting in Sitting Bull's killing and, two weeks later, the massacre at Wounded Knee. Though Standing Rock agent McLaughlin wanted to wait for colder weather to arrest him, word that Sitting Bull planned to witness the dancing at Kicking Bear's camp caused the agent to expedite the arrest. McLaughlin dispatched the Indian Police, who arrived to arrest Sitting Bull at his cabin on the Grand River in the early hours of December 15. As Indian Police forcibly removed him from his cabin, one of his allies fired a shot, at which the Indian Police killed Sitting Bull, his son, and other members of his household. In the end, eight of Sitting Bull's community and six Indian Police were dead. Members of Sitting Bull's camp fled, a large number joining Big Foot's camp on the Cheyenne River, fearful of further violence and reprisals.[51]

Misdirection after Wounded Knee

Sitting Bull's killing created a challenge in representation for sensational dailies. Papers continued to publish his image not only as a symbol of resistance to the Sioux Act and allotment but also as a striking character whose death seemed to bring a long-standing drama to its inevitable conclusion. Not surprisingly, illustrated dailies glossed over conflicting accounts about how Sitting Bull was killed and instead built on their earlier visualizations to include a broader range of images that offered narrative closure. No longer a threat, the "Sitting Bull of the Custer Massacre" photograph gave way to a richer array of images representing him as the defeated warrior returning from exile or the show

Indian from Buffalo Bill's *Wild West*. The *Chicago Tribune*'s illustration, based on an early photograph of Sitting Bull, was most obviously a mass-produced souvenir, including what appeared to be an authentic reproduction of Sitting Bull's autograph below it. This drawing was faithful in all details to a photograph, dating to his imprisonment at Fort Randall in 1881–83, in which he wore a fur-trimmed shirt and beaded necklaces; a single feather adorned his hair, which hung in two braids on either side of his chest, and he held a peace pipe in his lap (figs. 3.18 and 3.19). The photograph was both "authentic" and equivocal. It showcased a nonthreatening, defeated warrior in a positive and peaceful aspect that reminded viewers of his defeat and exile in 1877. Sitting Bull's traditional presentation was typical of images of Native Americans taken by photographers in this period, who conducted a booming business documenting a "declining" race for settlers and tourists. These were sold for profit by the *Wild West* show and by Sitting Bull himself to visitors at Standing Rock as a source of income for his family and community.[52]

FIGURE 3.18: "Sitting Bull," *Chicago Daily Tribune*, December 16, 1890, 1. Library of Congress.

FIGURE 3.19: Sitting Bull, seated: full-length portrait with pipe and signature, 1884, Item # A2250–0001, [Palmquist and Jurgens]. State Historical Society of North Dakota (SHSND).

FIGURE 3.20: "Sitting Bull," *New York World*, December 16, 1890, 1. New York State Library.

FIGURE 3.21: Sitting Bull studio portrait with one feather, 1884–1886, Item # 1952-7444, [David F. Barry]. State Historical Society of North Dakota (SHSND).

All images of Sitting Bull after his death published in the illustrated dailies were similarly true to source photographs. It was as if fidelity to the original, and accuracy in reproduction, somehow canceled out the fact that Sitting Bull was the inadvertent victim of the government's determination to stop the Ghost Dance. So, the *World* published a portrait based on a similar souvenir photograph (figs. 3.20 and 3.21). Such photographs were readily available to illustrators in Chicago and New York: many had appeared in the Custer histories of the 1880s; others resided in newspaper "art" files or personal collections. The exactness of the reproduction is a strong indication of the editorial value placed on "authentic" images. They conveyed conflicting messages, however:

FIGURE 3.22: "Sitting Bull (from a photograph)," *San Francisco Examiner*, December 17, 1890, 1. Reprinted with permission from ProQuest.

FIGURE 3.23: "Sitting Bull," 1885, II-83091, Wm. Notman and Son. McCord Museum, Montreal.

they recovered Sitting Bull's celebrity but also reminded readers of his status as a defeated warrior in federal custody.[53]

Souvenir imagery from the early 1880s blurred the line between Sitting Bull's killing and the many historical revisions of the Custer story, but newer imagery from the 1885 *Wild West* tour brought the Ghost Dance crisis into the realm of popular entertainment. The *Examiner's* portrait of Sitting Bull on December 17, 1890 (crediting the *Illustrated American* as source), was based on a photograph from a series taken in 1885 with Buffalo Bill at the Notman studio in Montreal, Canada (figs. 3.22 and 3.23). Taken about halfway through his four-month tour with Cody's *Wild West* show, the portrait depicted Sitting Bull in his "traditional" performance costume, as a Lakota warrior. The image underscored the headline's dramatic message that his death was inevitable: "'I Will Die Fighting.'" But it also established him as public figure of some note. More significant, none of the papers published illustrations of the most famous photograph from that shoot,

FIGURE 3.24: "Sitting Bull and His Family," *New York Herald*, December 17, 1890, 3. Library of Congress.

FIGURE 3.25: Sitting Bull family portrait, 1882, Item # A2952, [photographer unknown]. State Historical Society of North Dakota (SHSND).

with Sitting Bull and Buffalo Bill (both in their show costumes) standing side by side—as peers. Perhaps such an image would do too much to recall Sitting Bull's standing as a storied character in popular culture.[54]

Wild West images of Sitting Bull suggest ambivalence about his role in the Ghost Dance crisis. Was he instigator of the dance or a victim of the army? Was he a killer or a victim of murder or assassination? Warrior or entertainer? Had he abused U.S. soldiers, dishonorably "murdered" Custer, or had he fought a fair fight to defend his people and way of life? Underlying these questions was the unpalatable problem of whether his killing had been justified—or planned. A day later, the *Herald* now published a portrait of Sitting Bull and his family (figs. 3.24 and 3.25) that reflected a similar ambiguity. The source for this illustration was another of the earlier 1881–82 photographs (dating from his imprisonment) also sold as a souvenir in the 1880s.[55] It conveyed a humanizing message.

By contrast, the *World* published what at first glance appeared to be a political "cartoon," a drawing captioned "Five Types of American Civilization," which conveyed a lesson in social Darwinism. In reality, this image was adapted from yet another publicity photograph also taken at Montreal's Notman studio in 1885: a group portrait of Sitting Bull, his interpreter, Buffalo Bill, and two others (figs. 3.26 and 3.27). The *World*'s reframing transformed this group portrait into

FIGURE 3.26: "Five Types of American Civilization," *New York World*, December 21, 1890, 1. New York State Library.

FIGURE 3.27: "Buffalo Bill and His Troupe," 1885, II-94132, Wm. Notman and Son. McCord Museum, Montreal.

a metaphorical assertion of scientific racism. (The *World* offered a more complicated perspective [in text form], in an editorial, "Our Indian Wards," which excoriated the federal government's mishandling of the "Sioux Outbreak.") Overall, this visual outpouring in the illustrated dailies reflected confusion about how to comprehend Sitting Bull as a symbol of the Ghost Dance specifically and westward expansion more generally. In their fidelity to the original details, such illustrations inadvertently demonstrated the ease with which realistic, photograph-based images could be transformed—with something as simple as a caption—and given new meanings, as circumstances dictated.[56]

After Sitting Bull's death, Hearst's *San Francisco Examiner*, the most boosterish of the dailies, continued to produce images that showed unqualified support for the Indian police and U.S. soldiers. Notwithstanding its earlier criticism of the Harrison administration, the paper expressed no visual ambivalence about the outcome. On the contrary: it published a group portrait of the the Indian Police—identified as "survivors" of the abortive arrest of Sitting Bull, rather than his killers. The text emphasized that these "friendly Indians" had made the sacrifice to bring the crisis to its inevitable conclusion, reporting with satisfaction the disrespectful burial of Sitting Bull and subsequent desecration of his remains.

Such boosterish coverage brought results. A few days later, the *Examiner* boasted that it was competing economically with the other three dailies: it was now fourth in the nation in terms of pages of advertising sold, according to the *World*'s statistics, a formidable accomplishment for the twenty-seven-year-old Hearst and his first popular newspaper.[57] The commercial success and lessons learned in visual journalism during the "Ghost Dance war" prepared Hearst well for his move to the East Coast with the purchase of the *New York Journal* a few years later.

Visual coverage of the "Sioux Outbreak" in the four dailies subsided in the two weeks following Sitting Bull's death. Dailies printed without illustration wire reports that identified Big Foot, leading his own dancers from Cheyenne River along with refugees who had fled Standing Rock after Sitting Bull's killing, as the new warrior to capture. This development was significant but hard to visualize, and consequently, the "crisis" receded from view, supplanted by Christmas imagery, advertisements, and holiday fare.[58] Brief and conflicting stories of battles, skirmishes, raids on settlers, alongside shrinking estimates of Indians still on the "war path" (in other words, dancing and refusing to "come in"), moved from the front pages to the interior sections.[59] Behind the scenes, American military leaders sought to entice the remaining dancers from the "Stronghold" and to capture Big Foot's followers. Lacking familiar characters and existing imagery for effective sensational coverage, however, the four papers included no images with these reports.

It was only when Big Foot's negotiations with military leaders broke down that the drama resumed. After a misunderstanding with army leaders, and fearful for the safety of his followers, Big Foot abruptly withdrew, taking his band and refugees from Sitting Bull's camp on a heroic fifty-mile trek to Pine Ridge. Headlines characterized this as another example of Indian treachery, a bid to join the Stronghold dancers, in Christmas Eve stories that told of "Sitting Bull's Refugees Escape." The drama seemed to fade quickly when, after a few days of new negotiations, Big Foot (gravely ill with pneumonia) agreed to surrender at Wounded Knee Creek. With the conflict apparently over, the Democratic-leaning dailies stepped up their earlier critique of the government. "The surrender of Big Foot and his band practically ends the Indian trouble in the Northwest," said the *Examiner*. "It is to be hoped that the blunders which brought on the crisis will not be repeated. The united testimony of all competent witnesses is that the Indians were driven to revolt by starvation."[60] The paper's editorial empathy for the Lakota (in the form of political critique) did not extend to positive visualization, however.

On New Year's Eve, 1890, wire stories reported a new "battle" in the Indian War. It had almost seemed that conflict would be avoided: most of the dancers had left the Stronghold and were heading toward Pine Ridge; Big Foot had surrendered. However, General Miles sent orders that Big Foot's people at Wounded Knee, surrounded though they were by troops and weapons, must be disarmed; it was a risky order, given that tensions were very high. When only a few older weapons were produced, soldiers searched the entire Indian camp and the surrounded men. One man resisted, perhaps urged on by an elder's chanting, or possibly not wanting to surrender a prized weapon without compensation; when someone seized his gun, it went off into the air. Immediately, the commanding officer ordered the encircling troops to fire. Big Foot and his son were killed instantly, and in a confusion of crossfire both Lakota and some soldiers were killed; troops lobbed shells from their Hotchkiss guns into the camp, catching their own men in the process. Women and children who fled were hunted down by soldiers and executed. In the end, 146 bodies (eighty-four men, forty-four women, eighteen children) lay dead in the immediate vicinity; nearly three hundred Lakota would be found dead before the count was complete. Hearing the news, Stronghold dancers led by Kicking Bear and Short Bull, who had been moving toward Pine Ridge agency, retreated to their camp in the Bad Lands. The conflict was not over.[61]

Instead of representing the actual events at Wounded Knee, sensational dailies recast the massacre as the scene of a battle. Headlines spoke of acts of "treachery" committed by "reckless braves." Text praised the troops and Indian Police, blaming the Lakota for the deaths at Wounded Knee.[62] Each of the two New York (Democratic-leaning) dailies flogged the war angle with available imagery: the *Herald* paired its headline "Reckless Braves Slaughtered by the Score" with flattering group portraits of Indian police and U.S. Cavalry. The *World* complemented its headline "Hemmed In by Savages" with a small image of an "Indian scout." The *Chicago Tribune* declined to illustrate the situation at all, perhaps because of its potential to hurt president Harrison politically. While also blaming "Indian treachery," the *Tribune* excoriated the Democratic dailies for "exaggerating the situation in their eagerness to assail the Republican administration."[63] And then, despite the reality of actual fighting, many deaths, and high drama at Wounded Knee, the *World*, the *Herald*, and the *Tribune* abruptly ceased their attempts to visualize what was happening in the Plains West. Their visual blackout indicated the challenge they faced in presenting a massacre as a heroic fight; it also quite effectively screened the massacre from public view.

Hearst's *Examiner*, by contrast, continued its boosterish coverage, publishing more images in the ten days following than in all the months leading up to Wounded Knee. With a keen attention to drama, the *Examiner* focused on the tension over whether the last holdouts in the Stronghold would return peaceably to Pine Ridge. Still at a distance from the action (and relying on wire reports, the paper began a new strategy, copied from the weeklies, of attesting to image sourcing in its captions. For the time, and for a daily newspaper, the *Examiner* produced a stunning array of images that surpassed the competition in covering the aftermath of Wounded Knee. It illustrated a story headlined "Buried the Boys in Blue" with another group portrait, based on a photograph, of the famous Seventh Cavalry (of Little Bighorn fame) just prior to their deployment

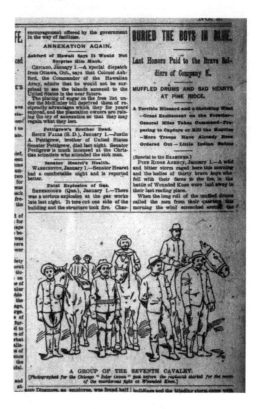

FIGURE 3.28: "Buried the Boys in Blue," *San Francisco Examiner*, January 2, 1891, 1. Reprinted with permission from ProQuest.

to Wounded Knee (fig. 3.28). A few days later, multiple drawings accompanied its feature story about "Miles's Old-Time Tactics": images of General Miles and his staff; an array of friendly and "hostile" Indians (including, for the first time, a portrait of Kicking Bear, standing, in war regalia). The *Examiner* also introduced additional scenes, including the river crossing to Sitting Bull's camp on the Grand River and a view of Fort Niobrara, where troops were stationed (fig. 3.29). In passing, the paper mentioned Miles's deployment of Emma Sickels as a negotiator with her old friend, Little Wound, to establish terms for the return of the last dancers to Pine Ridge.[64] The *Examiner*'s array of portraits and traditional Indian imagery (produced from photographs and sourced in the captions) set a new standard for creating dramatic "news" images that were not interpretive reenactments of what happened at Pine Ridge but rather scenes and a cast of characters for readers at home.

Ironically, the *Examiner*'s extensive visual coverage of the aftermath of Wounded Knee was even more effective than the blackout in the other dailies in screening out the massacre. Its images provided effective post facto justifications for the carnage there. For example, it published another (distorted)

FIGURE 3.29: "Miles' Old-Time Tactics," *San Francisco Examiner*, January 7, 1891, 1. Reprinted with permission from ProQuest.

INDIA.:S AGAIN AT THEIR GHOST DANCING.
[From a sketch in "Frank Leslie's Illustrated Newspaper."]

FIGURE 3.30: "Indians Again at Their Ghost Dancing," *San Francisco Examiner*, January 13, 1891, 1. Reprinted with permission from ProQuest.

Ghost Dance image, "Indians Again at Their Ghost Dancing," sourced to an illustration in *Frank Leslie's Illustrated Newspaper*, that was well designed to remind readers of the putative savagery of the dance (fig. 3.30). A day later, in a contradictory image, under the headline "Hostiles Returning to their Reservation," the *Examiner* concluded its narrative arc with an image of a Lakota wagon train approaching in the snow (fig. 3.31), an image sourced to another pictorial weekly, *Collier's Once a Week*. Though small, the image paid visual homage to a familiar *Harper's Weekly* illustration from 1881 of Sitting Bull's return from exile and surrender, which had been reprinted in many popular histories of the Custer saga. This final image of surrender closed the *Examiner's* visualization of the Ghost Dance and the Massacre at Wounded Knee. The paper immediately reverted to more familiar serial coverage—Jack the Ripper, Whitecaps—and the next novelty sensation.[65]

The *Examiner's* selective imagery demonstrates the illustrated dailies' newfound power to shape the visual narrative, even when using so-called "authentic" evidence and sourcing information. While the paper blamed the government and the military for the tragedy, it found an eye-catching and crowd-pleasing way to conclude the story. After the illustrated dailies moved on to other news, pictorial weeklies reasserted their dominance in visualization of the Ghost Dance and Wounded Knee. At first, they depicted the crisis as the "Last Indian

REDSKINS AT PINE RIDGE.

The Hostiles Have Come In and Are Camped Under the Guns.

GENERAL MILES WILL NOT DISARM THEM IMMEDIATELY.

Great Caution Thought to Be Necessary, for the Young Bucks Are Anxious to Fight—It Is Not Believed That the Trouble Is Over Yet—There May Be An Attack at Any Time—Or Peace.

[Special to the EXAMINER.]

PINE RIDGE, January 13.—It is the beginning of the end. To-night the undisputed outlook was that with a few more days of patience the Indian war will be over. The official bulletin from General Miles says:

"All the Indians are now in. They came in under our guns and made camp as directed, without other terms than that they were to return and submit to law and order."

General Miles is being already compli-

perched on the hill behind the earthworks, is an eight-inch rifle, which is trained on the camp. For a while yesterday everybody at Pine Ridge waited anxiously, feeling every moment that the roar of that gun might be heard, and everyone was expectant.

THEY CAME.

Suddenly two Indians were seen on the crest of the hill but a short distance beyond the other pickets. Then others appeared on the hills to the northwest, and then a body of more than 100 bucks rose to the crest of the hill behind which the hostiles were.

The number steadily increased to 400 by the accession of bands ranging in number from five to twenty-five. Captain Dougherty was immediately notified. He dispatched a courier to headquarters to notify General Miles of the movement. Then hurrying to the fortifications he had the gun prepared for action. The range-finder adjusted his sights and the cave in which the ammunition was stored was opened. A line of skirmishers was sent out beyond the fortifications on the crest of the hills.

The activity at headquarters was stirring. Orders were sent to the cavalry to saddle and be in readiness to move southwest of the camp. General Miles, accompanied by his staff, made a circuit of the camp, extra ammunition was issued and when everything was in readiness the troops waited.

LIKE TO TALK WITH HIM.

After two hours General Miles received word that the Indians did not mean to make any advance, but they would like to talk with him. The General sent them word to go quietly into camp and he would receive

HOSTILES RETURNING TO THEIR RESERVATION.
[From a sketch in "Once a Week."]

FIGURE 3.31: "Hostiles Returning to Their Reservation," *San Francisco Examiner*, January 14, 1891, 1. Reprinted with permission from ProQuest.

War" rather than a massacre of cold, starving refugees. Even *Harpers' Weekly*, which had published the most accurate rendering of the dance weeks before, now illustrated its coverage with a Remington image depicting not the massacre at Wounded Knee but, rather, a drawing based on his apocryphal (1890) painting, "The Last Stand." Although not an image of Custer, the drawing's caption alluded to the many "last stand" images of his demise and implied that the massacre was justified. Subsequently, *Harper*'s reimagined events at Wounded Knee as a defensive battle rather than a massacre.[66]

As the Ghost Dance and Wounded Knee receded from view, the idea of preemptive warfare as a necessity in dealing with the "irreconcilable" Indian remained a commercially viable component of popular lore.[67] Buffalo Bill Cody lobbied successfully to recruit a new group of Show Indians for his European tour, winning permission to sign up Kicking Bear, Short Bull, and the other "hostile" leaders of the Ghost Dance imprisoned at Fort Sheridan (Wyoming), to perform "savagery" in the *Wild West* pageant. Years later, Cody consulted on the battle scene for the 1913 film *The Last Indian War*, which depicted soldiers, rather than the Lakota being killed. The film established a paradigm for the movie Western, while further obscuring events at Wounded Knee.[68]

In their desire to produce dramatic news stories and images, sensational illustrated dailies amplified yet also undermined Ghost Dancers' efforts to memorialize a traditional way of life through religious practice. A few weeks after Wounded Knee, Bright Eyes (Suzette LaFlesch) blamed the tragic outcome of the Lakota Ghost Dance on the corruption of Indian Affairs agents, the plunder by settlers and traders, and sensational news reporting. "The whole Indian question has been wrong," she said bitterly. "The Indians have been [abused], starved and murdered."[69] The Ghost Dance, a powerful form of communication among Native American tribes, did not communicate well through prevailing media forms. Partly because the dance translated poorly into dramatic visuals, sensationalism as a genre had no incentive to portray the Ghost Dance accurately. Instead, daily newspapers used source-based and interpretive line illustrations—the most powerful media tools of the period—to urge and then justify military force to stop a peaceful religious ceremony. In later years, away from the limelight, the Ghost Dance would continue for decades after Wounded Knee. In 1890, however, lacking in an illustrated press of their own, the Lakota were vulnerable to misrepresentation. As the next chapter will show, African Americans in the 1890s used their own illustrated publications with somewhat greater success.

CHAPTER 4

"A Song without Words"

Anti-Lynching Imagery as Visual Protest in the 1890s Black Press

THE PRACTICE OF LYNCHING was a regular feature of American culture in the decades following the Civil War. In November 1895 an illustrated African American newspaper called the Indianapolis *Freeman* directly confronted that reality when it published an anti-lynching image over a simple caption: "A Song without Words" (fig. 4.1). In the late nineteenth century, African American newspapers for the first time published such images as part of a larger strategy to challenge racial discrimination, inequality, and violence.[1] Some years later, lynching photographs and postcards published in African American newspapers repurposed the propaganda of the lynch mob and turned it into an oppositional message.[2] The anti-lynching illustrations and cartoons of the late 1880s and 1890s, by contrast, were explicitly created by African American artists and editors for the black press. Such images supported the community's arguments about the need for federal protection of fundamental rights laid out in the Fourteenth Amendment. They strove to redefine the popular narrative about lynch mobs and their victims, laying the groundwork for later visual activism.

"A Song without Words" was also a sensational image, in the sense that it caught the eye and deliberately appealed to emotion. Its catalog of lynching's various forms—shooting, hanging, burning, and dismembering—made a mute but powerful appeal to readers. Like the blues music emerging in the same decade (or Billie Holiday's Depression-era protest song "Strange Fruit" two generations later), such images evoked a range of feelings—loss and anger, sorrow and resistance—in response to the trauma of lynching.[3] As was true of earlier sensational imagery, "A Song without Words" resonated differently than words did. While African American newspapers, including the *Freeman*, also made legal, constitutional, and moral arguments against lynching, the publication of

FIGURE 4.1: "A Song without Words," Indianapolis *Freeman*, November 2, 1895, 1.
Library of Congress.

anti-lynching imagery accessed a more elemental quality—feeling—to raise
consciousness and inspire activism. Though constrained by threats of violence,
discrimination, and disenfranchisement, black editors attempted to harness
sensationalism's capacity to move readers into action.

In early 1889 Henry Jackson Lewis, by then the period's foremost African
American illustrator, joined the *Freeman*. Much of his background remains a
mystery, but apparently Lewis was born in slavery in Mississippi in the late 1830s
(the exact year is unknown) and lived much of his life in Pine Bluff, Arkansas.
Despite having been severely burned as a child, which left him blind in one eye
and crippled in his left hand, he served in the Union Army during the Civil
War and subsequently mastered the craft of engraving and illustration. In the
1870s and 1880s he contributed illustrations to various publications, including
Harper's Weekly and *Frank Leslie's Illustrated Newspaper*, and he illustrated the
Smithsonian's "Mound Survey" of prehistoric Native American sites in Arkansas
and elsewhere. Many of his illustrations and cartoons for the *Freeman* focused
on themes of economic, social, and political rights for African Americans.
Lewis's tenure at the *Freeman* was brief (less than two full years), but even after
his death in 1891 the *Freeman* continued to republish many of his images, with
new captions, through the end of the century.[4]

The *Freeman* was a weekly illustrated publication that became, under the leadership of Edward E. Cooper, one of the nation's most important African American newspapers. Cooper envisioned the *Freeman* as a politically independent paper, an unusual feature for an African American publication at that time (most others were subsidized by the Republican Party). Perhaps to achieve economic independence, the paper's innovation was its generous use of illustrations and its self-presentation as the "*Harper's Weekly* of the Colored Race." In the style of Pulitzer and Hearst, between 1888 and early 1889 Cooper's expansion of illustrations transformed a rather humble publication—text based, with a rare portrait or two—into a competitive and nearly self-supporting commercial venture. Until he sold it in 1892, Cooper's *Freeman* employed some of the nation's first African American illustrators, artists, and cartoonists—including Lewis, Moses Tucker, and Edward E. Lee. Their drawings critiqued prejudice, inequality, and the government's failure to protect the principles of due process and equality under the law.[5]

Interpretive illustrations, cartoons, and news images in the *Freeman* and other African American newspapers protested racial violence in a number of ways: they documented atrocities, evoked emotion to fuel activism, and advocated a strong, federal government response. The black press played a significant role in the African American community and promoted a national, civic culture for readers all over the country, from Northern cities like Cleveland and Detroit to small, rural Southern towns like Huntsville, Alabama.[6] Building on the work of the National Afro-American Press Association, a few publishers began to produce a range of visual alternatives to negative racial stereotypes.[7] Missing or incomplete runs of these papers make it difficult to generalize, but a close examination of three (the *Richmond (Va.) Planet*, the *Cleveland Gazette*, and the Indianapolis *Freeman*) with more complete runs, confirmed by other papers where available, reveals a clear trend. Through the 1890s African American newspapers published anti-lynching illustrations in an effort to counter stereotypes, using both interpretive and "realistic" news images to sensationalize—and thus challenge—mainstream representations of lynching, for their own readers and sympathetic white allies.

The Emergence of the Illustrated Black Press

Positive images of people and places that highlighted respectability and achievement proved most popular in African American newspapers, few of which directly tackled racist stereotypes. Visually static images of "representative" types were common, typically wood-cut portraits of people and newly constructed buildings suitable for reproduction on a flatbed press for a small circulation, reflecting financial and technological constraints. Portraits of popular race spokesmen appeared often; former abolitionist and civil rights activist Frederick Douglass, for one, appeared frequently in a wide variety of papers. Positive achievements and sources of pride—professional, political, economic, and cultural success stories—constituted the preferred iconography. Stories and images of notable African American leaders allowed papers "to show [the] progress . . . being made among us in religious, literary, financial and industrial pursuits."[8] Uplifting news, they believed, could mitigate some of the negative stereotypes and challenge white supremacist propaganda. Images of institutions, particularly schools like the Tuskegee Institute and its president Booker T. Washington, were also common. Others featured portraits of Christian leaders, along with drawings of new churches and charitable institutions.[9] These photograph-based illustrations were anything but sensational; they provided realistic visual complements to text reports about civic and community life.

Articles about cultural and entertainment icons offered another way to counter negative stereotyping. Sports heroes, particularly boxers Peter Jackson and George Dixon, though rarely illustrated in the black press, regularly appeared in brief text reports. Not all editors approved. "The movements of Peter Jackson are announced by telegraph the same as those of any other distinguished citizen," the *Huntsville Gazette* commented dryly. "If the Afro-American would rise to the sublime height of the Caucasian he has only to enter the prize ring." While disapproving of prizefighting, the *Cleveland Gazette* commented more favorably on George Dixon's success in the ring: "Even in his line, he is doing much to elevate the race in the opinion of a large class of Americans, and therefore is a credit to his race."[10] Portraits of more "respectable" types, such as businessmen, Republican politicians, or YMCA officials, were more frequent. Literary figures, such as poets Paul Laurence Dunbar and Phyllis Wheatley, appeared occasionally.[11] Images of women highlighted their cultural leadership as singers, authors, and especially teachers.[12] Portrait galleries of war heroes and drawings of veterans' parades celebrated African American contributions to the nation, the more necessary because "history has unpardonably neglected the Negro."[13]

In creating this alternative visual archive of African American respectability, editors also praised their own newspapers as both agents and exemplars of positive black culture. They emphasized the achievements of the black press itself, accompanied by illustrations of editors and journalists in a self-reflexive hall of fame. As just one example, *Richmond Planet* editor John Mitchell Jr.'s portrait appeared even in competing publications, which praised his skill as a writer, followed his political career in Richmond, Virginia, and admired his reputation as a "fighting editor."[14] Portraits of such journalism celebrities were more than just self-promotion; they consciously affirmed the power of crusading journalism to report news, expose abuses, and shape public opinion.

African American editors understood their role as community leaders and advocates but were also acutely aware of their vulnerability to white mobs: they were targets because they took strong positions on the record. Praise for publications that defied intimidation and violence to serve readers was a common theme in the black press. For example, when the *Southern Christian Recorder* (Philadelphia) reappeared a few weeks after being suppressed by local whites in 1889, the *Detroit Plaindealer* welcomed the paper back into print, noting with pride that "the Recorder has lost none of the fearless tone which characterized it before its suppression." Kansas's *Parson's Blade* likewise praised a competing publication in nearby Coffeyville, Kansas: "Long live the Afro American Advocate."[15] Mutual encouragement, even though mitigated at times by fierce competitiveness and scathing criticism, reflected a sense of service to the black community and commitment to values supporting a free press.

Readers were less appreciative of satirical imagery, another form of visualization in the black press, when they saw it as reinforcing negative stereotypes. Some took offense after Cooper began publishing the work of cartoonist Moses Tucker in the *Freeman* in mid-1889. Little is known of Tucker's history, but in the late 1880s and early 1890s he produced a range of satirical and allegorical images for the *Freeman*. Cooper introduced Tucker to readers as an engraver, illustrator, and caricaturist from Atlanta, Georgia, whose expertise in lampooning his subjects derived from his prior experience with a humorous newspaper in Atlanta, the *Georgia Cracker*. While *Freeman* readers appreciated Tucker's civil rights drawings (discussed below), they panned his negative portrayals of rural African Americans. Caricatures of African Americans in the nation's only illustrated black newspaper, they felt, were "degrading to the Negro." The *Freeman* also published Henry Lewis's satirical cartoons: on one occasion, a competing editor found one of his drawings such a "grotesque and brutal mockery upon the race" that he doubted the artist was in fact a black man. Cooper defended his caricaturists as talented artists whose satirical views had a subversive quality and whose work indirectly served the goal of racial uplift.[16]

Tucker's allegorical drawings proved less controversial than his satire and were far more popular in the black community. For example, the *Freeman* frequently republished one drawing, with varying captions, that depicted an Atlas-like figure standing atop a rocky hill. His torso bare, and wearing a simple cloth covering below his waist, he lifted onto his shoulders an enormous globe, representative of his various burdens: poverty, brutal treatment, and oppression, among others (fig. 4.2). The image made clear the range of Tucker's contribution to the *Freeman* under Cooper's editorship. Its visualization of both struggle and strength highlighted the reality that the burdens African Americans carried were too great for any individual to surmount.[17]

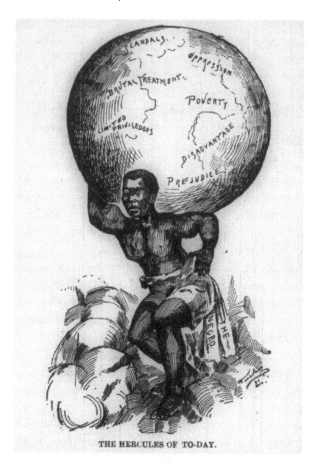

FIGURE 4.2: "The
Hercules of To-Day,"
Indianapolis *Freeman*,
March 22, 1890, 4.
Library of Congress.

THE HERCULES OF TO-DAY.

Both Lewis and Tucker included Uncle Sam as a recurring symbol for federal responsibility—or weakness—in their visual protests against political and
economic terrorism. The practice of lynching was on the rise (it peaked in
1892), and within this violent climate few images advocated self-protection as
a "remedy for Southern outrages," at least not in print. Aware of the broader
public they addressed, most of their images emphasized federal enforcement
of civil rights to guarantee fair trials, equal opportunity, and voting rights in
the face of Jim Crow segregation (enforced by violence). In late summer 1889,
for example, the *Freeman* responded to a Gouldsboro, Louisiana, massacre of
African American families on an excursion, and to the burning of a church, by
publishing an image that invoked Uncle Sam as a symbol of federal protection.
Drawn by Lewis, the image showed members of the Ku Klux Klan cowering
behind a tree, from which one lynching victim hung, as another man fled to

SOME DAILY OR RATHER NIGHTLY OCCURRENCES IN THE SOUTH.

FIGURE 4.3: "Some Daily or Rather Nightly Occurrences in the South," Indianapolis *Freeman*, September 21, 1889, 4. Library of Congress.

safety (fig. 4.3). Caption text emphasized the persistence of violence in the South, noting its "daily or rather nightly occurrence." Uncle Sam and a Union soldier (possibly meant to denote president Benjamin Harrison) advanced with rifles and bayonets in hand, a reference to the government's brief commitment, during Radical Reconstruction, to upholding the rule of law by suppressing mob violence.[18]

"Ethiopia," a second recurring figure, this one female and African American, represented a moral rather than federal figure of justice, and an emblem of race pride. In the same issue that responded to the Gouldsboro massacre, a second drawing by Lewis showed Ethiopia as a robed figure, standing majestically before an impotent Uncle Sam. Indicating the shooting of innocent African American men and women, and a burning church, she made a strong appeal to conscience in the caption. "See how my people are murdered, maltreated and outraged in the South," Ethiopia said, "and you, with a great army and navy, are taking no measures to prevent it" (fig. 4.4). Ethiopia's place in the *Freeman*'s visual lexicon was so central that for many years she figured prominently on the paper's front-page masthead. Her presence symbolized both race pride and a moral imperative along with firm advocacy for equal protection and due process.[19]

FIGURE 4.4: "Ethiopia to Uncle Sam," Indianapolis *Freeman*, September 22, 1889, 8.
Library of Congress.

Icons such as Ethiopia and Uncle Sam provided the *Freeman* with a way to
put dry legal and constitutional arguments into evocative visual form. They also
created a visual counternarrative to stereotypes of the black rapist that sensational illustrated newspapers used to justify lynching. Over the 1880s, images
in crime weeklies like the *National Police Gazette* exaggerated the sexual threat
posed by African American men and downplayed white sexual crime, except
in deviant cases of tramps or dissolute elites. As discussed in chapter 1, these
images reinforced prevailing prejudice among whites that rape was an inherent,
expected practice for African American men—"The Negro Crime"—while
erasing white sexual aggression and the rape of African American women. This
"rape/lynching narrative" asserted that interracial sexuality could be *only* forcible
rape of white women by black men, and it legitimated mob retaliation. By 1890
the "black rapist," or his subsequent lynching, was sensationalism's dominant
symbol of African American men.[20]

Lewis and Tucker produced interpretive images in the *Freeman* to counter
such distorted news illustrations. Tucker's visual response to the killing of
black prisoners by a white mob in Barnwell, South Carolina, and a race war
in Georgia during the winter of 1889–90 visually protested the violence. One

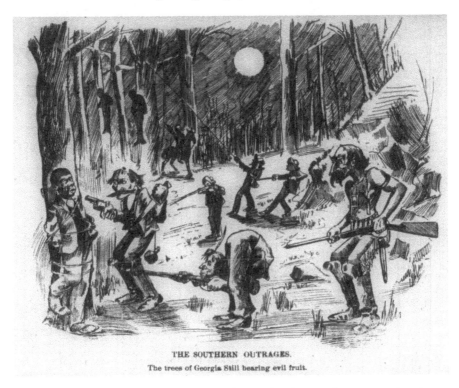

THE SOUTHERN OUTRAGES.
The trees of Georgia Still bearing evil fruit.

FIGURE 4.5: "The Southern Outrages," Indianapolis *Freeman*, January 18, 1890, 8.
Library of Congress.

such image (fig. 4.5) made a pointed visual critique of Southern "chivalry." In carnivalesque style, this drawing depicted hideous cavaliers, abetted by backwoods rustics, as they lynched African American men for sport; the subtitle read: "Trees of Georgia Still Bearing Evil Fruit."[21] The drawing encapsulated the belief that the federal government had failed to protect citizens' rights to due process and equal protection under the law, and that mob rule operated unchecked in the rural South.

Through such images, the *Freeman* created a visual language for the critique of president Harrison's Republican administration that resonated throughout the black press. "The chivalrous (?) white brutes have been at it again," commented editor Harry C. Smith in the *Cleveland Gazette* at the time. "President Harrison has not a word to say in condemnation of these affairs, either in an interview or his [annual] message [to Congress]. *Just remember this.*" Smith, a staunch Republican, did not take such a stand lightly. Later, as a Republican Ohio state legislator, Smith promoted civil rights legislation and a strict anti-lynching bill that became a model for other states.[22] Like the *Freeman*, he

OUR NATIONAL CEMETERY.

The defeat of the Blair Educational Bill has set the Afro-American press to talking. Visions of the Black Laws, the Force Bil', the Civil Rights and other measures come to view. When a Republican Congress and such men as Sherman and Ingalls go against the Negro, what is he then to do or expect.

FIGURE 4.6: "Our National Cemetery," Indianapolis *Freeman*, September 27, 1890, 8. Library of Congress.

found the Harrison administration's failure to support black civil rights and education efforts inexplicable. When the Republican Party failed to support the Blair Education Bill, which would have provided federal funds to states by proportion of illiteracy rates, Moses Tucker represented this as the party's latest betrayal of its founding ideals. The image showed Uncle Sam as a gravedigger (fig. 4.6), tending the failed legislation of generations.[23] Through such allegorical imagery, the *Freeman* channeled emotion—the community's frustration at the Republican Party and the federal government's broken promises.

By 1892 the *Freeman* had lost both artists[24] but continued to recycle their crusading images and their insistence on the notion of federal responsibility for individual civil rights—a principle that the black press extended to other marginalized groups. For example, editors denounced the Harrison administration's inaction after the lynching of eleven Italian men in New Orleans in 1891. The men were accused of orchestrating a Mafia assassination of the city's police chief, David Hennessy, but their guilt was unclear. The lynching occurred at a time when Italians were feared as "savage," innately criminal and racially distinct from whites. When the Italian government demanded federal prosecution of the lynchers and protection of Italian immigrants from "Anglo-Saxon" violence, President Harrison declared himself powerless to intervene, on states' rights grounds. The *Detroit Plaindealer* urged the Italian government to "impel our National government to use every means in its power to secure the trial and conviction of the leaders of the mob." By extending this idea of protection to other oppressed communities, the *Freeman*'s images sought to forge a wider understanding of due process and equal protection.[25]

Memphis and the Expansion of Lynching Imagery

Events in March 1892 made anti-lynching imagery in the black press even more important as a community resource. A triple lynching in Memphis proved that "respectability" and economic achievement could not protect lynching victims from mob violence—or subsequent slander. Memphis editor Ida B. Wells was a former schoolteacher with a history of activism; she had once successfully sued a railroad for discrimination (though the decision was overturned on appeal). In her newspaper, *Free Speech*, Wells exposed the lies misrepresenting the lynching of the three African American men, co-owners of a grocery store that directly competed with a white-owned business. When white newspapers insinuated that the lynching was justified because the men were desperadoes or rapists, Wells, who knew the men personally, pointed out the folly of accepting lynchers' excuses without evidence or trial. She urged her readers to boycott white businesses, and even to leave town, prompting an exodus that had a lasting economic impact on the city of Memphis. She used her paper to correct the record and challenge the rape/lynching narrative, going so far as to assert that some white women might have voluntary sexual relations with African America men. A white mob retaliated, destroyed her press and, with threats against her life, forced her into exile in the North.[26]

African American communities all over the country rose to protest the Memphis lynchings, and many endorsed Wells's challenge to the rape/lynching narrative. While a few leaders were alarmed by the rising anger, most shared Wells's belief that distorted reporting in white newspapers perpetuated Southern lynching. African American editors compiled weekly digests of Associated Press clips to catalog the widespread nature of lynching and to correct factual inaccuracies in wire stories. Under headings like "The American Pastime," "Outrage Column," "The Bloody Record of Crime," and "The Record of Shame," editors published a substantial (text) record of violence.[27] Many editors confronted the double standard in mainstream crime reporting, its exaggeration of black criminality and erasure of white sexual crimes. As Wells put it, "the details of these horrible outrages seldom reach beyond the narrow world where they occur. Those who commit the murders write the reports, and hence these lasting blots upon the honor of a nation cause but a faint ripple on the outside world."

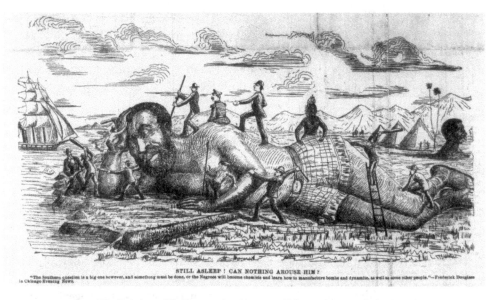

STILL ASLEEP ! CAN NOTHING AROUSE HIM ?
"The Southern question is a big one however, and something must be done, or the Negroes will become chemists and learn how to manufacture bombs and dynamite, as well as some other people."—Frederick Douglass in Chicago Evening News.

FIGURE 4.7: "Still Asleep," Indianapolis *Freeman*, May 14, 1892, 1. Library of Congress.

As the *Coffeyville (Kan.) Afro-American* put it, mainstream newspapers "have encouraged and shielded, have aided and abetted these mobs all along."[28]

African American publishers used creative strategies to visualize the injustice of lynching, which allowed them to harness the community's growing sense of outrage. They walked a fine line between raising consciousness and exposing readers to traumatic imagery. When, in 1892, Frederick Douglass warned whites of the dangers of "reaping the whirlwind," the *Freeman* recycled an oft-used illustration by the late Henry Lewis, depicting a sleeping African American Gulliver, a gentle giant at the mercy of club-wielding Lilliputian oppressors (fig. 4.7). "Something must be done," said Douglass in the caption, "or the Negroes will become chemists, and learn how to manufacture bombs and dynamite, as well as some other people." The image challenged viewers to question the notion of superior white civilization; imperialists, explorers, and slave traders of various nationalities scaled the prone figure, which represented Africa or possibly the African American man. "Still Asleep," said the caption: "Can Nothing Rouse Him?" The image combined themes of victimization and colonial oppression with an exhortation to resist. Few African American editors openly advocated retaliation against mob rule, but all felt the need for action. "I do not endorse Hon. Fred. Douglass, when he advises the Negro to resort to violence unless a change is brought about, yet something must be done," wrote one correspondent to the *Detroit Plaindealer*. "Patience has ceased to be a virtue."[29]

Allegorical cartoons in the *Freeman* represented a new kind of sensational-ism, whose goal was moral rather than commercial: it attempted to drum up indignation and channel it into constructive action that would force a concrete federal response. A quiet militancy in these images echoed broader feeling in the African American community. As Ferdinand Barnett's *Omaha Progress* put it, "the government's silence and utter disregard of these repeated outrages seems not only to consent to their continuance but to sharpen the inappeasable appe-tites of those Southern bloodsuckers." When President Harrison remained silent, editors encouraged communities to organize. "Indignation meetings" sprang up to protest lynching, some openly, others secretly. Congregations demanded law and order and federal protection of civil rights, in Columbus, Ohio; Chat-tanooga, Tennessee; Coffeeville, Alabama; Detroit, Michigan; Oberlin, Ohio; St. Paul, Minnesota; and Pittsburgh, Pennsylvania. One A.M.E. congregation protested against singing "My Country 'Tis of Thee," offering a rousing chorus of the anti-slavery anthem "John Brown" instead. In Northern states, open ad-vocacy was possible; in some places, such as Kansas City, Kansas, organizations met secretly. Perhaps the clearest evidence of this spirit of collective resistance can be seen in the massive turnout for the May 31 "Day of Prayer and Fasting" to protest government inaction on lynching. The May 31 (1892) events allowed African Americans in all areas of the country to grieve for the dead, mourn their loss of rights and citizenship, and bear witness to the suffering they endured.[30] Such actions highlighted the fact that lynching violated state and federal gov-ernment authority and emphasized moral grounds for federal intervention.

Anti-lynching images reinforced this moral imperative and amplified wide-spread assertions of a constitutional right to protection from violence. As an Alabama writer to the *Coffeyville (Kan.) Afro-American Advocate* explained, "the injustice perpetrated upon hundreds of colored citizens every day by butcher-ing, intimidating, brutalizing and denying the right of trial by jury, which is the great safeguard of personal liberty, is beyond human endurance, and in open violation of the Constitution, of this land for the free, and home of the brave."[31] Popular white political cartoonist Thomas Nast captured this sentiment in an image, whose caption read "Our Republic Can Only Exist So Long as Its Citizens Respect and Obey Their Self-Imposed Laws"(fig. 4.8). This image, widely reproduced in the black press, showed the symbolic figure of Justice simultaneously raising her hand to halt a lynching and discouraging retaliatory self-protection by the militant African Americans in the frame. "Take not the law into your own hands," she warned the lynch mob, "for where will that end?" Only due process and equal protection under the law, the image implied, could avert a downward spiral of retributive violence.[32]

Occasionally, editors in the black press seeking to visualize African American frustration and set the record straight resorted to putting lynching imagery

FIGURE 4.8: "Our Republic," *Detroit Plaindealer*, June 3, 1892, 1. Library of Congress.

into print. Many felt that Wells's exile from Memphis was a symptom of a larger suppression of the truth. "Free speech and free press are guaranteed by our fundamental law," said the *San Francisco Elevator*, "[yet] some citizens are prohibited from free expression of opinions founded on truth."[33] That June, the *Freeman* republished an earlier drawing by Henry Lewis that combined these themes in one of his most militant protest images (fig. 4.9). The cartoon lamented the need for negative and combative imagery in the black press but explained its necessity. "Some day the inspiration for such representations will have passed," the caption read. "Some day, America will extend equal rights and justice to all men." The central figure in the image exhibited anger, carrying a large club that represented a determination to defend himself and his community. A sign affixed to the whipping post read "Give the Negro an equal chance with other men, and there will be no race problem."[34]

Underlying these arguments against mob rule was the understanding that the rape accusation provided cover for lynching for other purposes. To make this clear, editors prominently displayed evidence of the voluntary relationships between African American men and white women. They also documented cases of white women crying rape to disguise intimacy with African American men.[35] Editors explained how the stereotype of the inherent criminality of black men made blackness a code for criminal behavior, causing public sympathy for African Americans to evaporate.[36]

FIGURE 4.9: "Some Day," Indianapolis *Freeman*, June 25, 1892, 5. Library of Congress.

African American editors also wanted to correct the visual record to include cases of white sexual violence against African American women, both during slavery and in the present.[37] When six white men gang-raped an African American woman in Columbus, Ohio, the *Cleveland Gazette* published their profiles on its front page (fig. 4.10). This seemingly realistic illustration, which included the names of the accused, provided something rarely seen in mainstream newspaper accounts of interracial rape: the faces of white sexual criminals. The incident prompted one editor to note the double standard: "Very few of the Northern papers gave any account of it, while if such a villainous outrage had been committed in the South by colored men upon a white woman the matter would have been spread before the whole country in a most sensational and partial manner." This image, published during the year documenting the highest number of lynchings in American history, constituted a daring visual intervention.[38]

Visual intervention became particularly important in fall 1892 as the presidential election drew near. Benjamin Harrison faced a tough rematch against his Democratic challenger, Grover Cleveland. Despite growing disillusionment with the president, most African American editors continued to support the Republican Party (the "party of Lincoln") and urged African American voters to the polls. Some, like the newly Republican *Freeman*, put aside frustration with Harrison's silence on lynching and visually equated the president to Lincoln, screening out the continuing reality of mob violence. An image (unsigned),

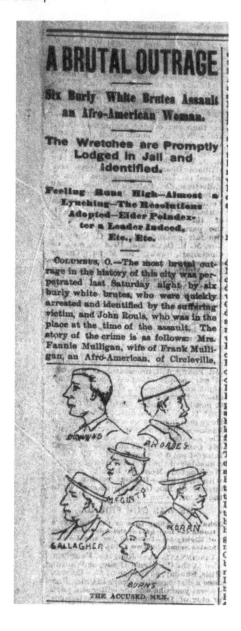

FIGURE 4.10: "The Accused Men,"
Cleveland Gazette, October 1, 1892, 1.
Library of Congress.

roughly drawn and difficult to decipher, sketched out four phases of African
American progress: a slave being whipped in 1860; Ku Klux Klan violence in
1870; and a lynch mob shooting a man in 1880. The fourth, and focal, image
showed a domestic scene of an elderly man in a parlor, gesturing toward two
portraits, one of Lincoln and the other of Harrison, while saying to a young boy,

FIGURE 4.11: "The Great Southern Exodus," Indianapolis *Freeman*, November 5, 1892, 1. Library of Congress.

"These are two of the best friends your old grandfather ever had." This rhetorical shift reflected the perspective of the *Freeman*'s new publisher, George L. Knox. Well-connected with the state Republican Party, Knox's *Freeman* went all in for Harrison and later became a staunch supporter of Booker T. Washington's philosophy of economic uplift.[39]

Visually, however, the *Freeman* continued to recycle its earlier militancy, in the form of images by Lewis and Tucker repurposed from the years of Cooper's editorship. On the eve of the presidential election the paper published images to remind readers that moving away was a form of protest against Democratic local and state governments that failed to punish lynching, perhaps to bolster the exodus that Wells's campaign had begun (fig. 4.11). A reprint of a drawing by Lewis showed a crowd of African American families in a train station, departing the South. Smaller insets showing whippings, lynching, and pursuit by dogs explained the mass exodus. After the election, African American editors attributed President Harrison's loss to his passive response to the Memphis lynching, which had cost him the black vote. Such images also reminded readers that placating the Democrats' desire for victory did not quell violence in the South—if anything, it encouraged greater atrocities.[40]

Representing Atrocity as Protest

A gruesome lynching in Paris, Texas, in February 1893 sparked a renewed visual campaign against federal inaction in the black press. In what has been called the first "spectacle lynching," the public torture of Henry Smith set a new low for mob violence. Smith, a known "imbecile," was accused of murdering a child, Myrtle Vance, daughter of a local police officer who had mistreated Smith in custody. It was a horrible crime, and Smith's guilt was clear. However, false rumors that he had sexually assaulted and dismembered the young girl (both found untrue after the lynching) spread in local white newspapers, and a crowd of ten thousand people, some from out of state, came to watch as Vance's family tortured and slowly burned Smith alive. In impassioned words, African American editors railed against the excuses of lame-duck Republican Harrison and his Democratic successor Grover Cleveland, that states' rights prevented them from prosecuting the lynchers. Images proved more potent.[41]

A powerful image in the *Detroit Plaindealer* represented one attempt to find visual language to condemn such exhibitions of atrocity. The *Plaindealer*'s editor Benjamin Pelham highlighted the role of the mainstream press in justifying the violence through false accusations. Lawful trials, rather than mob rule, were the only way to ensure that the accused had a chance to counter exaggerations and distortions with facts.[42] Overshadowing this reporting, and in a striking departure for Pelham's primarily text-based paper, the *Plaindealer* published an interpretive illustration on the front page, titled "Thirty Years of Progress." Its very presence indicated a high level of emotion—sorrow, outrage, anger, fear. But the core message concerned the Republican Party's failure to uphold the rule of law (fig. 4.12). At the image's center stood a statuesque President Lincoln, flanked by two smaller images to the left and right of his head. A banner-sized quote from his second inaugural address—"With Malice toward None, with Charity for All"—larger than the image title, joined the three frames. To Lincoln's left, a smaller image, designated "1863," showed him holding the Emancipation Proclamation while releasing an African American man from slavery. At right, an image labeled "1893" showed a white mob lynching a man by burning him at the stake, a clear reference to the torture of Henry Smith.[43] By contrasting Lincoln's leadership with the outgoing Harrison administration's failure to protect basic rights, the image registered outrage over the Republican Party's lost principles. Further, the juxtaposition highlighted the uncivilized nature of a government that condoned mob violence against any accused criminal but particularly against someone of Smith's limited mental capacity. Its concise visual language captured the failure of the Republicans and the immorality of mob rule.

Other editors were similarly moved to visualize their horror at the mob's torture of Henry Smith. "Free (?) America" read the terse, sarcastic caption

FIGURE 4.12: "Thirty Years of Progress," *Detroit Plaindealer*, March 3, 1893, 1. Library of Congress. Library of Congress.

to an illustration of Smith's torture published in Wisconsin's *Northwestern Recorder*. An illustration (fig. 4.13) of the mass lynching showed men torturing their victim on a platform surrounded by a sea of spectators. Next to the image, an account from an eyewitness to the lynching, Reverend J. P. King, provided details, including his attempts to stop the lynching and his own forcible eviction from town by the angry mob.[44] Such disturbing imagery rarely appeared in the black press, typically in times of extreme emotional response to racial terrorism of this kind. It expressed the community's outrage over the nation's betrayal of founding values and demanded a moral and legal reckoning.

"Isn't it strange that America, the home of the free and the blest," Kansas's *Parsons Blade* asked after the Henry Smith lynching, "can condole with the oppressed of foreign lands, while she, herself, is steeped with crime that would cause the most [barbarous] nations to blush with shame?" The *Blade*, a paper for exodusters—African Americans who had migrated to rural Kansas—compared lynch mobs to "a dangerous species of heathens" and sarcastically advocated sending "missionaries to the south, if we have to call them from darkest Africa." As Wells analyzed the case in her pamphlet, *The Red Record*, two years later, the

FIGURE 4.13: "Free (?)
America," *Northwestern
Recorder*, March 1893, 1.
Library of Congress.

Smith lynching directly contradicted the notion of white "civilization." "Never
in the history of civilization," said Wells, "has any Christian people stooped to
such shocking brutality and indescribable barbarism." In addition to representing the mob's savagery and the nation's moral weakness, coverage of Smith's
torture highlighted the complicity of the Northern press in suppressing details
and distorting the facts.[45]

Northern headlines focused instead on the nation's unfolding economic crisis.
As the depression of 1893 deepened, African American journalists were increasingly isolated in questioning the accuracy and authenticity of local reports of
lynchings and demanding national intervention. In 1893 Wells published two
lynching images (an early photograph and a drawing based on a photograph)
in a pamphlet designed to convince skeptics that the practice really occurred,
using visual evidence to assert truth. Journalist Jesse C. Duke, former editor
of the *Montgomery (Ala.) Herald,* who in 1887 had been driven out of town for

debunking the racist rape/lynching narrative, supported Wells's advocacy of truth and accuracy as the antidote to violence. He wrote,

> It must be left to the Colored Press to establish truth over such gross and intentional error. It is the duty of the people to seek out and give publicity to the truth. . . . Our noble deeds are omitted and our ignoble crimes grace the pages in double leaded columns. If we cannot effect arrangements with the Associated Press by which we may send our news and correct errors of statements relative to the race, we must seek out and find some other medium through which we can. *Let the world have the testimony of the other side.*[46]

In this spirit, in 1894 the *Cleveland Gazette* published a lynching image (fig. 4.14) to protest the murder of Roscoe Parker, in West Union, Ohio. The paper included a simple pen-and-ink drawing of Parker's lynched body and the white mob sketched in at the bottom left of the frame. In a separate frame the paper included his portrait (likely based on a photograph) as a way to retain his humanity and dignity.[47]

Where images were challenging to produce, other editors used words to move readers. Some tackled the excuse that overwhelming emotion led to lynching, that rape was a crime too shameful to its victims to be tried in open court. On the contrary, they argued, as a capital crime, the very seriousness of rape demanded the full exercise of the legal system, including lawful trials to ensure that the accused had a chance to face their accusers.[48] As the Detroit civil rights activist D. Augustus Straker said in 1894: "Southern [white] people know when they cry rape against their women, all sympathy, aye even justice for the Negro, is likely to be silenced for a time in wreaking vengeance against the wrong-doers. No better plan to place Northern sentiment against the helpless Negro than this." The underlying purpose of the rape/lynching narrative was, as Douglass put it, "to degrade the Negro" to the point of complete disenfranchisement.[49] The stereotype of the black rapist put the accused men beyond the pale of mainstream society, he argued, and its "perpetual reiteration in our newspapers and magazines has led men and women to regard him with averted eyes, dark suspicion and increasing hate."[50] Editors attempted to counter this misrepresentation by reporting on incidents of "blackface criminality" and false accusations against black men.[51] "A White man has but to Blacken his face and commit a crime," said Douglass, "to have some Negro lynched in his stead." Like other African American leaders, he knew that the representation in sensational, commercial newspapers of rape as a racial phenomenon, linked to blackness, had dire consequences for all African Americans. The emotional response arising from a presumption of guilt by association with blackness eviscerated the very principle of due process.[52]

Demands that the federal government enforce the rule of law permeated the black press in this period. The *Woman's Era*, a Boston paper edited by suffrage and

HORRIBLE!

That Lynching in West Union Most Disgraceful Indeed.

A Full Account of the Much Discussed Affair.

A Portrait of Roscoe Parker—A Picture of the Lynching—The Best Account of the Affair to be Secured.

WEST UNION, Adams county, O.—It was about the middle of January that the Afro-American youth, Roscoe Parker, *charged* with the murder of the aged couple (whites), Mr. and Mrs. Pit Rhine, was lynched and his body shot four or five times as it hung suspended from a limb of a tree. It was about 11 o'clock one Thursday night the jail was broken open and the 17-year-old boy dragged forth from his cell by a mob of 100 men, who were in the main masked, although a number made no effort to conceal their identity. It was near North Liberty where the barbarous act was committed. On the morning of the day Parker was lynched, Adams county's sheriff (Dunlap by name), brought the boy from the Portsmouth jail, where he had been taken by order of Sheriff McMannis before his retirement from office. Dunlap conveyed a crazy person to the Athens asylum the fore part of the same week, and made no secret of the fact that upon his return, on Thursday, he would bring Parker back with him. On the morning of that day he secured the boy at the jail in Portsmouth and boarded the morning C. P. & V. train, arriving at Peebles about 6 o'clock. On the depot platform he was accosted by a number of men of that village, who asked the sheriff if he intended to take Parker back to West Union, and in answer to their questions he said that he did. "Then he'll hang before midnight," warned the Peebles men. To this Dunlap shrugged his shoulders and smiled very knowingly.

The officers of the train on which the prisoner had been brought to Peebles spread the news at every station along the road from Peebles to Winchester. Shortly before the prisoner had left Portsmouth, a cipher dispatch was filed at the telegraph office there for delivery at Winchester, by a man who lives near Winchester, but who had been boarding near by the jail since Parker's confinement at Portsmouth, evidently being there to keep an eye out for his removal.

A young man, also of the same vicinity, had been visiting hereabouts ever since the preliminary trial of Parker, and soon after his arrival in the West Union jail returned to Winchester.

Sheriff Dunlap had not more than safely locked Parker in jail, than he, too, made a trip in the direction of Winchester. He returned before night, and was at home when the attack was made.

Shortly after dark, persons living along the Winchester pike noticed a number of men going in the direction

ROSCOE PARKER.

started on a swift and silent run to the jail.

Pickets were thrown out, guarding every possible avenue of attack, should one be made from the citizens of West Union, and then the prearranged plan was carried out.

Two men stepped up on the stone step in front of the jail door, and others stepped into the shadows of the building—the moon at that time making a dim, uncertain light. A loud knock was given, and to this Sheriff Dunlap soon responded.

"Who's there?" asked the sheriff.

"The marshal of Manchester," came the reply. "I have an important prisoner for you."

Unhesitatingly the sheriff unbolted the door and pulled it open. As he did so, he saw the men at the side of the building, and slamming it shut he ran the bolt to its fastening.

There was a halt of a second, then a man stepped up on the door step and swung an ax, hitting the door a hard, over-handed lick; the bolt cracked, jerked its holder from the door-jamb, and the wooden door flew open.

The men then swarmed into the corridor.

"Give us the keys, Marion," shouted a half-hundred excited men.

"Gentlemen, let me reason with you," said the sheriff.

"We want no reasoning; we want the boy."

Mrs. Dunlap appeared at the head of the stairs and implored her husband to give up the keys and not get hurt. She then threw down a key, which was tried in the lock of the front jail door, but it was not the right key.

"Bring on the sledge," came the order from the leader. Instead of a sledge, an ax was passed though, and soon stalwart arms were cutting the heavy lock from the grated door.

"What's that noise?" asked Parker of a guard, who was in the jail corridor.

"It's the fellows after you," was the guard's excited reply.

Grabbing his tin wash-basin the boy climbed upon his cage and prepared to fight for his life.

Clang, clang, clang, clang went the ax on the corridor door. The lock began to loosen from its fastenings, and words of approval came from the mob. With a bang the heavy door gave way, and the mob surged into the corridor. Now, only the cell door intervened between the mob and its prey. Like blood-thirsty beasts the now excited men seemed.

The ax was given into new hands, and the work of cutting off the lock of the cell began.

Deputy Sheriff McKee at this point came running across from where he roomed, and was promptly seized by a couple of stalwart men, who threw him to the ground and sat down upon him. They were soon joined by a third man, who also took a seat upon the prostrate form of the deputy sheriff, and here they sat and conversed upon the progress of the raid. The guard inside stood at the far end of the corridor and awaited the giving way of the door, which happened in a few moments.

A few licks and the door of Parker's cell flew open, and a half dozen men rushed into his compartment. An unearthly cry of despair broke from the lips of the boy when he heard the door give way.

A hand was reached up over the cage to grab him, but he dealt it a terrible blow with his wash basin. Again and again he wielded his weapon effectively, until at one time it seemed that he would yet save himself. Two men drew revolvers and pointed them at the crouching figure on the cage. Their arms were promptly knocked down by some of their comrades, who said: "Don't shoot him, he must hang."

At length a stalwart looking man pushed through the door and exclaimed: "Damn it, are you all afraid of a boy?" He climbed upon the cage and grappled with Parker. The struggle was a desperate one, a stripling of a boy, full well knowing that death was his portion, should he ever be taken from the top of that cage, engaged in a struggle with a man twice

FIGURE 4.14: "Horrible!" Cleveland *Gazette*, April 7, 1894, 1. Library of Congress. Library of Congress.

civil rights activist Josephine St. Pierre Ruffin and her daughter, Florida Ruffin Ridley, castigated the Cleveland administration for its complicity in violence.

> It is an astounding proposition that a great nation is powerful enough to stop white moonshiners from making whisky but is unable to prevent the moonshiners from murdering its citizens. It can protect corn but cannot protect life. It can go to war, spend millions of dollars and sacrifice thousands of lives, but cannot spend a cent to protect a loyal, native-born colored American murdered without provocation by native or alien in Alabama. Shame on such a government! The administration in power is *particeps criminis* with the murderers. It can stop lynching, and until it does so, it has on its hands the innocent blood of its murdered citizens.

Ruffin and Ridley rejected the excuse of temperance advocate Frances Willard and other white apologists who argued that lynching was necessary because the crime of rape would make a trial too horrible for its female victim. Rapists deserved punishment, they argued, "but it is the duty of the law, and not of the mob, to inflict this punishment. And every man, of whatever crime charged, has the right of a fair trial in the courts." This was particularly a concern in the South, as accusation alone was effectively a death sentence, they argued. Ruffin and Ridley emphasized the need for fact-based policies, based on the rule of law, rather than emotion: "All that is asked is that the law reign, and not the mob."[53]

The 1894 midterm election season approached amid a worsening depression, with widespread unemployment and economic protest. Black Southern editors, such as the militant *Richmond Planet*'s John Mitchell, walked a fine line to avoid antagonizing potential white allies in his state. In 1894 Mitchell organized a lecture for Isaac Jenkins, who had survived a group lynching at Clifton Forge, Virginia, in 1891, and reprinted an illustration to advertise the event (fig. 4.15). Based on a photograph taken right after that lynching, the illustration was an eerie, silent statement of outrage designed to bring an audience to Jenkins's lecture, an image Mitchell would republish through the decade. Mitchell also used the image in broadside advertisements for the *Planet*, under the words "You shudder at the picture. OF COURSE YOU DO!"—linking its traumatic impact on viewers with the importance of a militant black press. Yet given the political climate, Mitchell also exhibited caution; in the same issue, he urged readers to praise supportive white Democrats and allies.[54]

The now-Republican Indianapolis *Freeman* also struggled to address lynching in a divided political atmosphere. Its images explicitly sought to counter the Democratic Party's efforts in the Midwest to woo African Americans voters. When the National Negro Democratic Conference met in July 1894 in Indianapolis, the *Freeman* repurposed an older image (fig. 4.16) by the late Henry Lewis. The composite drawing depicted various forms of lynching and discrimination, including one frame showing a woman being evicted from a

FIGURE 4.15: "A Lynching Scene," *Richmond Planet*, June 23, 1894, 4. Library of Virginia.

FIGURE 4.16: "Notice!" Indianapolis *Freeman*, August 11, 1894, 4.
Library of Congress.

train (perhaps a reference to Wells's eviction from a train in 1883). It was an allegorical political cartoon, but at the same time each frame was realist in tone and referenced actual events. Lest there be any confusion about the purpose of the image, the caption singled out African American Democrats: "The attention of the National Negro Democratic Conference, to meet in Indianapolis next Tuesday, is respectfully directed to the above picture of real life," the caption read. "Gentlemen, cannot you persuade the White members of your party South, to cease these persecutions of your brethren?"[55] It was another attempt to channel emotion in support of anti-lynching activism.

Such imagery tied African American votes to a civil rights agenda and sought to make anti-lynching an issue in the 1894 midterm election campaigns. Several papers openly mocked President Cleveland's claim a year earlier that the federal government had power over property and resources but none to protect African Americans from mob violence. "The fishes of the sea, the birds of the air, the cattle on the western plains, everything is protected, except the Negro," said the *Parsons Blade*. It was hypocritical, many editors felt, that President Cleveland had dusted off a Reconstruction-era Enforcement Act to prosecute railway workers during the Pullman strike that July, yet he refused to intervene in lynching. As D. Augustus Straker put it, the government's "silence is consent to the wrong done the Negro."[56] An election-eve *Freeman* cartoon reinforced

FIGURE 4.17: "Prays for His Persecutors," *Richmond Planet*,
January 19, 1895, 1. Library of Congress.

this theme by recycling an image of Ethiopia speaking to Uncle Sam. (see
fig. 4.4). As before, she warned him of the political consequences of failing to
prevent mob violence. This time, Uncle Sam responded in backwoods dialect:
"The Republican party will never be caught again protecting property, hogs,
wheat, wool and sich likk above human life."[57] Republicans won in a landslide,
retaking both House and Senate (the Democrats lost one hundred seats, the
largest changeover in congressional history). Within a context of rising violence,
African American editors hoped that the election meant more than a reaction
to the depression and Cleveland's incumbency. They saw it as a sign of renewed
possibility for federal anti-lynching legislation and, more broadly, the principle
of federal protection from mob violence.

Early in 1895 John Mitchell published an unusual series of interpretive illustrations in the *Richmond Planet* that reflected the challenge he faced as an
African American Southern editor portraying an anti-lynching perspective. For
a few weeks, in place of the more typical portraits of famous leaders, institutions, and boilerplate Republican Party cartoons, he published illustrations that
he drew himself. Mitchell's drawings were less visually sophisticated than the
Freeman's images and less powerful as visual evidence than Wells's lynching
photographs (just republished in her new pamphlet, *The Red Record*), but they
reflected his belief that images were the most effective way to communicate his
anti-lynching message. Perhaps because of his location south of the Mason-
Dixon Line, Mitchell's emphasis diverged from other imagery in the black

Ohio Refused to Deliver Him

Judge M. L. Buchwalter of Cincinnati, O., refused to deliver Rev. A. H. Hampton, colored, charged with shooting and wounding a white man with intent to kill, to the Kentucky authorities, until he had assurance from the trial judge and the Governor of that state, that his life be protected and the prisoner guaranteed a fair and impartial trial in accordance with the provisions of the constitution of the United States.

Upon the failure of the Kentucky officers to furnish such guarantees, on Jan. 4, 1895, he discharged the prisoner. He stated that a prisoner, who had been sent into Kentucky from his court four months before had been lynched soon after he left the train.

Ohio refuses to act as an agent for murderers and rejects with scorn the plea for the delivery of the colored man into the hands of the lynchers

FIGURE 4.18: "Ohio Refused to Deliver Him," *Richmond Planet*, January 26, 1895, 1. Library of Congress.

press; he emphasized the importance of opponents to racial violence—black or white—rather than the lynching itself. His first drawing showed an African American man kneeling in prayer against a backdrop of lynched bodies (fig. 4.17), a reference to the recent murder of six men in Tennessee. The man appeared forgiving, even saintly, despite the violent backdrop. The least confrontational cartoon from this series, its central frame invoked nonthreatening, moral protest against violence, while the smaller frames drew attention to the lawlessness of the lynch mobs. Perhaps strategically, it advocated not self-defense but rather, like the popular "Day of Prayer and Fasting" three years earlier, appealed to the conscience of white allies and the federal government for support and protection.[58]

Mitchell's second drawing exhorted states to honor ideals of justice and due process. The image (fig. 4.18) contrasted two states' commitments to law and order, in reference to an Ohio judge who had refused to release an African American prisoner to Kentucky for fear that the man would be lynched in transit without a fair trial. The drawing portrayed the figure of Kentucky "justice" holding extradition papers while hiding the lynch mob and its work from view; meanwhile, Ohio justice wielded a sword and protected the prisoner from the

Firing at Long Range.

The Crusade in England against lynch-law in the United States has not been without its effect, and the reaction has had a tendency to create public sentiment in this country against the atrocity.

In the following cartoon may be seen the Anti-Lynching Society in England with Miss Catherine Impey assisting, directing the cannon of public opinion against the outrages. The kings and emperors of Europe have their attention attracted, and are gazing upon the Southern States where the bodies of colored men may be seen hanging to trees.

Miss IDA B. WELLS is lecturing to a crowd in the Northern States, while President CLEVELAND is endeavoring to call attention to the outrages in Armenia.

They are firing the cannon at long range. Its balls may not strike the object at which it is aimed, but its noise is directing to the South the attention of the civilized world.

FIGURE 4.19: "Firing at Long Range," *Richmond Planet*, February 2, 1895, 1. Library of Congress.

mob, allowing industry to thrive. "Ohio refuses to act as an agent for murderers," said the caption, "and rejects with scorn the plea for the delivery of the colored man into the hands of the lynchers."[59] The case brought to prominence Ohio governor William McKinley's strong advocacy for a Republican Party stance against lynching, which convinced *Cleveland Gazette* editor Harry C. Smith to support McKinley's candidacy in the 1896 presidential contest.[60] Mitchell's drawing emphasized the responsibility of state governments to prevent lynching, rather than the need for federal protection.

Mitchell also amplified Wells's appeal to white conscience in her anti-lynching efforts both at home and overseas. A third image highlighted her success in bringing British attention to U.S. government inaction in the face of Southern lawlessness. The drawing (fig. 4.19) showed the cannon of British "public opinion" firing across the ocean at the United States, Wells's opening salvo in a war over public opinion, a shaming device necessary because of U.S. government inaction. This time, the image's caption referred to the federal government's silence on lynching: "Miss Ida B. Wells is lecturing to a crowd in the Northern States, while President Cleveland is endeavoring to call attention to the outrages in Armenia." Ever conscious of the need to enlist sympathetic allies, another Mitchell cartoon praised liberal whites for their efforts to enforce law and order, and thereby protect Southern industry (fig. 4.20). "Lawlessness cripples business,

FIGURE 4.20: "White Men to the Rescue," *Richmond Planet*,
February 23, 1895, 1. Library of Congress.

and drives away capital," claimed the caption in a second plea for white action.
"Colored men's prayers are answered. Liberal-minded white men are coming
to the rescue."[61] Mitchell's strategic appeal to white allies, despite his known
militancy, likely revealed his consciousness that the paper was visible outside
the African American community.

Mitchell's final image, in March 1895, was his most controversial and overtly
critical of local failures to uphold justice in Virginia. It highlighted the double
standard that suppressed reporting and prosecution of white men's sexual assault
of African American women (fig. 4.21). The image portrayed a complex narrative that speculated on the disappearance of two witnesses for a trial against a
white man accused of raping an African American girl. A lengthy text caption
explained the situation:

> Thomas J. Penn a wealthy white man raped Lina Hanna, a ten year old col-
> ored girl at Danville, Va. She was fearfully injured, it being almost a miracle
> that her life was spared. The white people were much incensed against him,
> due to the brutality of the outrage. When the case was called for trial, Lina
> Hanna, mother and sister had disappeared as completely as though the earth
> had opened and swallowed them up. Whether they were carried to another
> state or murdered is the question.

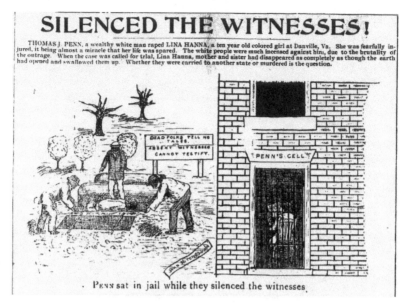

FIGURE 4.21: "Silenced the Witnesses," *Richmond Planet*, March 16, 1895, 1.
Library of Congress.

At the right, the image showed the accused man sitting in jail; at left, gravedig-
gers lowered a body into the earth. Next to them, a sign read "Dead folks tell
no tales—Absent witnesses cannot testify." The interpretive illustrations questioned the integrity of the Southern justice system and called for constitutional
protections for fundamental rights. Taking the five images together, Mitchell's
efforts to visualize a response to white violence shows his militancy, his anger
at injustice, but also his belief that white support was necessary for the success
of local anti-lynching efforts, especially in the absence of federal action.[62]

Political Oppression and the Limits of
Sensational Mobilization

Several things contributed to a decline in graphic anti-lynching images in 1895.
Often dependent for funds either on political parties, churches, or Booker T.
Washington, most African American editors took a moderate editorial approach to avoid alienating financial backers. That spring, Mitchell abandoned
his fledgling efforts at interpretive illustration and filled his front page instead
with photographs and drawings of a local murder case that took more than
a year to resolve. These photographs aligned with the new standards of visual
realism rather than interpretive illustration. Due to technological constraints
that made photographs difficult for most newspapers, the photographs were
blurry and hard to decipher, but they nonetheless represented Mitchell's desire

as an editor to innovate. It is unclear why he abandoned his efforts at interpretive illustration, but the photographs put his paper on the cutting edge of
visual journalism. The case established Mitchell's reputation as an editor and
the *Planet* as one of the nation's foremost African American newspapers, but
it also marked a shift on the front page away from anti-lynching illustration.[63]

Other events contributed to the retreat from anti-lynching imagery in the
black press. The movement lost two of its outspoken leaders in 1895. Frederick
Douglass died that February, leaving a leadership vacuum that made concerted
anti-lynching action more difficult. In June, Ida B. Wells married journalist
Ferdinand Barnett, became editor and owner of the Chicago *Conservator*, and
temporarily decreased her anti-lynching activities. That September, Booker T.
Washington stepped into the leadership void, delivering his famous speech
in Atlanta, Georgia, advocating nonconfrontational uplift through economic
advancement. Washington downplayed lynching, mentioning it only under
pressure from activists, leaving responses to local and ad hoc actions. Perhaps as
a result of these influences, even the most radical African American newspapers
toned down their anti-lynching images and editorials from 1895 through the
1896 election.[64]

As the economic depression continued, black editors also acknowledged that
their readers (like most Americans) and consumers seemed to prefer positive,
uplifting, or entertaining news. Lynching images reminded African American
voters of their vulnerability to white-supremacist Democrats in the South but
also subjected the community to a very negative visual culture. Editors covering
the subject recognized the danger of emotional overload. "It has been intimated
to us occasionally that our constant denunciation of mob law might become
wearisome to our readers," said the *Christian Advocate* somewhat defensively.
"Whether this is true we cannot say, but in any event our mind is made up. We
mean to fight it out on that line if it takes twenty years. . . . The very suggestion
that a mob is ever a necessity is a terrible indictment to the community." Most,
however, temporarily suspended confrontational anti-lynching arguments and
imagery in 1895–96.[65]

In May 1896 the Supreme Court handed down its landmark *Plessy v. Ferguson*
decision, dealing a demoralizing blow to the African American community.
Ruling on the constitutionality of a Louisiana state transportation law that
prohibited African Americans from white railway cars, the court's majority
held that segregated facilities were not unconstitutional, provided they were
equal in quality (the "separate but equal" doctrine). The *Cleveland Gazette* called
the decision just as "ridiculous" as the *Dred Scott* case (1857), and its ruling that
the "black men have no rights that white men are bound to respect." The *Freeman* took a more optimistic view. "If the race is debased in this latest tribute
of contempt it will be but momentarily," Knox editorialized, perhaps naively.
"Victory, somehow will be snatched from the teeth of seeming defeat." Few

echoed this optimism. Instead, some found solace in the minority opinion of
Justice John Marshall Harlan, which would provide the legal foundation for
twentieth-century challenges to segregation. "Nothing but profound respect
and gratitude can attach to Justice Harlan for such an honest opinion," said the
Omaha *Enterprise*. Most acknowledged that the decision set back civil rights
activism based on the equal protection clause of the Fourteenth Amendment.[66]

Instead, African American editors set their sights on the 1896 presidential
contest, strongly supporting the candidacy of Ohio governor William McKinley.
Many featured his portrait, spanning multiple columns, on their front pages. The
Cleveland Gazette's Harry C. Smith led the way, praising Governor McKinley
for crucial support of his anti-lynching bill in Ohio. And if McKinley said
nothing about lynching during the campaign, he did deploy Republican Party
chairman Mark Hanna to speak in general terms about Southern discrimination and outrages. "We Can Trust Him," insisted a recurring headline in the
Gazette through the election. Hope that government action would follow the
election supplanted cynicism, as editors urged African American voters to put
their trust in the GOP.[67] McKinley's victory in November sparked a sense of
vindication, celebration, and promise in the black press. "The colored people
throughout the country are rejoicing over the great Republican victory," said
Alexander Manly's *Wilmington Daily Record*, "and truly they have cause to
rejoice. A Republican victory means more to them than to any other class of
American citizens." McKinley was the "Great Protector," many believed, and
would take a strong federal stand against lynching. There was even speculation
that Booker T. Washington would be appointed to the McKinley cabinet.[68]
Upbeat stories and imagery anticipated the closure of a brutal, unfortunate era.

After the election, however, president-elect McKinley remained silent on
lynching. Some editors began to question their optimism, and reintroduce sensational anti-lynching imagery in their pages. In February 1897, even before
McKinley's inauguration, the *Richmond Planet* reintroduced lynching imagery in
a new, two-column-wide graphic sitting atop its regular tally of lynching victims.
This reproduced the image of three victims hanging from a tree in Clifton Forge,
Virginia (in 1891), used once before to announce a lecture (in 1894) (see fig. 4.15).
Now it became a kind of symbolic marker of ongoing atrocity, under the head-
line "The Reign of Lawlessness." This unsettling image, with its ever-expanding
list of names, remained a regular weekly feature in the *Planet* through President
McKinley's tenure in office—even as the paper curtailed most other images. Said
Mitchell, "The national government has done nothing to check lynching."[69]

African American editors were appalled when McKinley ignored the lynching of an Ohio man, "Click" Mitchell, in spring 1897. In a small interpretive
illustration (fig. 4.22), the *Freeman* depicted the mob scene, with insets showing the prisoner being removed from jail and lynched. "No lynching in the
south was ever more daring or atrocious," said the *Richmond Planet*, noting that

FIGURE 4.22: "Fair Ohio in Disgrace," Indianapolis *Freeman*, June 12, 1897, 1. Library of Congress.

the unmasked lynchers had murdered the innocent victim in broad daylight. Later coverage under the *Cleveland Gazette*'s "Not Guilty" headline featured a portrait of the victim while alive, a realistic-style image, probably based on a photograph (fig. 4.23). Headline and image rebuked President McKinley's silence and Booker T. Washington's explanation that lynch victims were "invariably vagrants"—troublemakers who deserved their fate. Early the next year, when a mob murdered postmaster Frazier Baker, along with his family in Lake City, South Carolina, the *Planet* noted that the GOP had sacrificed the idea of protection from mob violence, even for employees of the federal government (like Baker), on the altar of "national reconciliation."[70]

In 1898 a massacre of black voters and civic leaders by white mobs in Wilmington, North Carolina, made clear once and for all that the federal government did not intend to defend victims of mob violence—if they were African American. Democrats, fearing the growing power over state politics by the African American community in the Fusionist (Populist/Republican) ticket, ran an openly white supremacist campaign. In August 1898, in his paper the *Wilmington Record*, Alexander Manly published an editorial challenging the racist rape/lynching narrative. He was rebutting assertions of Rebecca Latimer Felton, a prominent white suffragist and wife of a Georgia Populist, who claimed that lynching was necessary to protect rural white women from black rapists.

NOT GUILTY.

"Click" Mitchell, the Unfortunate Afro-American, Lynched at Urbana,

Was Clearly Innocent of the Crime Charged, and His Willingly Surrendering Himself to the Officers

Goes Far Toward Establishing the Fact — His Side — The Truth at Last.

Special to THE GAZETTE.

URBANA, O., June 30, 1897.

Hon. H. C. SMITH, EDITOR GAZETTE—Dear Sir: As there has been considerable written and printed in the different newspapers of the country, and seemingly from the same prejudiced point of view, I deem it nothing more than right, in justice to the side of humanity and the friends of the Urbana victim of "Lynch Law," especially since the "mists are beginning to clear away," to present to the public a few things and comments from the opposite point of view. In the first place Mrs. Gaumer informed the public that a colored man had tried to force her to sign a check for $500 and that he threw a shawl over her face to conceal his identity and afterwards threw it over her face for the same purpose; that he had choked her and scratched her face. Later in the day she said that MITCHELL had raped her and the check story was false. She described her assailant as a "thick-lipped colored man who wore a checked coat and a brown derby hat." It is reported that upon the day of the alleged assault, etc., Mitchell left home wearing a cap. His lips were not at all "thick," and the newspaper cuts of him were simply horrible, to say the least. Mitchell was a very fine looking, stout-built, brown-skinned young man, being rather below the standard in height. From the description given, the officers supposed the assailant to be "CLICK" Mitchell, and they went in search of him, but failed to locate him. "Click's" friends learning that he was wanted for the alleged crime, went to him and told him that the officers were after him, and that if he was guilty he had better skip out. He told his folks that he was not guilty and that he would not go anywhere, and said if the officers wanted him they could get him. The next morning "Click" went down town and seeing Marshal Kiona hailed him and asked him if he was wanted. The marshal placed him behind the bars in the city prison. Mrs. Gaumer's "injuries" at first were only slight and Dr. Henderson reported her as suffering more from nervous prostration than from any injuries. Nevertheless she "grew worse" and the preliminary trial "had to be postponed," for several days, as she was "unable" to appear. As she "got no better" and "was getting worse all the time," it was decided to take "Click" before her for identification. The mayor had previously gone to Mrs. Gaumer's and she doubtless had been informed as to the appearance of the prisoner and that the marshal was coming with him. The marshal took "Click" down in a phaeton and there were present the members of the family (I think two brothers-in-law) and one or two others. Perhaps it is still fresh in the minds of the people how the identity of Walling and Jackson was established. "Click" was taken before her alone and she, having been previously informed that he was coming, had nothing to do but to say: "You brute, how dare you face me? Hang him!" On his ("Click's") return to the mayor's office two charges were preferred against him—one of assault with intent to kill and the other rape. "Click's" lawyer seeing being informed that the mayor intended to bind him over to court anyhow, waived examination and Mitchell was placed under bonds of $1,000 in each charge. In default of bail, in the evening he was taken to the county jail. Previous to his "identification" by Mrs. Gaumer, the report was current that the assailant had committed the crime of rape; that he had bitten her severely in the breast and side; had bitten off one of her nipples; had given her a loathsome disease and that it was impossible for her to recover. All of these rumors were calculated to and did serve to inflame and enrage the people. It was no uncommon thing to hear upon the streets the remark that "the

of execution. Here, amidst YELLS and HURRAHS, they threw a rope over a limb and began to pull him up and down, his head striking the limb above. After he was cut down, yeal after he was dead, the mob was so enraged that it began to spit upon him, stamp him and stick pins in him. BARBARIANS! WRETCHES! Mitchell's alleged victim was never so bad as reported. The fact is she got about two scratches on the back of the neck and one in the face and her side was scratched a little. It is now stated by good authorities that her nipple was not bitten; that her bruises in the side were a myth and that she was not hurt anywhere else as was reported by her friends. Furthermore she was never touched, let alone being ravished. Upon proper examination it was found that Mitchell was entirely free of any disease of a loathsome nature. Mitchell never confessed, neither was any crime satisfactorily proven against him. The act (assault) was not near as bad as reported in the different papers of the state and country. Even the white people here claim the lynching was not done on account of any atrocity of crime. The assault of Uliecy (white) upon the daughter of Z. T. Lewis (white) several years ago, was more aggravating than this one, yet the assailant was not lynched, but was only sent to the penitentiary for 18 months. Another phase of the matter that has been designedly kept from the public is that it has been reported upon good authority that a certain hardware store in town furnished revolvers to some members of Mrs. Gaumer's family for the purpose of shooting Mitchell on the spot provided he was identified. Mayor Ganson learning of this disarmed them. He is now being censured for not allowing the responsibility to be placed where it properly belonged if anywhere. For if it had not been the desire of Mrs. Gaumer and family that Mitchell be lynched he would never have been. In order to establish beyond a doubt the alleged assault of Mitchell, I understand that Mayor Ganson told a party of colored men that Mitchell confessed his guilt to her when he was taken before her. This was stoutly denied by some of those who were present. It is said that Mitchell never opened his mouth. It is said by one who was there that he did not think that Mrs. Gaumer saw Mitchell at all, but that the minute she heard him enter the door she began to yell "You brute, how dare you face me! Hang him." The same person says it was judging from her position that it was almost impossible for her to have seen him. Mitchell never confessed being guilty to any one. His lawyer advised him not to plead guilty if he was not. He used to get milk at Mrs. Gaumer's for the Hotel Sowles, but had not been there for that purpose since March. He wore a derby hat and a checked coat as a rule, at that time, but since then had worn a different hat and coat. Mrs. Gaumer's neighbors never heard any racket or any unnecessary noise, and they never knew anything of the matter until informed by her. She is reported to have said that if she had made a mistake in her identification, it was only a "nigger" less anyhow. When it becomes known that Mrs. Gaumer was not ravished and that she received only two or three scratches, and that Mitchell never confessed committing any crime as alleged, it will put an entirely different phase upon the horrible lynching and make it appear as it was—murder in the first degree. The desperate means now employed by the daily papers, the clergy (white) and the Christian (?) people (white) of this and other communities, to exonerate the members of the mob, are to be deplored and denounced in the strongest terms. On last Sunday one minister (white) in order to plead the cause of lynch law took his text in Deuteronomy. Just think of it! I feel sure that time will prove "Click" Mitchell innocent of any crime as charged.

"CLICK" MITCHELL,

The Innocent Victim of the Urbana Mob—Gov. Bushnell Could Have Saved His Life.

Manly's analysis echoed anti-lynching activists who insisted that courts of law were the appropriate venue for *all* rape cases (regardless of the race of the alleged rapist—a veiled reference to the rape of black women by white men). The more controversial part of Manly's editorial echoed Wells's argument that white women sometimes had intimate relationships with black men only to call it rape upon discovery by family or friends. White supremacists seized on Manly's challenge to the rape/lynching narrative to whip up support for the conservative Democratic party in the midterm elections and thus weaken the Fusionist ticket. In the days leading up to the election, armed white men paraded in Wilmington's black neighborhoods, suppressing the vote. After the election, white mobs destroyed Manly's press, drove him out of town, and murdered dozens and possibly hundreds of others in a two-day massacre. Federal troops, just returning from fighting in the Spanish-American War, wielded their automatic weapons—not to protect the victims but to threaten remaining African Americans—and assisted vigilantes in driving many from the city.[71]

Coverage of the Wilmington massacre in the black press blamed President McKinley's refusal to make good on his earlier support for anti-lynching legislation. Few papers attempted to visualize the massacre, and at first the *Freeman* theorized that the response to Manly's editorial was part of a deliberate campaign to whip up racial antagonism.

> The trouble in North Carolina is by no means to be attributed to Editor Manley's editorial, which perhaps, however, served to farther inflame the whites. Mischief has been brewing in that state for months and all methods that could incense these whites against the blacks were adopted. The Atlanta Constitution, a paper of no small influence, played a conspicuous part in arraying race against race.

A week later, the *Freeman* published a visual re-enactment, which depicted the offices of the *Wilmington Record* in flames; an inset drawing, based on a photograph, identified Manly as the editor. The relatively muted image (fig. 4.24) reflected the *Freeman's* ambivalence about the tone of Manly's editorial. However, Knox later condemned the racial violence and destruction of Manly's press, asking bitterly, "What do the white citizens of North and South Carolina show to the world by their lawlessness and mob spirit at the election polls?" For African American editors, McKinley's silence in the face of such violence spoke volumes. "In all this there is a lesson," said the *Cleveland Gazette*, "which should be seared into the very marrow of the bones of our children and that is that it is folly to look to any political party for protection for our lives, liberty and property in the South."[72]

Weeks passed, and McKinley said nothing to condemn the Wilmington massacre. When he echoed Booker T. Washington's advocacy of uplift rather than

FIGURE 4.24: "Editor Manley and the Office of the Wilmington
Record Destroyed by a Mob in North Carolina," Indianapolis
Freeman, November 26, 1898, 4. Library of Congress.

editors' calls for protection of basic rights, many African American supporters recoiled. The mention of McKinley's name—now "The Great Silent Man"
instead of the "Great Protector"—drew hisses at a Boston anti-lynching rally
that spring. In 1899 a Georgia mob tortured and burned Sam Hose, inspiring
mass protests as far away as Chicago. *New York Age* editor T. T. Fortune blamed
President McKinley: "The president has encouraged mob law by his silence."
African American editors had come to view President McKinley as inseparable
from local white supremacists and even questioned the administration's racial
motives in the Philippines. By 1900, support for McKinley's reelection in the
black press faded, and his victory brought no rejoicing. The dream of presidential
leadership in enforcing due process and equal protection, let alone promoting
anti-lynching legislation—goals that had motivated African American voters
in the election of 1896 and probably helped McKinley into office—had died.[73]

Anti-lynching representations in the 1890s black press used some of the
tools of sensationalism to expose truths, exhort action, and validate persisting
feelings of anger, hope, and grief. Their anti-lynching images did not convince
presidents—Republican or Democrat—of the need for federal anti-lynching
legislation or even for simple condemnation of mob violence. They served a
different purpose, spoke to a different audience, and represented a significant
emergence of black visual journalism. They projected a unified anti-lynching
message, portraying lynching as a violation of basic rights in ways that could
inspire both sorrow and anger. Indianapolis *Freeman* artists used the repetition of familiar characters—presidents, Uncle Sam, Ethiopia, Atlas, Justice, or
Gulliver—along with the symbolic use of lynching victims themselves, to foster

a sense of urgency and crisis and to call political parties to account. The *Cleveland Gazette*, by contrast, rarely showed the bodies of lynching victims, preferring to highlight their humanity. The paper continued to promote the national Republican Party until it refused to take up the anti-lynching cause. *Richmond Planet* editor John Mitchell's drawings strategically highlighted the importance of white support in local and state anti-lynching efforts. All three newspapers emphasized government action as essential to countering mob violence.

As they developed graphic news strategies for addressing lynching, the 1890s African American newspapers adapted emerging sensational techniques to create a symbolic lexicon that would become available to the next generation of civil rights activists. (During World War I, illustrations featuring Uncle Sam or President Woodrow Wilson made a similar case for federal action against mob violence.) The 1890s anti-lynching illustrations sought to counter the lynching photographs and souvenirs circulating in the white community, creating an oppositional iconography that captured oppression, trauma, and the denial of fundamental rights that were promised by the Fourteenth Amendment. While powerless to halt the racist rape/lynching narrative in mainstream newspapers and political contests, within their own communities anti-lynching images helped rally voters and inspire activism. Ultimately, the illustrations and cartoons laid a foundation for more successful civil rights activism and organizations.[74]

The task facing these illustrators and cartoonists was to distill the major arguments against lynching, widely disseminated in the black community, into visual form. Some of these images focused on the myth that lynching was a punishment only meted out to accused rapists, by visualizing cases (such as Henry Smith's) where rape was not even the alleged crime. Others made visible the rape of black women, both in slavery and under Jim Crow segregation. Most found ways to visualize the mockery of justice inherent in mob violence: the absence of fair trials, credible evidence, and equal justice. Finally, many images took the federal government to task for abdicating its responsibility to protect all citizens from acts of political and social terror.

Collectively, these protest images converted intellectual, legal, or moral arguments into visuals that recurred, like a tocsin sounding, with every new atrocity. A tenacious, if modest, community-supported newspaper tradition made this visual outpouring possible for African American editors. Other activists, lacking their own illustrated press, had to find other ways to reach their communities and touch an emotional chord. Women's rights activists who sought to challenge the double standard in prosecution of honor killings by engaging directly with stories in sensational daily newspapers, for example, quickly learned that unintended consequences undermined their larger agenda. Chapter 5 shows the benefits and pitfalls of using sensational news strategies to influence events and shape public opinion.

CHAPTER 5

"Wanted to Save Her Honor"

Sensationalizing the Provocation Defense
in the Mid-1890s

WOMEN'S ORGANIZATIONS in the 1880s and 1890s, lacking illustrated newspapers of their own, experimented with ways to use sensational daily newspapers to expand exposure of their own causes. It was a period of renaissance
for the women's movement, when organizations and clubs sprang up to offer
fresh arguments for the vote and expanded rights. Women's groups from across
the political spectrum had long rejected sensationalism's frontier-justice ethos
and specifically its glorification of male violence against women as an expression of "honor." They singled out the infamous sporting weekly, the *National
Police Gazette*, for pushing this theme, but they had little commercial leverage
over the paper, which staked its fortunes on a male readership. The growing
sophistication of illustrated daily newspapers changed this calculus, however.
Sensational dailies provided a new front in the battle over the representation
of women in the public sphere. Editors increasingly learned that sensational
narratives of intimate violence provided their advertisers access to a new kind
of news consumer—women.[1]

One of the most dramatic examples of this trend came in April 1895, when
New York's illustrated dailies (particularly the *Recorder*, the *World*, and—eventually—the *Journal*) exploded with the story of Maria Barbella (incorrectly
identified as Barberi by her appointed attorney, and thus the judicial system and
the press).[2] The facts of the case were not in dispute. Barbella, a young Italian
immigrant, had killed a man named Domenico Cataldo, who had drugged and
"seduced" her (in what today would be called rape). On April 26, 1895, despite
pleas from her family and following a heated argument, he had categorically
refused to "salvage her honor" by marrying her. Barbella followed him to a local
saloon, carrying his straight razor in her pocket, and approached him as he sat
with his back to her on a barstool. She asked him one last time if he intended to

marry her; he responded with an emphatic "no"—adding over his shoulder the contemptuous comment that "only pigs marry." Barbella then reached forward, pulled his head back, and cut his throat. Cataldo staggered from the bar and collapsed on the sidewalk across the street; he died within minutes. Barbella washed her hands in a bucket of water and returned to his apartment, where police found her throwing her bloodstained clothes into the alley. They arrested her immediately.[3]

In the days that followed, sensational dailies seeking ways to enlist women as readers and consumers presented Maria Barbella as a victim of male callousness and judicial overreach. Headlines, images, captions, and interviews sought to answer the central question of whether Cataldo's actions could justify her deadly attack. In keeping Barbella before the public eye, editors refined standards for news illustration to capture readers' imaginations. Images detailed her arrest, arraignment, trial, and sentencing—to death by electrocution (the first woman so sentenced)—followed by a successful appeal and a second trial that ended with her acquittal. Throughout, sensational dailies competed to demonstrate a spirit of crusading journalism with tactics that proved to be extremely popular.

By the mid-1890s, daily newspapers preferred realistic, source-based imagery to interpretive illustration, with exceptions that included political cartoons and courtroom reenactments. During the two Barbella trials, headlines and text reporting strove to make the details of her crime as vivid and visible as possible. They capitalized on public interest in detection and police procedures, producing daily illustrations of visual "evidence" that encouraged readers to draw their own conclusions. At first, a relative newcomer called the *New York Recorder* gave Pulitzer's *World*, the dominant illustrated daily of the period, strong competition. As the Barbella case progressed, the *World* successfully incorporated many of the *Recorder*'s innovative practices, and before long a new competitor—Hearst's recently purchased *New York Journal*—joined the fray. The competition drove the *Recorder* out of business before Barbella's second trial began, depriving her, and women's rights activists who supported her, of a sympathetic forum.

As newspapers jousted for the newly discovered news consumer, the Barbella case became a proving ground for new kinds of daily news illustration. The *Recorder* had been established in 1891 with money from the Duke family as a vehicle to assist their newly minted American Tobacco Company combination in marketing cigarettes to women. From the start, the paper had catered to women, featuring women's pages, household guidance, and society news that mimicked popular monthlies like the *Ladies' Home Journal*. By 1893, even though its owners were already trying to unload the paper, the *Recorder* boasted one hundred thousand women readers. The *World* soon adopted many similar features aimed at women.[4] Like the *Recorder*, the *World*'s visual coverage of Barbella's arrest and first trial (in 1895) emphasized points of evidence, setting,

FIGURE 5.1: "He Invited His Death," *New York World*, April 27, 1895, 14.
New York State Library.

and character: the saloon on East Thirteenth Street (where the attack occurred); portraits of Barbella, of an eyewitness, and of the victim (Cataldo). As the case moved forward, they supplemented these images with scenes from Barbella's prison cell, the courtroom, and her family home. Images saturated the Barbella reporting in both papers.

The image of Maria Barbella herself became the central visual signifier for the story's moral interpretation. The *World*'s first image of Barbella (fig. 5.1) showed her confessing to the crime, above the caption "The murderess telling the story of her crime (she was waiting for the police when they went to arrest her and told everything calmly, even smilingly)." The *Recorder*'s images (fig. 5.2) of the crime scene (and a small profile portrait of Barbella) were less visually arresting.[5] Both exhibited a realistic feel. Their placement on the page indicated how daily illustration had changed since the Ghost Dance in 1890: the images were larger, free-flowing, and cascaded across columns. As the case went on,

FIGURE 5.2: "He Spurned Her Love," *New York Recorder*, April 27, 1895, 4. New York Public Library.

the two papers published multiple (often contradictory) images of Barbella herself, which changed over time as editors struggled with the problem of how to represent her in print. Though changeable, this visual "evidence" made it possible for readers to *see* Barbella for themselves. The images also catered to popular notions about ethnicity, race, sex, crime, passion, and power, in a period when all of these categories were in flux. Representing Barbella's "person"—by which papers meant her antecedents, her biology, her contradictory stories, her many "faces"—became the key to making sense of the killing in both papers.

Women responded to the sensational dailies' focus on Barbella. Celebrity newcomers, veteran women's rights activists, and young women new to the movement mobilized in different ways to protest her sentence to death by electrocution and developed (successful) arguments for a retrial. Their support for Barbella marked a shift from arguments that had for decades animated the struggle for the women's rights and temperance movements. Instead of accepting Victorian ideology regarding women's inherent purity and passionlessness, they demanded equality before the law. It was a bold strategy, and one not without risk. To come to Barbella's defense, they needed to cast her as a victim of male aggression, and thus their defense of her emphasized her vulnerability, her naïveté, her ignorance of American ways, her passionate racialized "nature," and (especially) her youth. But they also had to concede to the idea of a woman's potential for "hot-blooded" violence. The act of supporting Barbella strained older arguments for women's moral authority in public matters.[6]

The fact that Barbella's victim, Domenico Cataldo, was also Italian likely made it easier for (white, Protestant) women's rights activists to support her defense. Both Barbella and Cataldo were part of a new wave of immigration to the United States, from Southern and Eastern Europe, known as the "new immigrants." Unlike Northern European immigrants, the new immigrants tended to be Catholic rather than Protestant, from rural/agricultural rather than urban/artisanal backgrounds. Their reception was comparable to what the Irish (also rural and Catholic) had experienced in preceding decades. Suspicion about Italian men, and specifically Southern Italian men, was widespread in the 1890s. This was true even in Italy, where positivist anthropologists from the north (most famously Cesare Lombroso, along with his protégée Enrico Ferri) used "scientific" techniques like the measurement of skull and facial attributes to argue that Southern Italians belonged to an inferior race, were inherently violent and prone to crime.[7] As a woman, Barbella was considered more docile and thus less suspicious; as an Italian, she still faced assumptions about her "natural" proclivity to violence.[8] This made her case ideal fodder for sensational dailies but also forced Anglo-American women to question long-standing assumptions about a woman's "nature" as moral, passive, and refined.

Crimes of Passion and Sensational News

With its focus on sex, crime, and violence, Barbella's story seemed made for sensational news, particularly as both the *Recorder* and the *World* emphasized a novel twist designed to appeal to female readers. Of the two, the *World's* headline—"He Invited His Death"—was perhaps the more forceful in arguing that Cataldo was partly responsible for his own killing. For the *World*, Cataldo's "violation of Barbella's sexual honor" was sufficient provocation for violence; he had "wronged the woman who trusted him and was slain," as the subhead explained. The *Recorder's* more modest headline ("He Spurned Her Love") likewise embraced the provocation angle, casting the case as a drama of a woman betrayed by a scoundrel, then "maddened by his refusal to marry her." The *Recorder* highlighted Barbella's "desperation" (suggesting an incapacitated mental state, a possible line of defense) after being seduced (or raped) and then rejected by Cataldo.[9] Both sensational dailies kept attention focused on Barbella's *motivations*—in ways that were more typical of sporting representations of cases involving a man's killing of a wife or lover.

In 1895 the "crime of passion" was an unusual defense for a sensational newspaper to offer a woman who had killed. It indicates how fiercely daily news providers competed to attract women as readers. The crime of passion, traditionally defined as a husband's killing of his wife's lover or seducer, under the influence of "hot blood," was the subject of fierce legal debate in late-nineteenth-century America. Sporting weeklies had long profited from publicizing "honor" crimes, with their underlying assumption that uncontrollable passions led men to kill in defense of sexual honor. Weekly crime newspapers like the *Police Gazette*, in particular, found crimes-of-passion stories irresistible. Their strong narrative arc and the immediacy of summary justice provided instant gratification to readers while reinforcing men's prerogatives and control over women. The serial nature of the slow and imperfect legal mechanisms of the state following these crimes, complete with recurring characters, courtroom scenes, and exciting new evidence, kept readers enthralled.

Fascination with crimes of passion in the daily press amplified the provocation defense. Also known as the "unwritten law," in the early nineteenth century the "crime of passion" defense applied only to men accused of killing their wives' lovers when discovered *in the act* of infidelity. The rationale was that the sight so violated a man's sense of honor that in the heat of the moment, he temporarily lost his sanity. From midcentury onward, however, the scope of this defense expanded to include men who also killed their (allegedly) unfaithful wives. Juries and judges increasingly upheld the husband's view of the wife as an agent of provocation. Gradually, such cases stretched the time frame far beyond the moment of discovery of infidelity. Three court cases (*Sickles*, 1859; *Coles*, 1867; *McFarland*, 1869–70) expanded the unwritten law, paving the way for what became known as the temporary or moral insanity defense. Thanks to these precedents, defendants employed the "crime of passion" defense even in cases of premeditation, passage of time (in other words, lack of "heat"), and without direct witnessing (or evidence) of infidelity. Some juries went so far as to accept a defendant's claim that he merely *believed* he was being betrayed or humiliated, accepting his perception as a valid form of evidence.[10]

Women's rights activists had long denounced the expanding definition of provocation that sensational newspapers had done so much to popularize. The idea that justice might depend on a perpetrator's sense of honor empowered society's worst assumptions about men's prerogative in (and even outside of) marriage, binding women to a possessive conception of male authority, many argued. (Such concerns continue to resonate in twenty-first-century debate about the impact of the expanded provocation defense on women's legal rights and safety.) Giving primacy to motivation in the provocation defense, while clearly a progressive development for defendants, boded ill for women, the typical victims of such crimes. It could be applied even in cases where the perceived provocation included simple rejection, as well as separation or divorce—far beyond the traditional "heat" arising from finding one's wife in bed with another man. Since men are far more likely to commit intimate homicide, the law's embrace of the expanded "heat of passion" defense tends to reinforce a man's right to control or dominate a woman. Over time, the heat of passion defense would come to include even cases where a relationship had been terminated (or cases where the "relationship" was nothing more than wishful thinking on the part of the killer).[11]

It is ironic, then, that Barbella's case temporarily encouraged female activists to rally around the idea of provocation as a defense for *women* who killed. They reasoned that a woman, too, could experience the "heat of passion" when her sexual honor was betrayed. Further, their support of Barbella upheld the expanded defense that certain kinds of provocation warranted a mitigated sentence, even when there was evidence of premeditation (as in the case of Barbella, who had brought the razor with her). Disregarding the longer-term risk to their arguments against male honor killings, they seized the opportunity to expand it further to include female defendants.

Women's rights activists had long protested the narrative pushed by the *Police Gazette*, one of the nation's most prolific chroniclers of male crimes of passion. It is unsurprising that honor killings filled its pages, given its distribution within male public spaces of barrooms and barbershops and its long history of illustrating sex, crime, and violence. These crimes-of-passion narratives neatly crystallized Victorian assumptions about men and women that were deeply held but often unspoken. As in other sensational images in the *Police Gazette*, the honor killing collapsed accusation, trial, "evidence," verdict, and (often) punishment into a single visual frame. The paper's tableaux of betrayal and retribution, of provocation and punishment, pushed highly gendered perceptions of the place of violence in intimate relations. Just as with the images of racial assault, these illustrations represented legal cases in a partial manner, to use both senses of the term: they provided an incomplete (and often distorted or fictionalized) account of events leading to violence, and they overwhelmingly favored the perspective of the killer (a man) over that of the victim (a woman). Corrections of factual distortions never appeared; accuracy was not the paper's purpose. The *Police Gazette*'s selective promotion of the "hot blood" or provocation explanation for men—but not women—effectively popularized men's retributive violence against women.

Jealousy provided the *Police Gazette*'s most frequent narrative explanation for wife killing. For example, an 1889 image, "A Message in Blood," highlighted jealousy as the husband's motivation and, by implication, the wife's responsibility for provoking the crime (fig. 5.3). The dead woman appeared in the frame, but the image's dynamic focus was on the man's act of writing (in blood) his motive for killing her: "jealousy." Based on a brief wire-service clip, an interpretive illustration of this kind took great creative license; its artistic rendering of a complex and controversial event was highly selective. Ambiguous and biased, it gave prominence to the husband's belief in his wife's infidelity, even though the facts told otherwise. The text (buried on another page) presented a more complex story, and detailed accounts from local papers indicated that neighbors and friends disputed the husband's suspicions, believing that the he "had not the slightest ground for his insane jealousy of his young wife." In the *Police Gazette*'s

A MESSAGE IN BLOOD.

FRANK COMPTON OF WEST PITTSTON, PA., KILLS HIS WIFE AND THEN CUTS HIS THROAT, AFTER WHICH HE WRITES ON THE WALL.

FIGURE 5.3: "A Message in Blood," *The National Police Gazette*, June 15, 1883. Library of Congress.

visualization of the case, the husband's subjective emotion dominated the frame, creating a closed narrative loop of cause and effect: a prop in the man's visual story, the wife's corpse appeared not as a victim but rather as a consequence of her own actions.[12] This was also the legal theory for the defendant at his trial.

By contrast, *Police Gazette* images of women as killers lacked such narrative closure and often disguised or ignored the "heat of passion" evident in the text stories that inspired the illustrations. For example, an 1893 image (fig. 5.4) showed a St. Louis woman shooting her husband as they grappled on the floor for a gun. "Killed her husband," the caption stated, without speculating on the cause; the smaller print continued in passive voice: "while struggling for possession of a revolver *John Minor is shot*." Both interpretive illustration and caption were silent on Mrs. Minor's motivation for killing her husband; her lethal violence appeared accidental, possibly even the result of clumsiness. However, the text (on another page) revealed that she had, in fact, shot her husband through the heart, allegedly because he was "said to have been supporting another woman."[13] The omission from the image and caption of any indication that Mrs. Minor's crime was a "hot-blooded" action prompted by jealousy or due to her husband's betrayal of her sexual honor erased women's capacity for violent vengeance. It transformed what might be seen as a woman's "honor killing" into just another random crime amid the paper's cacophony of violence.

Another case highlighted this gendered difference in portraying lethal violence even more clearly. An 1894 *Police Gazette* image (fig. 5.5) depicted the story of a sixteen-year old girl, Mary Yusta, who killed another woman, Maggie McDermott, in Deadwood, South Dakota. The two women, both allegedly prostitutes and rivals for the affections (or custom) of a gambler named Frank

FIGURE 5.4: "Killed
Her Husband," *The
National Police Gazette*,
November 25, 1893.
Library of Congress.

Debelloy, had confronted him in the back of a saloon to force him to choose
between them. When he refused, the two women quarreled, and in the ensuing struggle, Yusta used Debelloy's gun to shoot the older woman through the
heart, killing her. Though Debelloy was in fact arrested as an accessory—he
allegedly dared Yusta to kill McDermott and gave her the gun—*Police Gazette*
images exonerated him as a party to the shooting. In both the larger frame
and the smaller inset, the visual narrative focused on his (vain—and fictive)
efforts to prevent the shooting. Motivation can be inferred from the caption's
wording—"Shot Her Pretty *Rival*"—but in such a way as to downplay the
man's responsibility.[14] While the *Police Gazette* did represent women's lethal
retributive violence in this case, it portrayed the man's role as the unsuccessful
protector rather than the accomplice—or instigator—of the crime.

The *Police Gazette* frequently displayed women's *nonlethal* violence against
men, however. In such cases, captions included references to provocation in
phrases like "wronged wife" and "unfaithful husband."These images presented
a more coherent narrative loop of cause and effect than when a woman's violence turned fatal. For example, an image depicting Mrs. Henry, a wife in
Corinth, Kentucky, attacking her husband and his lover (Mrs. Bricey) adopted
the woman's vantage point, highlighting the victims' terror (fig. 5.6). The text
emphasized her "heat of passion": "With the fury of a tigress the wronged wife
beat both offenders until they sprang from the bed and rushed from the home."
Mr. Henry was believed to be badly injured and hiding out in Cincinnati, while
Mrs. Bricey "was considerably bruised about the face and arms."[15] The cumulative message of such imagery and caption wording was effective because it was
subtle. In the pages of the *Police Gazette*, nonlethal assault appeared to be a
woman's legitimate response to a man's infidelity, but killing went beyond the
limits of a woman's retributive justice for the paper's audience of men.

SHE SHOT HER PRETTY RIVAL.
A MEMBER OF THE DEMI-MONDE OF DEADWOOD, S. D., IS PERFORATED BY A BULLET FROM
A REVOLVER IN THE HANDS OF A JEALOUS FEMALE OF THE SAME TYPE.

FIGURE 5.5: "She Shot Her Pretty Rival," *The National Police Gazette*, January 13, 1893. Library of Congress.

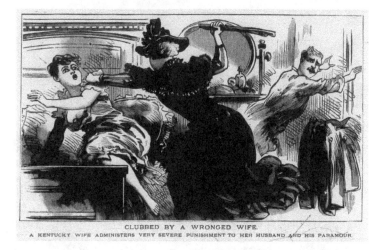

CLUBBED BY A WRONGED WIFE.
A KENTUCKY WIFE ADMINISTERS VERY SEVERE PUNISHMENT TO HER HUSBAND AND HIS PARAMOUR.

FIGURE 5.6: "Clubbed by a Wronged Wife," *The National Police Gazette*, October 14, 1893. Library of Congress.

By contrast, humorous accounts of ineffectual attacks by wronged wives on errant husbands abounded in the *Police Gazette*. In an 1897 case, a Nebraska woman stabbed her "unfaithful husband" in the chest with a sharp kitchen knife. "Knife for an Unfaithful Husband," read the caption: "An energetic wife ... disciplines her spouse with a bright, keen blade." In typical *Police Gazette* style, the framing emphasized the situation's humorous rather than tragic elements, wryly describing the woman as a wife "who doesn't believe in divorce." The text explained that she learned that he was "untrue to her, and as soon as she was sure of it she concluded to teach him a lesson he wouldn't forget." After stabbing him in the chest, she reportedly asked him, "Now will you go with other women?'" The paper facetiously noted that upon receiving his promise of future fidelity, she nursed him back to health.[16] Such satirical renderings precluded any real conception of female honor, casting the attack as a more extreme example of the domineering wife (or henpecked husband).

Over decades of selective culling of wire stories to illustrate such cases, the *Police Gazette* had developed a visual lexicon that seemed to justify some forms of lethal intimate violence. Women who killed men while defending themselves against sexual assault by ethnically or racially distinct strangers (to protect their "sexual purity") found acceptance, even approval, in *Police Gazette* images. Those women who used violence to defend their honor against cheating spouses or known seducers were lampooned or ignored. The paper's apocryphal "crime of passion" iconography can be seen in the image "She Was Untrue" (fig. 5.7). Its framing of the husband as protagonist, its reenactment of the shooting, and its

FIGURE 5.7: "She Was Untrue,"
The National Police Gazette,
February 1, 1896. Library of
Congress.

caption combine as a neat summary of the man's perception that his wife was the guilty party—a "provoker"—rather than a victim of murder. These visual narratives mirrored the expansion of the "unwritten law," which now invoked honor to mitigate sentencing for a man who killed his unfaithful wife (rather than her seducer, the traditional usage of the "unwritten law"). Captions similarly reinforced the killer's perspective that he was justified.[17] This was true not only for images depicting unfaithful wives; women seeking to leave or avoid a relationship with the perpetrator were also portrayed as provokers of male retribution. Emphasizing—and empathizing with—men's subjective motivation made women appear as accomplices in their own victimization.[18]

The frequent, almost normative nature of images of wife killings in the *Police Gazette*, framed as they were by the husband's internal rationale for the violence, reinforced an ethos of personal retributive justice—essentially, revenge—rather than temporary insanity. It was the popular culture analog to shifts in legal response. By contrast, *Police Gazette* images almost never portrayed a husband as implicated in his own death at the hands of a wife; no caption of "He Was Untrue" lent explanatory power to an image of a woman killing an unfaithful man. It was this perspective that women's rights activists, acutely conscious of the double standard in "crimes of passion" sentencing and sensational news reporting during this period, sought to challenge. The Barbella case seemed like the perfect opportunity.

Provocation and the Double Standard

Long before Barbella's case, women's rights newspapers had noted and debated the double standard in honor killings. Their text-based publications could not compete visually, but they did compile news stories about domestic violence, sometimes including elements of text-based sensationalism. Stories of violence against women in these newspapers bolstered their arguments for women's political and legal rights. In particular, they condemned the use of provocation as a mitigating factor in cases of fatal intimate violence, particularly when there was evidence of deliberation and premeditation. They disparaged sensational reporting, which they felt reinforced and perhaps encouraged men's efforts to evade responsibility for killing their wives and so-called "sweethearts." The notion that women were complicit in their own deaths in such news stories, they argued, contributed to the social stigma against victims of domestic violence, which deterred women from reporting ongoing marital abuse before it turned fatal. In their own papers, women's rights activists argued that holding women responsible for violence against them reinforced women's subordination.[19]

In the decades leading up to Barbella's 1895 case, women's newspapers had developed strategies to challenge the "crime of passion" justification for violence against women, as part of their broader effort to achieve equality for women. A sample of these newspapers reveals how overtly or indirectly they attempted to confront—and refute—the assumptions underlying crime-of-passion reporting. They opposed the idea that intense emotion, including jealousy, gave grounds to justify compassion in sentencing a man who killed his wife or lover. They pointed to the relative leniency in the sentencing of wife killers, compared to sentencing for other crimes, as the inevitable consequence of excluding women from the public sphere. Some attempted to alert readers to the broader political implications of the "hot blood" defense, lobbying for greater equivalency in remedies for violent crime and killing. A few insisted that only expanded political power for women—as voters, as jurors—and public demands for rights could lead to equitable legal outcomes.

The *Woman's Journal* (Boston) was perhaps the most outspoken and certainly the longest-standing critic of the double standard in domestic violence prosecutions. As early as the 1870s, its editors, Lucy Stone and her husband, Henry Blackwell, had documented "crimes against women," listing men's violence against women in a (largely unsuccessful) effort to get anti-battering legislation passed. In 1879, for example, Blackwell noted an average of six such assault cases per day in Boston alone. He attributed to class bias legislators' failure to support a law providing an order of protection for wives: "If it were the sister or the daughter of our legislators, whose rights to life, liberty and the pursuit of happiness were in question, there would be no denial." In 1882 the paper praised a Maryland law that sentenced wife beaters to public whipping, for example, and a similar corporal punishment law proposed in Pennsylvania two years later as mechanisms to deter domestic violence. (In keeping with its middle-class and ethnic bias, the *Woman's Journal* assumed in its reporting and editorials that mostly "foreigners" would be affected). Further, Stone and Blackwell used such cases to drum up support for protective legislation for women.[20]

When journalism failed to achieve anti-battering legislation, Stone and Blackwell recommended political action, tying their campaign to stop violence against women to their campaign for women's right to vote. For example, in 1879, when a woman of "low repute" was kidnapped and assaulted for days, and police allowed the suspects to escape, Blackwell emphasized women's powerlessness before the law. "Cannot any man or woman who is not as blind as a mole," he wrote, "see that the enfranchisement of women will make them a power to be conciliated by the officers of the law?" In 1884 the *Women's Journal* ran a story of an Ohio man, convicted of manslaughter for killing his wife a few years earlier, whose friends were lobbying the governor for a pardon, on the same page and just above resolutions from the Toledo Woman Suffrage Association condemning the effort. "The ease with which crimes against women are pardoned," Stone argued in an editorial, "and the frequency of cases where a sentence cannot be secured even in aggravated cases . . . should make [women] see their need of the power which the ballot gives."[21]

By the early 1890s, women's rights activists grew increasingly dismayed by the way popular reports of wife killers focused on the man's motivation and emotional state. In 1891 the *Woman's Tribune* (Beatrice, Neb.) dismissed the provocation rationale in a case where a thwarted suitor claimed to have killed a young woman out of frustrated love for her. "Say a man kills a girl for love of her and mawkish sentimentality is aroused at once in pity," wrote editor Clara Bewick Colby. "Designate that deed as it is in reality, and it is seen to be so hateful that it loses its attractive power to influence others and the perpetrator is disgraced and shunned." The *Woman's Tribune* pointed out the political implications of the jealousy defense, which denied a woman's ability to make her own choices in intimate relationships. "To shoot the girl who will not marry him is the protest of the savage against the self-assertion of what he has been accustomed to regard as his by right of brute force." Only full equality, Colby argued, would stop such "sex tragedies" from occurring.[22] Not all women's newspapers drew such broad political lessons from honor killings, however. In a similar case, the populist *Farmer's Wife* (Topeka, Kan.), though generally supportive of women's rights arguments, accepted violence as part of men's nature and reflected on jealousy's power to incite it. "More than half the murders in the world are committed through its influence," the paper said. But the editor declined to comment on the gender politics in reporting, or of possessiveness itself, saying merely that "the greatest curse in the world is jealousy."[23] This lack of unity among women's newspaper editors over the causes and justifications of men's violence against women made it difficult to challenge violence against women in the wider public sphere.

Women's rights activists did agree that sensational imagery, particularly the illustrated crime weeklies, constituted a powerful form of propaganda for men's violence and promoted "greater levels of societal violence." It was a view shared by a range of reformers in the United States and England. Pacifists, for example, blamed images of violence in crime weeklies and sensational dailies for providing an "education in brutality" for the "vicious classes:"

> Men with wild, angry faces, standing with uplifted dagger ready to plunge it into the heart of a woman on her knees near him, or with pistol drawn and flashing its smoke and powder into the face of some enemy, or standing with club in hand over some victim of his wrath who lies crushed on the ground— these are samples of what may be seen every day posted up in conspicuous places in our American cities.

In the 1880s and early 1890s, activists in the Women's Christian Temperance Union (WCTU) lobbied for laws restricting the exhibition and sale of crime papers like the *Police Gazette*. To some extent, their concerns reflected the cultural anxieties and class interests of the white, Protestant middle class facing a growing immigrant population. Underlying these biases, however, was the assumption that violent imagery made some people more violent.[24]

Following in the path of Comstock two decades earlier, a variety of reform organizations agreed that viewing violence contributed to violence, so they developed strategies to curtail the publication, distribution, exhibition, and sale of illustrated crime news. Temperance activists in the 1890s now set their sights on the sensational *daily* newspapers, believing "in the power of words and images to suggest a new course of behavior to the innocent viewer." They also agreed with Comstock that a focus on divorce and adultery degraded morality. Emily Martin, superintendent of the WCTU's Department for the Suppression of Impure Literature, pressured daily editors "to recognize their role as powerful cultural influences, report on more philanthropic deeds, and voluntarily improve the moral tenor of their stories by excluding details on crime." The National Editorial Association credited women's organizations in 1894 when it adopted a "pledge to uphold 'good' morals." In 1898 the organization reinforced this call to rein in "inaccuracy of statement, sensationalism and undue space given to recitals of crimes and descriptions of brutal exhibitions."[25] Controlling what people could see in public print, they believed, would curtail violent acts.

At the same time, and with a few exceptions, women's rights activists and women in the WCTU tended to approach marital violence and murder only indirectly. Their condemnation of intimate violence came out typically in advocacy for other causes without explicitly viewing men's violence as a symptom of patriarchy. Consequently, their critique of men's brutality often associated marital violence with "rough" classes and "foreigners" as a subset of the excesses (and alcohol use) inherent in immigrant, working-class life. Reformers found ways to use evidence of spousal brutality to argue for a range of causes, from restricting immigration to expanding women's political rights.[26]

By the 1890s, women's rights activists used their own publications to challenge the gendered provocation defense. While their republished squibs and editorials had little *visual* power, their tiny headlines *were* sensational in tone. In 1891, for example, when a Boston woman was killed by her husband, the *Woman's Journal* headlined the story "Are Women Protected?" as a way to highlight women's vulnerability under the legal double standard that downgraded male punishment for violence.

> This brutal murder of a wife by her husband (both apparently sober)—a crime cold blooded, unprovoked, deliberate, malicious, the culmination of a series of personal outrages—is called 'manslaughter.' . . . If the victim had been a man and a voter, [the killer] would have been committed for murder in the first degree, punishable with death or life-imprisonment. *But alas! The victim was only his wife.*[27]

Yet the sole eye-catching strategy was a headline in roughly eight-point type. The *Woman's Tribune*, which also expressed concern about this story, published it without any headline at all, noting, "This will send him to prison for only a few years, whereas the crime called for the full penalty of murder in the first degree."[28] Either a shortage of funds, ethical objections, or lack of media experience made women's rights newspapers unable—or unwilling—to employ the tools of visual sensationalism.

Argument was the most interpretive weapon women's rights editors used in their campaign to halt the culture of violence against women. For example, Lucy Stone editorialized about leniency to wife killers in an 1892 case in which a Boston man who burned his wife and was sentenced to "one year in the House of Correction," and in a case a year later when a Lawrence, Massachusetts, man killed his wife and received only a two-year sentence, less than the six to eleven years for a man found guilty of theft. "Of so much less importance is the murder of a wife than is the breaking and entering of a house," Stone commented.[29] A few months later, when a Philadelphia man received a relatively short sentence for the brutal killing of his wife, Stone deplored the "noticeable fact that the most brutal cruelty and even murders committed upon women often meet with slight punishment, *especially if perpetrated by the husband*."[30] Editorial sarcasm, reasoned argument, critique, and some bitter language constituted the extent of Stone's forays into the emotional terrain of sensational news.

Reports of atrocities against women did, however, make it possible for editors of women's newspapers to push harder for political rights to help women protect themselves, specifically through new legislation and enforcement of existing laws. Blackwell challenged the assumption that domestic crimes posed no public threat. Comparing one wife killer, banished from New York to Colorado, to a wild animal that society should rightly cage, Blackwell wrote, "Here is a more dangerous character, who has murdered one [un]offending woman, and tried to murder several others, let loose upon the women of Colorado."[31] The inequality of sentences became a further argument for women's legal and political rights. In 1893, even the moderate *Farmer's Wife* pointed out a disparity in punishments meted out by the Topeka Police Court.

> A man pounds a woman, once his wife, breaks her bones and further maltreats her, and gets ninety days. On the same day another man gets the same number of days for vagrancy. In the eye of the law it is exactly as bad to have nothing to do as to beat a woman within an inch of her life.

Later that year, another women's newspaper, the *Kansas Sunflower*, clipped a similar case from a local paper: "Yet all the punishment law can inflict on this brute is a fine for assault. It's time women had something to do with making the laws."[32] These editors shared the belief that rational advocacy for women's rights would enhance justice: being able to vote and sit on juries would empower women, bring their white, middle/upper-class moral sensibilities into the polity, and perhaps challenge the unequal application of the provocation defense.

"Those Who Feel for Maria Barberi"

Women's rights activists' frustration with the expanding provocation defense and its distillation in the sporting weeklies is what makes the *World*'s headline in the Barbella case—"He Invited His Death"—such a significant departure. Unlike sporting weeklies, whose interpretive illustrations visually re-enacted crimes, the *World* and the *Recorder* relied on a different kind of visualization.[33] Their goal was to bring the *evidence* and the *proceedings*—the crime scene, courtroom, and cast of characters—into public view. They also (at least initially) brought a women's rights perspective on the double standard in prosecution of honor killings to their reporting. Critics blamed the dailies for creating "an appetite for things abnormal,"[34] but in the Barbella case the dailies claimed the mantle of crusading journalism in pursuit of justice.

Once the trial opened on July 11, 1895, images and headlines in the *World* and *Recorder* were strikingly similar, in both cases designed to emphasize the latest details of the hearings and place readers in the position of jurors and spectators in the courtroom. Both papers produced composite sketches of the trial and its major characters, including Maria Barbella; the so-called "Tombs Angel" (a woman named Mrs. Foster who accompanied her throughout the ordeal); an array of witnesses; and glimpses of the courtroom scene. Both dailies noted the judge's refusal to consider Cataldo's betrayal (in other words, Maria's motivation) as exculpatory evidence: "It matters not,' said he, 'whether Cataldo was a sadist or a devil, the only question before the jury is did this defendant kill him and kill him with premeditation.'" Both noted the unfairness to her defense resulting from having her testimony inexpertly translated from Italian. Both lamented the jury's verdict of "Guilty."[35] The similarity in coverage suggests that both sought to make the story appealing to a wider (and female) audience.

The *World*'s initial trial coverage was entirely typical of the sensational style, focusing on Barbella's mental state and especially her alleged lack of emotion following her conviction for first-degree murder. At the time, some editors saw this as an indication of her depraved nature (today, it might be considered an indicator of post-traumatic stress). "Is Maria Barberi Mad?" asked the *World*'s headline, and the accompanying text described the contrast between her tear-ravaged face during the trial and her impassive countenance on hearing the guilty verdict: "The expression of her face had ceased to be harrowing and agonized; it had become dull, lethargic, almost lifeless." The paper documented this claim visually with a small illustration of a "catatonic" Barbella being embraced by her sobbing mother in her cell. Wording and image represented her as a "non-woman," even inhuman, in ways that corresponded with more general media patterns of depicting women accused of murder as somehow outside the scope of "normal" womanhood. But the broader story showed her to be susceptible to some emotion: visited by missionaries who sang hymns, at one point she "crouched down upon the stone floor and huddled herself into a shapeless little bundle, burying her face in her knees" (fig. 5.8). The meaning of this little scene is unclear—perhaps Barbella simply wanted to evade the scrutiny of her observers—but it presented women readers with a pathetic scene. The *World*'s image showed a distressed but affectless woman unable to face up to her crime.[36]

The *Recorder*'s coverage took a different and more sympathetic approach that highlighted Barbella's betrayed honor, a focus that proved to be both dramatic and humanizing; it changed the nature of her coverage, public perception, and, very likely, her fate. The paper began by scooping the *World* with a clever device: a candid interview with Barbella, conducted in Italian, by one of the paper's women reporters. "Maria Barberi did not mean to kill," claimed the *Recorder*'s headline, while the subhead, "*Wanted to Save Her Honor*," sketched out a new line of defense: "The Child-Woman, Barberi, had no intention of Taking Her

MARIA BARBERI HEARS A HYMN.

FIGURE 5.8: "Is Maria Barberi Mad?" *New York World,* July 17, 1895, 3. New York State Library.

Lover's Life." As these headlines make clear, the *Recorder*'s central focus was not Barbella's mental fitness but rather the motivation for and legitimacy of her action.

> Is a woman justified in taking any step, however extreme, to avenge the loss of honor?
>
> That is the question that seems to be in the mouths of everybody who is at all interested in the case of little Maria Barberi, the child-woman, who has been convicted of murder in the first degree for cutting the throat of Domenico Cataldo, the man who betrayed her.[37]

Interviewing her in her native language, the "Recorder woman" (unnamed) gave Barbella the opportunity to speak directly to the public in her own words. In this way, the *Recorder* attempted to retry the case in the press.

In this interview, Barbella revealed details about Cataldo's seduction and betrayal that had been suppressed by the judge, revelations that were now possible because "her questioner was a woman, [who] addressed her in her own tongue." Barbella confided that she had not meant to kill Cataldo but instead to inflict "a little gash that would bring the blood and have us both arrested," believing that if they were both brought before a judge, Cataldo would be forced to marry her. An illustration of the two women deep in conversation in the prison cell (fig. 5.9) featured a childlike and animated Barbella, explaining her actions to the professional journalist, who was easily recognizable by the tools of her trade—her notebook and journalist's characteristic boater hat.[38] The interview and image cemented the *Recorder*'s reputation as a women-friendly

FIGURE 5.9: "Maria Barberi Tells Her Story to a Recorder Woman," *New York Recorder*, July 17, 1895, 1. New York Public Library.

paper, staffed by professional female journalists, sympathetic to a woman's perspective, attentive to women's interests, and aware of their relative powerlessness within the legal system.

The *Recorder*'s interview set the tone for subsequent sensational coverage. Boasting that it had created "Hope for Poor Maria," the paper's front-page headline a day later took credit for prominent New Yorkers' renewed interest in the case: "The Recorder Has Aroused Strong Sympathy for the Convicted Italian Girl." The paper also took credit for the arrival of a new character in the drama—a defender for Barbella—namely, the Contessa di Brazza Savorgnan, a New Orleans native who had married an Italian count and was well connected with New York's social and cultural elite. To her new supporter (also fluent in Italian), Barbella repeated her claim that she had acted on friends' advice to give him "a little cut . . . but, ah! *Madonna mis*, it was too deep." The article concluded (and somewhat undermined) this claim with a statement from her lawyer, expressing surprise at this "present story of the girl," which, he noted, had not come up earlier in preparation for trial. He nonetheless restated his faith that the killing was not premeditated and announced his determination to pursue executive clemency—"not for commutation of sentence, but for pardon."[39]

Not to be outdone, the *World* found ways to match the *Recorder*'s women-friendly coverage with front-page copy and imagery well-designed to attract female readers. Next to a sympathetic, two-column illustration of Barbella seated in a chair, facing the reader, the *World*'s front-page opinion piece ratcheted up the sensation by predicting that Barbella would never be electrocuted, even if sentenced to death (fig. 5.10). The piece reported the author's assurances to

FIGURE 5.10: "Miss
Maria Barberi," *New
York World*, July 18, 1895, 1.
New York State Library.

Barbella that she was safe from execution because no doctor would be "willing
to make himself the executioner of a woman." The author offered a second, more
"delicate" reason why Barbella "will never be cooked or shocked in the electric
chair": female modesty. "She cannot be killed with her legs decently covered,
because if her skirts were down the electrode might then blaze up and catch
fire," the article explained. "When a State like this makes up its mind to kill a
young woman weighing 115 pounds, speaking no English, understanding nothing of her rights, badly defended and otherwise ill-fitted to cope," it violated
not only women's rights but basic standards of decency.[40]

On July 18, 1895, however, Barbella received her sentence to death by electrocution. Both the *Recorder* and the *World* now expanded their populist, honor-
based approach to the story. This was particularly true of their visual coverage.
Alongside a headline, "MARIA'S DOOM SPOKEN," the *Recorder*'s visual
commentary occupied three columns at the top of the page. It was an effective
political cartoon (fig. 5.11), showing a disheveled female prisoner, hands bound
or held behind her back, guided by a towering man in uniform, labeled "Jailer."
The man reached for the knob of a heavy wooden door, above which a sign read
"Entrance to DEATH CHAMBER"; a paper floated below the knob that said
"Death Warrant, MARIE BARBERI." An enormous hand blocked entrance
to the door, with the end of a jacket and shirt cuff visible: the words on the
cuff read "Public Sentiment." A simple caption below summed up the scene:

York Recorder.

MORNING, JULY 19, 1895.—12 PAGES.   PRICE TWO CENTS.

esidences Than Any Other New York Newspaper.

MARIA'S DOOM SPOKEN

Recorder Goff Has Sentenced the Hapless Girl to Death by Electricity.

TAKEN TO SING SING AT ONCE

FIGURE 5.11: "STOP!" *New York Recorder*, July 19, 1895, 1. New York Public Library.

"STOP!" The image emphasized specifically the need for women, as readers, to put their feelings for Barbella into action.[41]

Following sentencing, the *World* (and later the *Recorder*) began to publish columns of letters from women denouncing the execution sentence for Barbella. "Women Would Save Her," said the headline over the published letters, titled, "Distinguished Members of Her Sex Plead for Maria Barberi's Life." The third and fourth headlines, all in capital letters, now posited that the provocation defense applied to a woman; they explained the killing by virtue of the "unwritten law" as "Frenzied Revenge for Honor" and pointed to the double standard: "Men Who Murder upon This Impulse Escape the Capital Penalty—Why Not She?" Letters published that day and the next echoed this theme, including a statement from veteran women's rights activist Elizabeth Cady Stanton. The *World*'s headlines summarized their arguments: "Women Say a Man in a Like

Case Would Be Treated Leniently: Might Even Go Free with Honor." The paper gave headline status to Stanton's insistence that Maria was "not tried by a jury of her peers" and, further, that "until women do court duty . . . justice need not be expected."[42] A circulation war between the *Recorder* and the *World* for women readers had transformed one woman's legal jeopardy into a lively forum for debate over the rationale for the provocation defense and, by implication, women's rights.

The *Recorder* soon moved beyond letters and editorials demanding commutation, pardon, or appeal, by encouraging women to organize resistance to the death sentence. "FOR MERCY!" the headline read: "Commutation of the Death Sentence Won't Satisfy *Those Who Feel for Maria Barberi*." Text commentary lamented the "new era" of "human torture" known as "solitary confinement," and a sample "MERCY/Petition" to New York's governor offered guidance for women to rally signatures and demand that he commute Maria's sentence: "We protest against a legalized outrage which will bring disgrace upon the people of the Empire State," the sample petition read.[43] The *Recorder*'s stance contrasted with a staid, text-based, patrician newspaper like the *New York Tribune*, which deplored the "sympathy run mad" that was "making a heroine of [Barbella] and letting maudlin emotions run riot." Instead, the *Recorder*, having taken credit for drumming up "public sentiment" against electrocution, now began to channel it into calls to activism. The petition campaign capped coverage that had begun with headlines, images, letters, and interviews: all elements of the sensational toolkit employed to rescue Barbella from execution—and to sell newspapers (and products, such as tobacco).[44] Women's rights arguments about equality before the law had arrived in sensational news.

Engendering the Provocation Defense

Sympathetic headlines and images in sensational daily newspapers proved effective in generating a powerful "wave of sympathy" among women, and notably among veteran women's rights activists. Their campaign for "Mercy for Maria Barberi" soon moved to mass meetings, fundraisers, and petitions to the governor; it filled the pages of women's rights newspapers. In letters to the press, Barbella's supporters emphasized the double standard evident in her death sentence in contrast to leniency shown to male defendants in cases of spousal killing in the "heat of passion." "Horror at the loss of her good name," one advocate wrote, "at becoming an object of scorn for her neighbors and being practically classed among the dishonored outcasts who are hounded from lair to lair by society, *frenzied the mind of this harmless creature and turned her into a fiend for the moment.*" As a writer to the *World* put it, "We have many times heard and read of cases where men murdered their wives and betrothed *in jealous fits* caused by unfaithfulness and betrayal and who were declared 'not guilty' and were set free as men who loved honor and virtue."[45] Just as sensational crime weeklies had normalized honor killings for men, sensational dailies now allowed Barbella's supporters to make the same case for women.

Supporters blamed the judge for barring testimony that would prove Barbella's seduction, and they began a campaign for commutation of her sentence, a pardon, or (as would eventually prove successful) an appeal. "The tenderest compassion should be felt for a woman condemned to death for *a deed committed when she was driven to despair* by the cruelty of the man who should have been her husband," Lillie Devereux Blake, a woman's rights activist, wrote. Elizabeth Cady Stanton agreed:

> The jury who convicted the poor little Italian woman, Maria Barberi, were not capable of judging the motives which actuated her crime. They know nothing of the *feelings of outraged womanhood*: they are not familiar with the instincts and *impulses* which would prompt such an act.

Though their goal was political rights for women, Barbella's victimization by Cataldo, her very vulnerability, these supporters argued, was ample provocation for the killing. "Enticed from her home, she was drugged and ruined, abused, and her life threatened, and when the brutal seducer refused to marry her, as he had promised, and thus save a little of the disgrace she was suffering, *in her frenzy she took his life*," one correspondent wrote to the *New York Tribune*, complaining about the paper's unsympathetic coverage. "Who could wonder that she did it?"[46]

Until this case, women's rights advocates had viewed the provocation defense as little more than an excuse for retributive violence, a negative outcome of masculine power, and a second victimization for murdered women. Their new support for the provocation defense now aligned them with Barbella's Italian supporters, including the Italian vice-consul, who (though hesitant to comment on a particular case) viewed such an act as a traditional Italian method to "safeguard the family's honor." Some women's rights reformers viewed Barbella's violence as a consequence of cultural or racial difference; a few posited that her Italian heritage alone, her "impulsive southern blood," should be considered a mitigating factor. "This young Italian girl had never been trained to control her emotional nature," argued Elizabeth Grannis, president of the National Christian League for Social Purity. "She had been raised in an atmosphere of passion and impulse." Rosalie Loew, a lawyer, agreed that Barbella embodied the "inherited vindictiveness that we frequently find in people of her race and class."[47] Such arguments blended "scientific" racist views about Southern Italians with progressive faith in the power of nurture to inculcate self-control; together, they came very close to condoning vengeful killing by women, and, by extension, also by men.

As women's rights reformers began to consider the virtues of honor killing, they upended Victorian notions that women were inherently spiritual, passive, passionless, and weak. One rationale for this challenge was that fact that the much-touted "gallows chivalry," believed to protect women from excessive sentencing, had failed to protect Barbella. "A man killing the seducer of his wife is pardoned," a correspondent to the *Woman's Journal* pointed out, "but a 'little girl' inflicting upon her seducer revenge, must pay the full penalty of the law. [Those who oppose Barbella's commutation] talk of the weakness and tender heartedness of juries when women are concerned, but truly it is not apparent in this case!"[48] Far from being protected by a paternal state or sympathetic jurors, Barbella had been victimized twice, such writers argued: first by her seducer/betrayer (Cataldo) and second by a patriarchal state. Under these circumstances, some women's rights activists argued, the killing was not just understandable, it was justified. "If ever a wretch deserved death it was this man, and Maria . . . was just as much defending her honor as if she had killed him in the act," argued the Nebraska *Woman's Tribune*. The WCTU's newspaper, the *Union Signal*, likewise saw the killing as justified. "The conviction and sentence places a premium on immorality," wrote the editor. "It is not commutation that Maria should have, but full pardon. It is not mercy that her case calls for, but justice."[49] In arguing for *justification* rather than merely provocation in Barbella's case, women's rights supporters went even beyond language used to mitigate sentencing in honor killings by men.

Barbella's sentence—death by electrocution—heightened women's rights activists' awareness of their own powerlessness in law. "Let women beware before they allow themselves to be influenced against the movement to accord suffrage to women!" one argued. For these suffrage activists, Barbella's case highlighted the gendered difference in legal treatment. "No woman has ever had a fair trial, from my point of view," as Stanton put it, "nor will she have until she is tried by a jury of her peers. Laws are made by men, administered by men and executed by men." Male jurors could not possibly understand the psychic toll of Cataldo's seduction of and refusal to marry Barbella; their determination that she was guilty of first-degree murder only underscored women's powerlessness before the law. "What manner of men are these jurymen," one writer asked, "that they find the proper punishment to be meted out to this wretched woman—who has already suffered and will suffer, even if she go free, all she has merited—is death? What right had these to judge?" In a statement, Susan B. Anthony, too, found the punishment unfair, adding cultural incompetence to the double-standard argument: "I [am] opposed to the State's murdering a young woman who cannot understand our language and for a crime that is condoned in a man, young or old, with scarce a reprimand." The *Union Signal* agreed: "If the girl had been one of a family of wealth and influence, or anybody but a poor Italian so ignorant of the English language not to know what her sentence was, the act would not have been condemned." In this way, Barbella's death sentence proved a unifying moment for suffrage activists and reformers across generations and along the breadth of the political spectrum.[50]

As many of the preceding quotations establish, Barbella's defenders also emphasized (wrongly, as it turned out) her youthfulness as a mitigating factor in sentencing. This focus on youth was consistent with a trend in news coverage of intimate violence that increasingly reported rape as a crime primarily against very young women. At first, Barbella's alleged youth unified female activists, who believed that as a young "child/woman" and thus more clearly a victim and less able to control her emotions, she was even less responsible for her actions. A death sentence for a "child of fifteen" was, according to one writer to the *Woman's Journal*, "judicial murder." Alice Stone Blackwell, daughter of Stone and Blackwell, viewed Barbella as "an Italian child, 15 years of age, reared in the slums, ignorant of our institutions, unable to speak our language, poor and illiterate . . . [who] has not yet reached the age of mental maturity." Emphasis on Barbella's youth proved an effective way to enlist popular support (as the assistant district attorney complained) and reinforced the sense of her victimization by a heartless state. (There was much confusion over Barbella's age. Court documents variously listed her age as fifteen, nineteen, and twenty-two; evidence suggests that she was in fact twenty-four years old at the time of the killing).[51]

In mobilizing to defend Barbella as a young, disenfranchised, immigrant woman, women's rights activists embraced the provocation defense they had long deemed reprehensible. They viewed her case as a perfect example of the double standard: while they did not condone retaliatory violence, they believed in equality before the law; if the legal system saw provocation as a mitigating factor in sentences for men, it should do so equally so for women. The case was "an object-lesson for woman suffrage," Henry Blackwell argued in an editorial for the *Woman's Journal*. "Had Maria been a wife and her husband the avenger, he would have been applauded for the deed. . . . Here is the odious contrast: For a man and a voter pity and acquittal, followed by preferment; for a disfranchised woman, even though a child, condemnation and electrocution!" Referring to the "extreme provocation and outrage" that led her to kill, Barbella's sentence threw into stark relief earlier women's rights arguments about women's powerlessness under the law. Woman suffrage, with full and equal citizenship, Blackwell argued, was the only remedy. Blackwell penned this editorial as a tribute to the long campaign of his late wife, Lucy Stone: "I think it is what Lucy would have said if she were living," he wrote privately to a friend. In this specific case, he and other women's rights activists lobbied the governor to commute Barbella's sentence from death to life in prison.[52]

In April 1896, nine months after Barbella was sentenced to death by electrocution, the new legal arguments, relentless coverage, and petition campaigns, as well as funding for better legal representation, led to a reprieve. Women's legal activists had developed an argument for prosecutorial misconduct, and her defense team successfully convinced the New York state court of appeals that suppression of evidence in the first trial made the verdict illegitimate. Most significant was that they convinced the appeals court that the judge in the first trial, Recorder Goff, after excluding evidence of provocation, had incorrectly instructed the jury to consider no verdict other than murder in the first degree, effectively sidelining a "heat of passion" defense.[53] In its unanimous decision in favor of a new trial, the court of appeals found (paraphrasing the "heat of passion" language from Blackstone's legal dictionary [1890]) that

> the defendant was not guilty of murder in the first degree, unless the act was premeditated, not only with the intent to kill, but also with deliberation and premeditation. If the defendant inflicted the wound in a sudden transport of passion, excited by what the deceased then said and by the preceding events which for the time disturbed her reasoning faculties and deprived her of the capacity to reflect, and while under the influence of some sudden and uncontrollable emotion, excited by the final culmination of her misfortunes as indicated by the train of events prior to that time, the act did not constitute murder in the first degree.

Judge Goff, the appeals court explained, had biased the jury in his instructions during the trial. The appeals court's decision upheld the defense's reasoning that evidence of seduction, betrayal, and other circumstances leading to the murder were facts relevant to Barbella's mental and emotional state prior to the killing, and that their exclusion was prejudicial to the jury.[54] Maria Barbella had been granted a new trial.

Sensational dailies amplified Barbella's victory in gaining a retrial. "Says Goff Was Unfair" ran the *World*'s headline for a story covering the appeal, with full details of the judge's instructions from the July 1895 trial. A large image of a forlorn and penitent Barbella (fig. 5.12) sitting alone in her cell in Sing Sing prison lent pathos to this story. In reporting the successful appeal, the *World* closed the narrative loop but also ignored the question of whether a woman was justified in killing her betrayer or seducer to defend her honor. Yet women had gained a victory of sorts—not the elimination of the provocation defense for men that held women's lives cheap, as objects in men's struggles for control and power, but instead its application to a woman as defendant. In other words, a woman's emotional state was relevant to her defense. The appeals court had implicitly upheld the new position put forward by some women's rights activists that women should not be treated differently through mercy (the "gallows chivalry" argument) but rather should receive equal access to the "hot blood" defense available to men. Yet when the new trial began in November 1896,

FIGURE 5.12: "Maria
Barberi in Her Cell at
Sing Sing Prison," *New
York World*, April 22,
1896, 5. New York State
Library.

Barbella's legal team abandoned this reasoning altogether, opting for a new
line of defense that Barbella's predisposition to epileptic attacks caused of her
(accidental) killing of Cataldo, sidestepping the opportunity to put a simple
female honor defense on trial.[55]

"Her Ancestors Were a Race of Epileptics"

As the second trial began in November 1896, sensational daily newspapers jet-
tisoned the female-honor narrative, taking their cue from Barbella's defense
team. Portrayals of Barbella that had emphasized her vulnerability as a young
woman and an immigrant caught in a biased legal system all but disappeared.
In their place, the illustrated dailies now published images that emphasized
her physical traits, floating speculation about a range of possible mental and
physical infirmities. More significant, perhaps, was the demise of the *New
York Recorder*, which had done so much to influence coverage about Barbella's

right to defend her honor the previous summer. Driven out of business by the increasingly competitive marketplace for sensational news, the *Recorder* folded a month before her second trial began.[56] Without the *Recorder* leading the way, sensational dailies turned from female honor to other methods to make the case visually striking.

Taking the *Recorder*'s place was a new competitor, William Randolph Hearst's *New York Journal*. Having achieved some success with the *San Francisco Examiner*[57] (making the paper financially solvent by 1890), Hearst was looking for ways to break into the East Coast market. This became more urgent as the economic depression, beginning in 1893, began to cut into the *Examiner*'s revenue. Hearst set his sights on New York's larger market, purchasing the New York *Morning Journal* in September 1895. The paper already catered to a working-class, female readership (it was known as the "chambermaid's delight"). Hearst quickly added new techniques to the repertoire he had honed at the *Examiner*, launching his revamped *Journal* on November 7, 1895.[58] Having missed the first phase of Barbella's ordeal, Hearst found other causes to champion on the *Journal*'s front page. Late in 1895, Hearst took credit for defending and securing the release of a (different) woman falsely arrested, for example.[59] Over several months in 1896 Hearst used Pulitzer's own methods against him, buying out the *World*'s entire Sunday staff and his famous artist of the "Yellow Kid" cartoons. The *Recorder* folded that October, leaving the *Journal* well positioned to challenge the *World* for dominance of Barbella's sensational second trial.[60]

When the trial began in November 1896, the *Journal* downplayed the idea of honor killing, instead taking up the defense's argument of degeneracy and foregrounding Maria's physical attributes. Under a caption reading "Features of Maria Barberi and of a Typical Degenerate," one such image (fig. 5.13) placed shaded drawings of Barbella's hand, ear, and profile (from two angles) next to those of a typical "degenerate," drawing from a book on criminology. As presented, the crudely rendered drawings could easily persuade a casual observer that the text supported the images' suggestion of her degeneracy; in fact, it did not.[61] The *Journal* emphasized two new controversial claims introduced by her legal team: a witness, suppressed in the first trial, to testify to Barbella's drugging and seduction by Cataldo, and expert witnesses testifying to a family history of epilepsy. This second claim ultimately succeeded in getting Barbella acquitted of the murder charge. "Every one of the surviving members of her family is an epileptic," her lead lawyer asserted in his opening statement, after describing the killing in gruesome detail. "*Her ancestors were a race of epileptics. She knew no more of that deed than a babe unborn.*" Although even at the time physicians questioned this understanding of epilepsy's effects, the *Journal*'s visual evidence echoed the defense, notably with a "Chart Showing Heredity of Maria Barberi Now on Trial for Murder" that filled the page.[62] This gave the

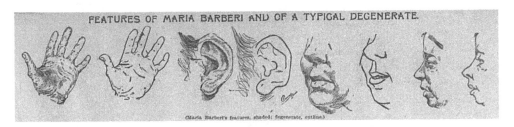

FIGURE 5.13: "Features of Maria Barberi and of a Typical Degenerate," *New York Journal*, November 20, 1896, 3. New York Public Library.

appearance of providing "scientific" evidence connecting her family, epilepsy, and Cataldo's murder.

The *World* expressed some editorial misgivings about the idea of a "homicidal trait," but its front page reporting and illustrations were quite similar to the *Journal*'s. The *World*, too, used headlines ("Taints in Her Blood"), a family tree, and images to emphasize Barbella's physical features: her profile, her eyes, her heredity, including even a foray into palmistry, analyzing whether her palm resembled that of a "typical degenerate." Illustrations of the family, details of her mother's impassioned testimony, and exaggerated familial differences (often steeped in ethnic stereotypes) served to establish the Barbella family's "natural tendency" to violence. In a later Sunday edition the *World* used illustration (fig. 5.14) to invoke biological theories about "natural" criminality in a gallery of "criminal types" under the heading "Barberi's People," attributed to criminal anthropologist Enrico Ferri.[63] Together, illustrations in both the *Journal* and *World* did a great deal to reinforce—and popularize—the defense's new strategy that Barbella was physically and mentally predisposed to violence. Both mentioned the epilepsy claim and threw in a hodgepodge of prevailing racialized theories about biology and crime. Neither mentioned justifiable honor killings or gender equality before the law.

Public interest in the trial kept the papers busy providing coverage, and both the *World* and the *Journal* gave generous space to Barbella's own description (now in English) of the events leading to her action: her seduction via a drink (or a drug in a drink) that had enticed her from her home in the first place, and Cataldo's callous treatment of her in the bar. After his final insult that "only pigs marry," Maria now said, her "head grew hot," she "saw black and red," lost consciousness, and had "no knowledge of the killing until she found blood on her hands." As her testimony unfolded, the *Evening World* (a late edition pitched more specifically to women) provided an interpretive illustration (fig. 5.15) for the case in a visual reconstruction of the events she described; drawn in a cartoon-like way, it did not reenact the crime so much as attempt to visualize the series of events and actions described in her testimony. Defense expert

FIGURE 5.14: "Barberi's People," *New York World*, November 29, 1896, 29.

witnesses disagreed on the exact nature of her condition, but they united in the conviction that she was not responsible for her actions.[64]

The *Journal* took greater pains to make clear that Maria's seduction provoked not a "hot blooded" killing in the traditional sense but rather a sudden epileptic fit, in the throes of which the killing took place. The distinction avoided the question of whether a woman might kill when her honor was violated. Its il-

FIGURE 5.15: "The Tragic Story of Maria Barberi," *New York Evening World*, November 27, 1896, 2. New York Public Library.

lustrations, too, emphasized her family's physical history, as they took the stand to describe a litany of physical and mental defects in order to save her life (fig. 5.16). Defective heredity, the *Journal* seemed to affirm, rather than female honor, inspired her action. The new strategy was effective, eye-catching, and—unlike the female-honor defense argument—noncontroversial. (Jurors apparently found it convincing; they acquitted Barbella in less than an hour.) Neither the *World* nor the *Journal* offered a political argument about equal justice for women. Instead, their images gave visible form to prevailing wisdom about the "taints in her blood."[65]

As portraits of Barbella shifted from trial to trial and image to image, they conveyed conflicting meanings. The Italian-American newspaper, *Echo D'Italia*, commented on the visual inconsistency. The editor singled out the *World* ("always an evil beast when it concerns [Italians]") for its wildly different illustrations of Barbella. It pointed to the transformation of her image published after her arrest—when she was portrayed as having "an almost beastly face"—to her image during the second trial showing a "beautiful young lady" resembling a noblewoman. The paper wondered sarcastically whether the implication was that Italians were better off in prison, because it was "an institution of physical improvement for the fine race of delinquents." A few weeks later, after the acquittal, the paper commented again on her improvement, that she was "more well-mannered, more educated, and finer in appearance." It dryly noted that through the "pity and aid of thousands and thousands of people" Maria

FIGURE 5.16: "Members of the Barberi Family Testifying," *New York Journal*, November 23, 1896, 16. New York Public Library.

FIGURE 5.17:"Maria Barberi While Undergoing Cross-Examination," *New York Journal,* November 28, 1896, 3. New York Public Library.

Barbella "obtained by means of a crime those satisfactions that others never reach by the ways of virtue."[66]

Shifting images in the *World* and the *Journal* that mirrored the defense's new strategies, combined with the *Recorder*'s demise, leave us no way of knowing whether a straightforward "crime of passion" defense might have remained popular during Barbella's second trial. (It is clear that the defense team thought it prudent to proceed with a different theory of the crime.) Even as the two sensational dailies amplified the defense's strategy, focusing on an epilepsy-induced fit of violence, their visual coverage remained equivocal. For example, one *Journal* drawing depicting Maria's "many faces" on the stand showed not just her features but also her changing expressions. It conveyed a complex and far less flattering portrait of a woman who was by turns distressed, angry—and perhaps deceptive (fig. 5.17), which highlights the paper's ambivalence about her case. The image also laid bare, perhaps unintentionally, the subjective nature of even "realistic" illustration—its ability to convey multiple (and contradictory) messages from a single subject, its potential for manipulation to suggest innocence or guilt. In many ways, the "realist" style of the sensational daily was no less interpretive than earlier reenactments of the *Police Gazette*.[67]

The media circus surrounding Barbella's trials was a show within a show, a kind of spectacle in its own right. Its carnivalesque quality gave the *World* and the *Journal* a new reason to thrive. The *Evening World* lampooned this phenom-

FIGURE 5.18: "The Latest in Matinees," *New York Evening World*, December 9, 1896, 4. New York Public Library.

enon in an image of women clustering at the courthouse in fine clothing, with the caption "The Latest Thing in Matinées Is the Barberi Murder Trial."[68] The ambivalence conveyed by the caption—was this a pursuit of justice or merely the latest fad?—was perhaps a sign that, even as the case gained public attention and sold papers, sympathy for Maria waned (fig. 5.18). Some of Barbella's most outspoken women's rights defenders from the previous trial, such as Lillie Devereux Blake, now disparaged the "absurd hysterical sympathy" during her second trial.[69] Mainstream newspapers—the *New York Tribune* and *New York Times*—had long expressed similar views. By contrast, sensational dailies like the *World* could have it both ways; even as they whipped up emotion and galvanized public interest, they could mock it as well.

The new argument for Barbella's retrial—that circumstances provoked the epileptic seizure under which the attack occurred—diminished the case's significance for women's legal rights, and did little to challenge the gendered nature of the provocation defense, either in court or in sensational news. Sensationalism's enthusiastic—if fleeting and opportunistic—embrace of the "crime of passion" defense for Barbella temporarily drew women's rights activists to embrace the provocation argument, but the case ultimately weakened women's critique of the double standard, removing one of the last major obstacles to the broad expansion of the crime-of-passion defense in subsequent decades.[70] The Barbella trials simultaneously revealed the potential benefits and inherent pitfalls involved when women borrowed from the sensational toolkit. As the Epilogue reveals, the media frenzy surrounding the case also inspired a backlash against "yellow journalism."

Epilogue

Legacies of Visual Journalism and the Sensational Style

GRAPHIC NEWS PRACTICES, and their power to "attract the eye," became central to commercial media in the nineteenth century. Long thought to have begun in 1897, they date back at least to the founding of the penny press in the 1830s and advanced with the rapid growth of visual journalism after the Civil War. Critics who denounced the media circus surrounding the Maria Barbella case, described in chapter 5, saw it as merely the latest in a long line of offensive episodes. In January 1897, just weeks after Barbella's acquittal, a *New York Times* editorial revealed, with disgust, a gimmick proposed by a "new journalist" for one of the sensational dailies. The scheme was to offer a friend of Barbella's a hundred dollars to take her back to Sing Sing prison, strap her into the electric chair in a mock execution, and share her sensations—her "manifestations of horror"—with a reporter. It is not difficult to imagine the "witnessed" illustration planned to accompany this story, had it succeeded. A few days later, Adolph S. Ochs visibly branded the *Times* as sensationalism's antithesis, affixing on the masthead the slogan "All the news that's fit to print." Meanwhile, religious leaders, social organizations, and political clubs encouraged their members to boycott sensational dailies, mobilized to ban them from their reading rooms, and lobbied (unsuccessfully) for an "anti-cartoon" bill in the New York state legislature. Debate over declining standards in journalism filled a variety of news and opinion publications, and one concerned editor coined a new term—"yellow journalism"—to disparage the sensational style.[1]

Pejoratives, slogans, bans, and boycotts, however, did nothing to counter the boost to circulation and advertising revenue that graphic news provided. Amid the outcry over yellow journalism, in fact, the *New York Journal* published its misleading illustration of the strip-search of a female Cuban prisoner on the American steamship, the *Olivette*, discussed in the Introduction. The publication of this image defied critics, and affirmed that—at least for some dailies—graphic news had become essential to commercial success.

In 1897, critics accused the new dailies of exploiting "carnivals of crime," of profiting from sensations such as the Barbella case and the *Olivette* strip-search coverage.[2] Yet sensational innovations, designed to shock readers, provoke a reaction in the service of a cause, or simply satisfy the public's right to know, grew out of long-established traditions in popular news production. New technologies simply enabled new ways to provoke. A good example is the *Journal's* promotion of the "headless torso" case. Over several weeks in summer 1897, the *Journal* published details of a mysterious case about a body, missing limbs and head, found by police in New York's East River. Offering a $1,000 reward to enlist the public's help in solving the crime, the *Journal's* innovation was its *color* reproduction of the oilcloth that had been found wrapped around the torso (an image that, in fact, led to the identification of the perpetrators). But Hearst's boast that his paper had solved the case was nothing new: after all, in 1884 Joseph Pulitzer had claimed that the *World*'s publication of a criminal's portrait had led to his arrest in Montreal; in 1878 Richard K. Fox had insisted that the *National Police Gazette*'s crime imagery improved morality; in 1857 Frank Leslie had taken credit for exposing, through his weekly's illustrations, poor sanitary conditions in milk production.[3] Crusading visual journalism was by 1897 more *accessible* to daily readers—and lucrative enough to entice other dailies to adopt at least some aspects of the sensational style—but it was not *new*.

Sensational visual journalism was also not a neutral form; as the cases in this book demonstrate, it could serve a variety of masters but was at its most persuasive when it promoted stories of honor, adventure, and swashbuckling heroism. Hearst's most famous crusade in August 1897, to free Evangelina Cosio y Cisneros, the daughter of imprisoned Cuban rebel Augustin Cosio, fit this narrative well.[4] Hearst's coverage amplified a theme pushed by émigré Cubans who sought U.S. intervention to further their independence movement. For two years, using lectures, entertainments, and carefully placed stories in the *Journal*, the *World*, and the *Recorder*, they had generated broad public support for *Cuba Libré*. Their efforts reinforced highly gendered ideas well-suited to the sensational style—of Cuban rebels as chivalric knights defending idealized, feminine Cuban damsels from Spanish abuses. Evangelina Cosio (misidentified at the time as Cisneros) had been arrested on charges of inciting an uprising among prisoners against the island's Spanish military governor. The *Journal* emphasized her claim that she had been defending her honor from his sexual assault and was now confined in a prison for prostitutes in Havana, threatened with transfer to an infamous Spanish prison off the coast of Africa.[5] Hearst publicized Cosio's predicament as a symbol of Spanish oppression but also to further his jingoist agenda—and sell more papers. Many in the United States saw the Cuban struggle for independence as analogous to their own revolutionary tradition and condemned Spain's *reconcentrado* policy of relocating refugees to inhumane camps, where many died from neglect and starvation. But sympathy for Cuban rebels was also compatible with a variety of other interest groups: annexationists who sought U.S. control over the island; sugar planters and financiers who sought the benefits of an expanded sugar economy; Protestant missionaries who sought new converts; martial enthusiasts who held that a war would strengthen U.S. men and make the nation as a whole more "manly."[6] Rival newspapers disputed many details, but Hearst used the entire sensational toolkit to maximize the romantic possibilities of Cosio's predicament.

Hearst began his quest to free Cosio with a petition drive, hoping to recapture the recent outpouring of support for female honor in the *Recorder's* campaign for Maria Barbella two years earlier. The *Journal's* Sunday headline—"Women of America Will Save Her"—echoed the *Recorder's* 1895 headline in the Barbella case ("Women Would Save Her"). Cosio served as the perfect avatar for the sensational themes of chivalry and honor, as well as the mystique of *Cuba Libré*. Written as a tale of romance, Hearst's crusade captured public interest: over several months, the *Journal* ran more than 250 stories about Cosio, which generated fifteen thousand letters and telegrams in response. The paper published a roll call of well-known women who signed the *Journal's* petition to the Spanish minister and the pope, demanding Cosio's freedom.[7] It was a clever—if familiar—strategy, one that allowed him to make further inroads into the as-yet-untapped and lucrative market for women as news consumers.

Before the excitement waned, Hearst manipulated events to intensify the story's romantic effect. First, he authorized a journalist to engineer Cosio's rescue from prison. Impressionistic portraits (embellished from photographs, based on a doctor's opinion) and full-figure drawings represented the toll taken on Cosio by her suffering, further reinforcing the message of Spanish tyranny (fig. E.1). Once she was free, Hearst paid her expenses to travel to New York and arranged for her introduction to New York society and to President McKinley. Significantly, both portraits and meeting with the president appeared on the front pages of the *Journal's* women-friendly Sunday editions, on October 10 and October 24, 1897 (the latter issue included a two-page series of interpretive illustrations reconstructing her rescue).[8] Hearst had gone from heightening, exaggerating, and even misrepresenting the news to creating—literally—a tailor-made narrative for a specific audience. It was an expensive undertaking, yet it resulted in soaring circulation for the *Journal* and catapulted the paper—and Hearst—into national prominence, paving the way for the expansion of his media empire. In the process, he transformed Cosio, a woman who had proved her heroism as a rebel and a political actor in her own right, into a dime-novel damsel in distress. Like the women and children whose alleged victimization

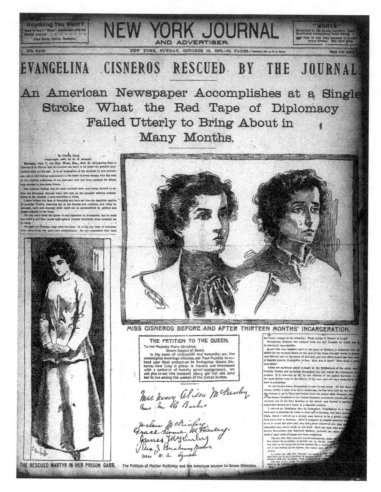

FIGURE E.I: "Miss Cisneros before and after Thirteen Months
Incarceration," *New York Journal and Advertiser*, October 10, 1897, 1.
New York Public Library.

helped justify violent attacks on African American and Chinese men, Cosio's
story made a persuasive argument for the nation to go to war for a woman's
honor, this time against Spain.[9]

Visual coverage following the destruction of the *Maine*, the U.S. warship
stationed in Havana harbor, on February 15, 1898, provided more evidence of
the power of graphic news to catch the eye in order to persuade. In headlines
and images claiming that the ship had been sunk by enemy attack, killing
266 officers and men on board, sensational dailies continued the pattern of
maximizing the dramatic effect of news stories. "*Destruction of the War Ship*

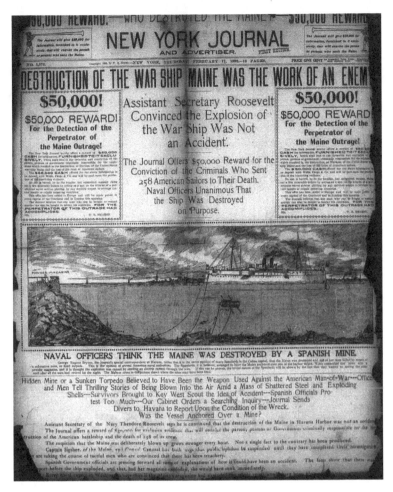

FIGURE E.2: "Naval Officers Think the Maine Was Destroyed by a Spanish Mine," *New York Journal and Advertiser*, February 17, 1898, 1. New York Public Library.

Maine Was the Work of an Enemy," read the *Journal*'s February 17, 1898, headline (citing Assistant Secretary of War Theodore Roosevelt as authority) in a font that spanned the width of the page in text and was as tall as the name of the paper itself. Below, a crime-scene-style reconstruction showed the opinion of unnamed "naval officers" that the *Maine* had been attacked; a "powder magazine" on the shore at the left, connected by wires to an underwater mine, set off the explosion under the hull, the picture and caption alleged. The *New York World* also used headline and image to bypass official hedging, insisting that an external cause—"Torpedo or Bomb"—had caused the explosion (figs. E.2

FIGURE E.3: "Maine Explosion Caused by Bomb or Torpedo," *New York World*, February 17, 1898, 1. New York Public Library.

and E.3)[10] Despite differences in interpretation and style, both front pages contained a moral imperative, a cry for retribution, similar to that of opium dens, reenactments of interracial rape, anti-lynching imagery, and honor killings of women. Both the *Journal* and the *World* built on decades of interpretive illustration to dramatize news to further a cause.

Newspapers that rejected interpretive illustration turned to photographs and other evidence-based images to convey more factual (and less dramatic) news coverage. For example, images published by the patrician *New York Tribune* contrasted sharply with those in the "yellow" dailies, above.[11] A group photograph showing the "Officers of the Maine" (fig. E.4) was technically advanced, reflecting the *New York Tribune*'s edge as the first newspaper to develop a high-speed printing press capable of publishing regular news photographs. Like group portraits of the Seventh Cavalry after Wounded Knee, the portrait

THE OFFICERS OF THE MAINE.

FIGURE E.4: "The Officers of the Maine," *New York Tribune*, February 18, 1898, 2. New York Public Library.

was evocative of loss, even though it conveyed neither the kinetic verve of the *World*'s explosion nor the *Journal*'s visual reconstruction of the alleged method of attack. The *Tribune*'s schematic drawing of the *Maine* was less emotional; it scrupulously declined to suggest the explosion's cause, showing instead the ship's layout, including the berths where many crew members had been sleeping when the explosion occurred. Such evidence-based imagery, preferred by anti-sensationalist newspapers, eschewed visual hype; they provided an alternate standard for visualizing daily news.[12]

Other newspapers tried to have it both ways, combining "realistic" evidence of the *Maine*'s destruction with headlines and captions that conveyed drama. Such images built on now familiar visual strategies of transforming evidence-based images for emotional effect, with greater deniability and less vulnerability to protests than interpretive illustration. A good example of this appeared in the *Chicago Tribune* in a schematic drawing of the *Maine*'s hull, from the side rather than from above (fig. E.5). The caption hedged—"Side View of the Maine—How the Disaster *Might* Have Occurred"—but the image's visual speculation on the blast's cause supported the theory of Spanish treachery. Readers rewarded drama, even as they increasingly expected authentic evidence: images that provided both might have more success in "proving" a hypothesis of Spanish aggression that was at the time (and remains to this day) a subject of fierce debate.[13] As news visualization began to shift to photography, and interpretive illustrations like the *Maine* images in the *World* and the *Journal* became increasingly suspect, many papers opted for this third way of framing and adapting evidence-based images for sensational effect.

The period long associated with the beginning of "yellow journalism" in some ways marked its zenith. As this book demonstrates, news producers had used

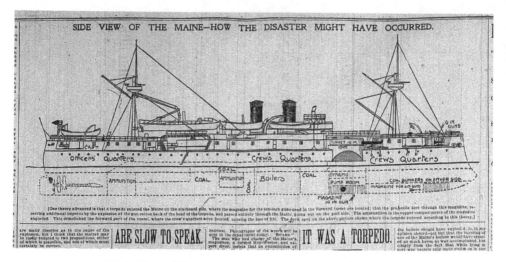

FIGURE E.5: "Side View of the Maine—How the Disaster Might Have Occurred," *Chicago Daily Tribune*, February 18, 1898, 2. Library of Congress.

interpretive illustration in highly charged, emotional situations for decades—to remove ambiguity, justify specific actions, and create narrative coherence from confusion.[14] Sensational images of the *Maine*'s destruction, alongside editorials critiquing the McKinley administration for refusing to fight, provided an effective cudgel for Democrats in a congressional election year.[15] The images did not necessarily propel the nation to war, but they provided emotional support for those inclined to push for a military response, making it harder for opponents to resist.[16] Sensationalism's appetite for narratives that feature honor, jingoism, retribution, manly response, and moral outrage formed part of the climate that made the *Maine* images persuasive and the war itself more palatable—and therefore more likely.[17] This remained true even as audience demand for authenticity grew and interpretive illustration gave way to realist, evidence-based imagery.

News images shifted again once the wars in Cuba and the Philippines were underway, as editors (echoing the McKinley administration) recoiled from the real possibility that the independence movements in both places might succeed. Interpretive illustrations and political cartoons sympathetic to *Cuba Libré* gave way to depictions of rebel insurgents as ineffectual, ungrateful, or simply invisible—even when their actions paved the way for military victories for U.S. troops. Newspapers replaced group photographs of heroic Cuban rebel forces with group photographs of U.S. soldiers at the front as "knightly rescuers." Cartoons mocked anti-interventionists at home as weak, unwomanly (if female), effeminate (if male), and altogether lacking in honor and the martial spirit. Similarly, after the United States went to war against Filipino insurgents in early 1899, photographs valorized U.S. troops deployed in the Philippines as uncomplicated heroes and liberators, much as they had done (recreated as line illustrations) after Wounded Knee. Once the U.S. "liberating force" turned into an army of occupation, dailies published now-familiar stereotypes of the indigenous population—as children, as "savages," as "rapine"—to show their "unfitness" for self-government. (Only after reports of atrocities committed by U.S. soldiers in the Philippines filtered into public print did such images lose sway.)[18] Graphic news images of the two wars did not invent these themes, they simply did what sensational newspapers had always done: they converted actual events into eye-catching, melodramatic tales.

By the late 1890s, even as Hearst and Pulitzer continued to profit from interpretive illustration, many newspapers celebrated the photograph as the best form of visual evidence available—and even as the remedy for sensationalism. Subscribing to the "regime of realism," editors upheld photographs as the gold standard in "objective" news visualization, supplanting illustration and "earlier notions of picture-enhanced storytelling." But the long tradition of incorporating visuals to dramatize the news adapted easily to the advent of photojournalism. Editors had already found creative ways to turn photographs into emotionally charged illustrations, to manipulate even the most detailed and "accurate" photographic evidence. News illustration had relied on sourcing from photographs to bolster the legitimacy of their emotional messages for a long time; whether "realistic," interpretive, or fictive, news images had become effective purveyors of sensational narratives since midcentury. Photojournalism did not fundamentally change the dynamics of graphic news.[19]

Chosen well, evidence-based images, including photographs, told dramatic stories.[20] Reproductions of Sitting Bull's portraits showed painstaking fidelity to the details in the original photographs, but this did not make them accurate (or neutral) documents of the Ghost Dance. On the contrary, Sitting Bull's portraits were efficient visual capsules that contained narratives about colonialism and the imagined threat to settlers (particularly women) that infused the period's popular culture. Even editors of the "yellow" dailies (Hearst, Pulitzer, and others), despite their continued preference for interpretive illustration for visualizing the news, had already found ways to evoke drama through "realistic" imagery. Others did the same. In the early 1900s, activists such as W. E. B. Du Bois (as editor of the NAACP's *Crisis*) found ways to repurpose lynching photographs to engage readers and stimulate activism; suffragists staged controversial direct actions to break into the front pages of daily newspapers.[21] Sensationalism survived the transition to the "realist regime" because photographs, like images based on photographs (and interpretive illustrations), carried emotional appeals.

As a form, sensationalism was never purely cynical—its crusading spirit sometimes promoted jingoism, "manliness," racism, or imperialism but also fostered Cuban independence, anti-lynching activism, and women's rights. Sensational images as they developed in the U.S. context contained their own logic of victimization and rescue, honor and heroism; they favored certain themes, particularly those relating to sex, crime, and violence. If photojournalists were constrained by what they could capture on film, their editors continued to select images to "attract the eye." Images that evoked stories of captive women being rescued from tyrants (or "savages") or of "unprovoked" attacks on American military forces served that purpose well. "Realist" images, in other words, could further fantasies or push an agenda. As the twentieth century began, and even as newspapers championed greater objectivity in visual journalism—made possible by the latest technological advances—many publications found new ways to sensationalize the news.

Notes

Introduction

1. W. Joseph Campbell, "Not Likely Sent: The Remington-Hearst 'Telegrams,'" chap. 3 of *Yellow Journalism: Puncturing the Myths, Defining the Legacies* (Westport, Conn.: Praeger, 2001), 71–96.

2. The image accompanies the story headlined "Does Our Flag Protect Women?," *New York Journal*, February 12, 1897, 1. The *World*'s rebuttal appeared in "Tale of a Fair Exile," *New York World*, February 15, 1897. The image diverged from Remington's characteristic style—he was famous for picturing the American West, the renowned expert at capturing horses in motion—and most of his Cuban drawings (based on sketches he had made "on site") conveyed the evils of the *reconcentración* camps and the plight of fleeing civilians, rebel soldiers, and miserable refugees. Remington was back in the United States before the image was published. See Frederic Remington to Poultney Bigelow, January 28, 1897, reprinted in Douglas Allen, *Frederic Remington and the Spanish-American War* (New York: Crown, 1971).

3. "Spaniards Search Women on American Steamers," *New York Journal*, February 12, 1897. "Tale of a Fair Exile: Seniorita Arrango's Own Story," *World*, February 15, 1897. Richard Harding Davis, the *Journal* story's author, condemned the image as a distortion of his reporting. The Hearst telegram legend originated in James Creelman, *On the Great Highway: The Wanderings and Adventures of a Special Correspondent* (Boston: Lothrop, 1901), 177–78. In fact, Creelman had by that time been banished from Cuba by the Spanish for his pro-rebel reporting. See John D. Stevens, *Sensationalism and the New York Press* (New York: Columbia University Press, 1991), 94–96; Ted Curtis Smythe, *The Gilded Age Press: 1865–1900* (Westport, Conn.: Praeger, 2003), 187. "Because the evidence is so persuasive that the purported exchange did not take place, the anecdote deserves relegation to the closet of historical imprecision—at least until proven otherwise," argues Campbell in *Yellow Journalism*, 86. On persisting accounts of the alleged strip search, see Ben Procter, *William Randolph Hearst: The Early Years, 1863–1910* (New York: Oxford

University Press, 1998), 104–5; Ferdinand Lundberg, *Imperial Hearst: A Social History* (New York: Equinox, 1936), 69.

4. Editorial, *New York Times*, February 16, 1897; YMCA quote in *New York Times*, March 4, 1897. "Yellow journalism" may have been an adaptation of "yellow kid journalism"—referring to the "yellow kid" comic series duplicated by both the *Journal* and the *World* after Hearst enticed away Pulitzer's cartoonist in late 1896. Campbell argues that Ervin Wardman, the editor of the conservative *New York Press*, probably coined the term "yellow journalism" as a shorthand for sensationalism's excesses. Campbell, "Yellow Journalism: Why So Maligned and Misunderstood?," in *Sensationalism: Murder, Mayhem, Mudslinging, Scandals and Disasters in Nineteenth-Century Reporting*, ed. David B. Sachsman and David Bulla (New Brunswick, N.J.: Transaction, 2013), 5. I discuss Comstock and other anti-vice activists in more detail in chapter 1. A full-page list of institutions banning "yellow journalism," and condemnations from the clergy, can be found in "Yellow Journalism Denounced Everywhere," *New York Press*, May 3, 1897.

5. On crime reporting, see William E. Huntzicker, "Pushing the Boundaries of Propriety: The Rise of the Penny Press, Flash Papers, and Illustrated Newspapers," in Sachsman and Bulla, *Sensationalism*, 241–52; Stevens, *Sensationalism and the New York Press*, 77. On the movement of advertising pages to the interior after the Civil War, see David R. Spencer, *The Yellow Journalism: Sensationalism and America's Emergence as a World Power* (Chicago: Northwestern University Press, 2007), 84; Kevin G. Barnhurst and John Nerone, *The Form of News* (New York: Guildford, 2001), 88–90. On contemporary critiques of sensationalism and emerging professional standards, see Hazel Dicken-Garcia, *Journalistic Standards in Nineteenth-Century America* (Madison: University of Wisconsin Press, 1989), chap. 6; Spencer, *Yellow Journalism*; 83–84. On the significance of headlines, see G. C. Bastion, *Editing the Days' News* (1923), cited in Alfred McClung Lee, "The Editorial Staff," in *The American Journalism Reader* (208), in his *The Daily Newspaper in America* (New York: Routledge, 2000 [1937]).

6. Walter Lippmann, *Public Opinion* (New York: Macmillan, 1922).

7. Scholars of sensational journalism acknowledge the presence of images but rarely analyze their delivery of meaning. Campbell, "Yellow Journalism," 4–5; Bella and Sachsman, *Sensationalism*, xxi; Spencer, *Yellow Journalism*, 85; Dicken-Garcia, *Journalistic Standards*, 91–96. Texts in journalism history tend to downplay or ignore illustrations as communicators. See, for example, Bonnie S. Brennen and Hanno Hardt, eds., *The American Journalism History Reader* (New York: Routledge, 2010).

8. For nineteenth-century critics, see Dicken-Garcia, *Journalistic Standards*, 202–3. Tabloidization can be defined as a more extreme version of sensationalism. For example, S. Elizabeth Bird identifies tabloidization as evident in style (short, punchy, non-analytical); emphasis (personal stories); visuals (images, reenactments, dramatization); content (trivial, gossip, human interest). Bird, "Tabloidization: What Is It and Does It Really Matter?," in *The Changing Faces of Journalism: Tabloidization, Technology and Truthiness*, ed. Barbie Zelizer (New York: Routledge, 2009), 41–42. Critics of "tabloidization" include G. Djupsund and T. Carlson, "Trivial Stories and Fancy Pictures? Tabloidization Tendencies in Finnish and Swedish Newspapers, 1982–97," *Nordicom Review* 19, no. 1 (June 1998): 101–14; Frank Esser, "Tabloidization of News: A Com-

parative Analysis of Anglo-American and German Press Journalism," *European Journal of Communication* 14, no. 3 (1999): 291–324; Howard Kurtz, *Media Circus: The Trouble with America's Newspapers* (New York: Three Rivers, 1994); David Paletz, *The Media in American Politics: Content and Consequences* (New York: Longman, 1999), 75–76; Graeme Turner, "Tabloidization, Journalism and the Possibility of Critique," *International Journal of Cultural Studies* 2, no. 1 (1999); John Langer, *Tabloid Television: Popular Journalism and the 'Other' News* (New York: Routledge, 1998); J. Gripsrud, "The Aesthetics and Politics of Melodrama," in Peter Dahlgren and Colin Sparks, eds., *Journalism and Popular Culture* (London: Sage, 1992). On its "regressive" tendencies, see Colin Sparks, "Introduction," Colin Sparks and John Tulloch, eds., *Tabloid Tales: Global Debates over Media Standards* (New York: Rowman and Littlefield, 1999); John Tulloch, "The Eternal Recurrence of New Journalism," in Sparks and Tulloch, *Tabloid Tales*; Dean Alger, *Megamedia: How Giant Corporations Dominate Mass Media, Distort Competition, and Endanger Democracy* (New Yotk: Rowman and Littlefield, 1998); Neil Postman, *Amusing Ourselves to Death* (New York: Penguin: 1986).

9. See for example John Fiske, "Popularity and the Politics of Information," in Dahlgren and Sparks, *Journalism and Popular Culture*, 45–62; Catharine Lumby, *Bad Girls: The Media, Sex and Feminism in the '90s* (St. Leonards, NSW: Allen and Unwin, 1997); Andrew Ross, *No Respect: Intellectuals and Popular Culture* (New York: Routledge, 1989); Jim McGuigan, *Cultural Politics* (New York: Routledge, 1992); Barbie Zelizer, "Why Journalism's Changing Faces Matter," in Zelizer, *Changing Faces of Journalism*, 1–10; Herbert J. Gans, "Can Popularization Help the News Media?," in Zelizer, *Changing Faces of Journalism*, 24–25; Carolyn Kitch, "Tears and Trauma in the News," in Zelizer, *Changing Faces of Journalism*, 30; Serena Carpenter, Stephen Lacy, and Frederick Fico, "Network News Coverage," *Journalism and Mass Communications Quarterly* 83, no. 4 (2006): 903.

10. Methodological and research challenges partly explain this lack of attention. Even today, few cheap dailies have been digitally indexed, and crime weeklies that are indexed typically do not identify images as distinct elements, separate from news stories they illustrate. Production costs for scholarship containing high image content are higher than text-based research publications.

11. Joshua Brown, "Seeing the Civil War through Nineteenth-Century Eyes," School of Arts and Sciences Lecture, SUNY College at Old Westbury, November 2018.

12. See Roland Barthes, "Myth Today," in *Mythologies* (New York: Hill and Wang, 1972 [1957]).

13. Joy Wiltenberg, *Crime and Culture in Early Modern Germany* (Charlottesville: University of Virginia Press, 2012); Joy Wiltenburg, "True Crime: The Origins of Modern Sensationalism," *American Historical Review* 109, no. 5 (December 2004): 1377–404; David Bulla and Heather Haley, "Sensational Journalism in the Mid-19th Century," in Bulla and Sachsman, *Sensationalism*, 77; Jack Breslin, "Naughty Seeds of Sensationalism: Gossip and Celebrity in 19th-Century Reporting," in Bella and Sachsman, *Sensationalism*, 115." Gregory Borchard, Stephen Bates, and Laurence Mullen, "Publishing Violence as Art and News: Sensational Prints and Pictures in the 19th-Century Press," in Bulla and Sachsman, *Sensationalism*, 53, 58–59. See also Karen Halttunen, *Murder Most Foul:*

The Killer and the American Gothic Imagination (Cambridge, Mass.: Harvard University Press, 1998).

14. Friedrick Koenig patented the first steam press in 1811 (the Koenig press), which could print 1,100 prints per hour. Beau Riffenburgh, *The Myth of the Explorer: The Press, Sensationalism and Geographic Discovery* (Oxford: Oxford University Press, 1994), 18–20. On the *Herald*'s "sprightly manner" and "sensory details," see Warren Franke, "Sensationalism and the Development of the Nineteenth-Century Reporting: The Broom Sweeps Sensory Details," and Donald L. Shaw and John W. Slater, "In the Eye of the Beholder? Sensationalism in American Press News, 1820–1860," both in *Journalism History* 12, nos. 3–4 (Winter–Autumn 1985): 80–85, 86–91. On crime in the penny press, see Patricia Cline Cohen, *The Murder of Helen Jewett* (New York: Knopf/Doubleday, 1999); William E. Huntzicker, "Sex, Sin, and Sensation: Two Major Crime Stories in Antebellum New York," in Sachsman and Bulla, *Sensationalism*, 201–22; Amy Srebnick, *The Mysterious Death of Mary Rogers: Sex and Culture in Nineteenth-Century New York* (New York: Oxford University Press, 1987); Andie Tucher, *Froth and Scum: Truth, Beauty, Goodness, and the Ax Murder in America's First Mass Medium* (Chapel Hill: University of North Carolina Press, 1994).

15. Joshua Brown, *Beyond the Lines: Pictorial Reporting, Everyday Life, and the Crisis of Gilded Age America*, (Berkeley: University of California Press, 2002), 11, 14; Riffenburgh, *Myth of the Explorer*, 58. Illustrations caused ink clogs. They were also labor intensive and thus slow to translate onto carved wood blocks. Although the *Herald* introduced a faster press in 1849, which increased printing tenfold using the stereographic transmission of text to paper, logistical difficulties led to the near-complete suspension of images by 1850. On the use of newsboys to hawk crime news in the *Herald* and *Sun*, see Stevens, *Sensationalism and the New York Press*, 27. On the significance of the Robinson-Jewett case, see Cohen, *Murder of Helen Jewett*. On the shift from subscription to individual sales, see Michael Schudson, *Discovering the News: A Social History of American Newspapers* (New York: Basic, 1978), 15–18, 25–26.

16. On struggles over decency standards in the antebellum flash press, see Patricia Cline Cohen, Timothy Gilfoyle, and Helen Lefkowitz Horowitz, *The Flash Press: Sporting Male Weeklies in 1840s New York* (Chicago: University of Chicago Press, 2012); Tucher, *Froth and Scum*. On the "crusading spirit" of sensational journalism, see Frank Luther Mott, *American Journalism, A History, 1690–1960* (New York: Macmillan, 1962), 442; Dan Schiller, *Objectivity and the News: The Public and the Rise of Commercial Journalism* (Philadelphia: University of Pennsylvania Press, 1981), 179.

17. Michael Denning, *Mechanic Accents: Dime Novels and Working-Class Culture in America* (London: Verso, 1987); Shelley Streeby, *American Sensations: Class, Empire and the Production of Popular Culture* (Berkeley: University of California Press, 2002); Jessica Dorman, "Inheritors of a Sentimental Mantle: The 19th-Century Roots of Progressive Era Muckraking," in Bulla and Sachsman, *Sensationalism*, 172.

18. Leslie began by working with P. T. Barnum to publicize singer Jenny Lind's successful tour in 1850–51. As Joshua Brown shows, Leslie innovated the mass production of woodcut images, cutting production time for a single woodcut from more than a week to roughly eight hours by a large team effort. The addition of a faster press in 1858

further sped up the paper's visualization of news. Brown, *Beyond the Lines*, 7, 14–28, 35–40. On *Leslie's* images of the Burdell murder, see Huntzicker, "Sex, Sin, and Sensation," 219. On audience demand for illustrations, see Patricia J. Anderson, *The Printed Image and the Transformation of Popular Culture, 1790–1860* (Cambridge, Mass., Oxford University Press, 1994); Borchard, Bates, and Mullen, "Publishing Violence," 60.

19. Jennifer E. Moore, "'Ours Has Been No Pleasing Task': Sensationalism in Frank Leslie's Campaign against Swill Milk," in Sachsman and Bulla, *Sensationalism*, 138. By contrast, *Leslie's* "staid rival," *Harper's Weekly*, avoided Leslie's penchant for advocacy of moral reform. Brown, *Beyond the Lines*, 41.

20. *Leslie's* abandoned its overt Democratic leanings during the Civil War to appeal to Northern readers. Brown, *Beyond the Lines*, 31, 53. *Harper's Weekly* by midway through the war took a pro-Republican stance. There is no definitive study of *Harper's Weekly*. On the paper's illustration of wounded soldiers during the war years, see Valerie DeBrava, "The Offending Hand of War in *Harper's Weekly*," in *American Periodicals*, 11 (2001): 49–64; on its showcasing of industrial progress, see Gib Prettyman, "*Harper's Weekly* and the Spectacle of Industrialization," in *American Periodicals* 11 (2001): 24–28; on the cultural significance of the paper's most famous cartoonist, see Fiona Deans Halloran, *Thomas Nast: The Father of Modern Political Cartoons* (Chapel Hill: University of North Carolina Press, 2012). "Wartime austerities" curtailed daily illustration. Barnhurst and Nerone, *Form of News*, 76. The war also created an appetite for regular "thrills." Borchard, Bates, and Mullen, "Publishing Violences," 60–61. On controversies over images available to soldiers during the Civil War, see Judith Giesberg, *Sex and the Civil War: Soldiers, Pornography, and the Making of American Morality* (Chapel Hill: University of North Carolina Press, 2017); Amy Werbel, *Lust on Trial: Censorship and the Rise of American Obscenity in the Age of Anthony Comstock* (New York: Columbia University Press, 2018).

21. According to Frank Luther Mott, magazines grew rapidly from about seven hundred in 1865 to more than three thousand publications in 1885. Mott, *A History of American Magazines, 1865–1885, Volume 3* (Cambridge, Mass: Belknap, 1967), 5. By 1882, all major newspapers in New York City had moved from cloth paper to wood-pulp stock, bringing down costs. The linotype, introduced by the *Tribune* as a labor-cutting measure, ultimately did not decrease the number (just the kind) of compositors needed. Story lengths grew with the expansion of pages (for advertising revenue). Bulla and Haley, "Sensational Journalism." Journalists blamed editors for pressure to embellish; editors blamed consumer demand. Smythe, *Gilded Age Press*, 123–27, 160–65.

22. Joel Wiener, "How New Was the New Journalism?" in *Papers for the Millions: The New Journalism in Britain, 1850–1914*, ed. J. H. Wiener (Westport, Conn.: Greenwood, 1988); Robert Park, *The Immigrant Press and Its Control* (New York: Harper, 1922); Charles Ponce de Leon, *Self-Exposure: Human-Interest Journalism and the Emergence of Celebrity in America, 1890–1940* (Chapel Hill: University of North Carolina Press, 2002). On the press as moral or social arbiter, see Gerald J. Baldasty, *Vigilante Newspapers: Tales of Sex, Religion, and Murder in the Northwest* (Seattle: University of Washington Press, 2010), 167. On the illustrator as a new kind of journalist, see Barnhurst and Nerone, *Form of News*, 110–13.

23. On the "newspaper crusades" of the 1880s, beginning with William T. Stead's public

campaign against "white slavery" in London's *Pall Mall Gazette* in 1885, see Gretchen Soderlund, *Sex Trafficking, Scandal, and the Transformation of Journalism, 1885–1917* (Chicago: University of Chicago Press, 2013), 24–66.

Chapter 1. "We Simply Illustrate"

1. I discuss the emergence of the illustrated dailies in the late 1880s in chapter 3.

2. Founded in 1873, the *Daily Graphic* innovated by introducing the half-tone process by 1880, which made it possible to reproduce photographs for publication. Due to technical limitations (printer speeds, paper quality), however, the *Graphic* more typically used a process called photolithography to reproduce images for publication.

3. Ida M. Tarbell, *All in the Day's Work* (Urbana: University of Illinois Press, 1939), 13–15.

4. "The Female Brokers of the Period," *Days' Doings*, February 26, 1870; "The Monster Scandal," *Days' Doings*, November 20, 1872. For a detailed discussion of Woodhull's visual and cultural meanings, see Amanda Frisken, *Victoria Woodhull's Sexual Revolution: Political Theater and the Popular Press in Nineteenth-Century America* (Philadelphia: University of Pennsylvania Press, 2004). On Woodhull's exposure of Beecher and the ensuing scandal, see also Richard Wightman Fox, *Trials of Intimacy: Love and Loss in the Beecher-Tilton Scandal* (Chicago: University of Chicago Press, 1999); Altina Waller, *Reverend Beecher and Mrs. Tilton: Sex and Class in Victorian America* (Amherst: University of Massachusetts Press, 1982).

5. The law passed, with little discussion in Congress, in March 1873. See Helen Lefkowitz Horowitz, *Rereading Sex: Battles over Sexual Knowledge and Suppression in Nineteenth-Century America*, (New York: Knopf, 2002), 358–85. If the late-nineteenth century constituted what David Rabban calls the "forgotten years" of the free-speech struggle, the 1870s arguably comprised a critical decade, one that set the terms for subsequent debate. David Rabban, *Free Speech in Its Forgotten Years, 1870–1920* (Cambridge University Press, 1999). For a more detailed discussion of sensational imagery and the rise of the radical free speech movement, see Amanda Frisken, "Obscenity, Free Speech and 'Sporting News' in 1870s America," in *Journal of American Studies* 42, no. 3 (2008): 537–77.

6. Frank Couvares, "The Good Censor: Race, Sex, and Censorship in the Early Cinema," in *Yale Journal of Criticism* 7, no. 2 (1994): 234. Rochelle Gurstein, *The Repeal of Reticence: A History of America's Cultural and Legal Struggles over Free Speech, Obscenity, Sexual Liberation and Modern Art* (New York: Hill and Wang, 1998), 50.

7. Nicola Beisel, *Imperiled Innocents: Anthony Comstock and Family Reproduction in Victorian America* (Princeton, N.J.: Princeton University Press, 1998). As Amy Werbel shows, the Comstock Law introduced two new adjectives, "lewd," and "lascivious," which had broader interpretive power than the 1868 New York law's focus on "indecent" images. Amy Werbel, *Lust on Trial: Censorship and the Rise of American Obscenity in the Age of Anthony Comstock* (New York: Columbia University Press, 2018), 72.

8. Anthony Comstock, *Traps for the Young*, ed. Robert Bremner (Cambridge, Mass.: Harvard University Press, 1967 [1883]), 20.

9. Julia Ward Howe, "The Influence of Literature on Crime," published in *Papers Read at the Second Congress of Women, Chicago 15, 16 and 17, 1874* (Chicago: 1874), 13, 15. On the

role of women in the anti-obscene literature campaign in the 1880s, see Beisel, *Imperiled Innocents*, 71–73, 132–34; Alison Parker, *Purifying America: Women, Cultural Reform and Pro-Censorship Activism, 1873–1933* (Urbana: University of Illinois Press, 1997), 56–57, 60–63; Paul Boyer, *Purity in Print: Book Censorship in America from the Gilded Age to the Computer Age* (Madison: University of Wisconsin Press, 2002), 17–18.

10. L.B.D. to *The Revolution*, July 22, 1869, reprinted in Cheris Kramarae and Lana F. Rakow, eds., *Revolution in Words: Righting Women, 1868–1871* (New York: Routledge, 1990), 224; Olive Logan to *The Revolution*, October 15, 1869.

11. *New Northwest*, October 6, 1871. Reprinted in Rakow, ed., *Revolution in Words*, 185; Duniway, "Obscene Publications," *New Northwest*, June 21, 1872.

12. Iconoclast, "Have We a Free Press?" *Truth Seeker*, January 1874.

13. It is unclear whether Comstock arrested Lant for publishing a poem, which described the Beecher-Tilton scandal in humorous naval metaphors, or a letter discussing physiology. Bennett, "Case of John A. Lant," *Truth Seeker*, January 29, 1876; "Another Outrage," *Truth Seeker*, July 1, 1876, emphasis in original. Earlier editions of Foote's book gave advice on preventing conception, but he had removed the relevant passages in response to the 1873 Comstock law; *Dr. Foote's Health Monthly*, October 1876; reprinted as supplement to December 1876 issue. Foote defended his work as educational, in opposition to "really obscene" publications. See also Horowitz, *Rereading Sex*, 405–9.

14. The U.S. Supreme Court endorsed this view in *U.S. v. Bennett* (1879), which established the Hicklin test as a precedent for subsequent prosecution under the Comstock Law. For Bennett's views on sex education, see his article, "Physiology for Women," in *The Word*, July 1872, 4. See also Horowitz, *Rereading Sex*, 433–35.

15. As Joshua Brown shows, *Leslie's* began in 1855 with a more sensational ethos and crusading spirit. Founding the sporting paper the *Day's Doings* in 1868 enabled him to tone down *Leslie's* to make it a more family-friendly publication. Brown, *Beyond the Lines*, 22–26, 43–44. The *Days' Doings'* circulation peaked at sixty-seven thousand copies in 1872, after which its sales diminished rapidly to twenty-five thousand copies in circulation by 1876, when it changed its name to the *Illustrated Times* (never rising again above twenty-thousand copies, it ceased publication in 1885). *Geo. P. Rowell's American Newspaper Directory*, 1872–1900. *N. W. Ayers & Sons' American Newspaper Annual*, 1880–1909. While the *Illustrated Times* claimed a more respectable and "elevated tone," it too published sensational content. Joshua Brown, "'The Social and Sensational News of the Day': Frank Leslie, the *Days' Doings*, and Scandalous Pictorial News in Gilded Age New York," *New York Journal of American History* 66, no. 2 (Fall 2003): 10–20.

16. *Frank Leslie's Illustrated News*, December 7, 1872.

17. Quote from Anthony Comstock, *Diary*, January 14, 1873. Entry quoted in Heywood Broun and Margaret Leech, *Anthony Comstock: Roundsman of the Lord* (New York: Boni, 1927).

18. For example, it is remarkable that her defiant lecture on January 9 (to a standing ovation) and her subsequent arrest by federal marshals did not make the paper's pages. After Comstock made his displeasure against Leslie known, the sisters never again received significant illustration in the tabloid. See Frisken, *Victoria Woodhull's Sexual Revolution*, chap. 3.

19. [Frank Leslie], "Special Notice," *Days' Doings*, February 1, 1873, 2. Emphasis added. Most illustrated papers followed a convention of post-dating their issues by one or two weeks to allow for the delays in production and intracontinental delivery services; he probably wrote this around January 20. Leslie did not publicly acknowledge his connection to the *Days' Doings*.

20. Anthony Comstock, *Traps for the Young* (Cambridge, Mass.: Belknap, 1967 [1883]), 17, 20.

21. [Frank Leslie], "Special Notice," *Days' Doings*, February 1, 1873, 2.

22. Records of the New York Society for the Suppression of Vice, vol.1 (1873): entry 51, page, 16, January 28, 1873, Manuscripts Division, Library of Congress. A brief report of the indictment appears in "New York," *New York Times*, January 29, 1873: "The Grand Jury of the Court of General Session before adjourning, yesterday, presented several important indictments, among which was one against Frank Leslie, charged by Mr. Comstock with issuing obscene publications." Brown interprets Comstock's diary entry as reflecting his "consternation" that the district attorney's office intervened. Brown, "Social and Sensational News of the Day," 11.

23. "Notice to Advertisers," *Days' Doings*, February 15, 1873, 2.

24. *Days' Doings*, January 25 and February 1, 1873, 15 (and most preceding issues). Such advertisements disappeared after February 15.

25. *Days' Doings*, February 8 and February 15, 1873, 15. For a more detailed examination of the shift in advertising, see Frisken, "Obscenity, Free Speech, and 'Sporting' News," 548–53.

26. "The Aviary," *Days' Doings*, July 22, 1871, 13. Other examples include "Musidora," *Days' Doings*, September 28, 1872, 6; "The Charmer," *Days' Doings*, October 12, 1872, 13. Beisel, *Imperiled Innocents*, 178.

27. "Leap Frog by the Sad Sea Waves," *Days' Doings*, July 27, 1872, 8; "A Conductor's Gallant 'Passage at Arms,'" *Days' Doings*, March 1, 1873, 13. See also "Impromptu Stilts," *Days' Doings*, January 25, 1873; "A Lady in Charleston, Va.," *Days' Doings*, September 28, 1872, 9.

28. "Episode of the Spanish Revolution," *Days' Doings*, May 22, 1873, 13 (poor image quality prevents reproduction here). On the perception of late-nineteenth-century Anglo-Saxon Americans that national others, including Spaniards, were racially distinct, see Matthew Jacobson, *Whiteness of a Different Color: European Immigrants and the Alchemy of Race* (Cambridge, Mass.: Harvard University Press, 1998), chap. 2.

29. It is unclear exactly when Matsell sold the paper, but it was apparently before July 1873, as the *New York Times* mentioned his *former* connection to the *Police Gazette* upon his appointment as superintendent of police (and later president of the Police Commission) in 1873. The *New York Times*, for example, blamed Matsell's editorship of the *Police Gazette* for the rise of "indecent houses" (of prostitution) and for "debauching the minds of the young," which it called "surely one of the most monstrous" crimes. *New York Times*, July 2, 15, 16, 1873. Matsell was replaced as superintendent in July 1874 and removed as president in December 1875. He (briefly) opened a law practice on Broadway, then retired to his farm in Iowa. He died in 1877. *New York Times*, July 26, 1877.

30. With the two proprietors, Fox slowly restored circulation to about twenty thousand

copies by early 1878, after which he revamped production, and the paper climbed to new heights in the next decade. *Geo. P. Rowell's American Newspaper Directory, 1872–1900.* Although historians generally date Fox's influence on the paper to the 1878 changes, the sole remaining issue for 1874 that I have examined lists him as the business manager, and his influence is evident in a numbers contest he introduced in that issue. *National Police Gazette,* December 5, 1874, 2. On Fox's arrival in New York and takeover of the *Police Gazette* in 1876, see Guy Reel, *The* National Police Gazette *and the Making of the Modern American Man, 1879–1906* (New York: Palgrave, 2006), 14, 43. See also David Welky, "'We Are the People': Idealized Working-Class Society in the *National Police Gazette* 1880–1900," *Mid-America, An Historical Review* 84, nos. 1–3 (Winter/Summer/Fall 2002): 101–27. For a more gossipy (if somewhat inaccurate) short biography of Fox that recounts his arrival and early months in New York City, see Walter Davenport, "The Dirt Disher," *Collier's,* March 24, 1928.

31. Records of the New York Society for the Suppression of Vice, February 16, 1877, 1:83, Manuscripts Division, Library of Congress.

32. Apart from the American Periodicals Series collection of the *National Police Gazette* on microfilm, now digitized, no copies for these years can be found in larger archives, including the American Antiquarian Society, the New York Historical Society, the New York Public Library, and the Boston Public Library. I have also consulted rare newspaper sellers and Ebay. The APS collection contains one issue for 1874 (December 5). I own a single issue for June 21, 1877. The APS collection for the years following Fox's dramatic adaptation and introduction of the pink pages in 1878 is more complete.

33. *Police Gazette,* December 5, 1874, and June 21, 1877.

34. *Police Gazette,* December 5, 1874, and June 21, 1877.

35. Advertisements shrank from four out of five columns in 1874 to two out of six columns in 1877.

36. Walter Kendrick, *The Secret Museum: Pornography in Modern Culture* (New York: Viking, 1987), 158.

37. Heywood defended English reformers Annie Besant and Charles Bradlaugh, arrested in 1877 for selling Charles Knowlton's physiology work, *Fruits of Philosophy.* See his editorial, *Word,* August 1877. He also defended Josephine Tilton, sister of Angela Tilton Heywood, arrested in Halifax, Nova Scotia, for selling his own critique of marriage, *Cupid's Yokes.* Heywood, "The New Inquisition," *Word,* November 1877. Bennett protested his good intentions in "It Has Come at Last!" *Boston Investigator,* November 28, 1877. Mattie Sawyer, "Invasion of Liberty and the Common Right to Knowledge," *Word,* January 1878.

38. [Angela Heywood], "Editorial Notes," *Word,* January 1878. Ezra Heywood, "The Impolicy of Repression," *Word,* January 1878; Chandler, "Correspondence," *Word,* January 1878; [Angela Heywood], "Editorial Notes," *Word,* August 1878; see also Elizur Wright, "Clandestine Publications," *Word,* February 1878.

39. Elizabeth Blackwell, "Counsel to Parents on the Moral Education of their Children" (1879), quotations, p. 109, 116, and 148, respectively. Blackwell's chief concern was that such literature implanted images in the young mind that encouraged masturbation.

40. "Seeds of Vice," *Alpha*, June 1 1877.

41. Underwood, "Free Thought in Sympathy with No Kind of Indecency," *Boston Investigator*, July 3, 1878. Abbott, quoted (and critiqued) in "Repeal! Repeal! Repeal!," *Word*, October 1878. The Free Thought convention in Watkins, New York, gathered to defend and support Heywood and Bennett, resolved in similar language that "[The association] hereby declares its emphatic approval of the use of all such means as may be within the legitimate scope of the Government to secure the repression both of the issue and circulation of such matter by the press." Freethinkers Association of Western New York, "Freethought Issues," *Word*, September 1878. On the internal split of the National Liberal Association and the formation of the NDA, see Rabban, *Free Speech*, 38; Horowitz, *Rereading Sex*, 410, 420, 422, 435–36; Beisel, *Imperiled Innocents*, 87, 92.

42. E. H. Heywood, "The Outlook," *Word*, January 1878. Seaver, editorial, "The Three Arrests at Watkins," *Boston Investigator*, September 11, 1878. Wright, "Correspondence," *Word*, January 1878. Seaver, editorial, "Obscene Literature," *Boston Investigator*, June 5, 1878. Seaver, editorial, "The Case of E. H. Heywood," *Boston Investigator* July 3, 1878. On Seaver's concerns about the perils of "blood & thunder" literature, see editorial, "Preamble to Dime Novel Heroes," *Boston Investigator*, January 23, 1878. For more detail on the debate among freethinkers, see Frisken, "Obscenity, Free Speech and 'Sporting News.'"

43. Welky, "We Are the People," 101, 107. Commercial newspapers typically expanded to accommodate more advertising, but that appears not to have been the *Police Gazette*'s motivation; space devoted to advertising had in fact shrunk since 1874 and was still in decline. From two columns on page 7 in 1877, advertising had shrunk to a single column by April 1878. *Police Gazette*, April 27, 1878, 7. It took a few years for the revamped paper to experience a significant growth in advertising sales, but by May 1882 advertisements filled all four columns of the advertising page. *Police Gazette*, May 20, 1882, 15. Revenue also likely rose due to increased circulation, which grew rapidly from twenty thousand in 1878 to fifty thousand in 1882, and to one hundred thousand in 1883.

44. The adjectives "lively and entertaining" conveyed a great deal of meaning to contemporary readers, being code words for material steeped in sexual innuendo and double entendre. "Our Enlargement," *National Police Gazette*, April 27, 1878, 2.

45. "Our Enlargement," *Police Gazette*, April 27, 1878, 2. Once the new paper appeared, it quickly became clear that it would neither base its illustrations on witnessed scenes nor its stories on its own correspondents' reports. Instead, it expanded its wire news coverage, by offering more comprehensive catalogs (without illustration) of crime news under headings like "Vice's Varieties" or "This Wicked World." For further discussion of the purpose of these columns, see Reel, *National Police Gazette*, 60.

46. "Salutatory," *Police Gazette*, May 11, 1878, 2.

47. "Shooting of Mollie Hickey," *Police Gazette*, May 18, 1878, 8; "A Parisian Romance," *Police Gazette*, May 18, 1878, 16.

48. "Tramp Horror," *Police Gazette*, May 18, 1878, 16. It is possible that Fox took such pains to prevent lawsuits. The victim was expected to die of the attack. The article predicted that the tramp would be lynched, once caught. However, in the actual case, three

possible tramps were discovered, and it was unclear whether the correct perpetrator would be identified. *Memphis Public Ledger*, May 8, 1878.

49. "Miss Stuart Murdered by Three Negresses," *Police Gazette*, My 18, 1878, 5. *Staunton Spectator*, May 14, 1878.

50. "The Negro Crime," *Police Gazette*, May 21 [possible typo in original; likely date May 25], 1878, 9 (image), 5 (text). The outcome is unclear; there is no existing copy for the Victor *Index* (the story's source identified by the *Police Gazette*) in archives at this time. No other available paper from Iowa or anywhere in the nation appears to have picked up the story.

51. "Brutal Outrage on Miss Carrie Wayne," *Police Gazette*, July 27, 1878, 8.

52. On the political significance of interracial sexuality during Reconstruction, see Hodes, "Sexualization of Reconstruction Politics." See also Hodes, *White Women, Black Men*, 176, 205–6. As I discuss in chapter 4, African American newspaper publishers devised their own counternarratives to combat this propaganda campaign. A typical Fox editorial praised lynching as the "virile" solution to the alleged crisis black rapists: "A Travesty of Justice," *National Police Gazette*, May 18, 1878, 2. As Estelle Freedman notes, such rape narratives "served to shore up white male privilege through constructions of dependent women and dangerous African Americans." Estelle Freedman, "'Crimes Which Startle and Horrify': Gender, Age, and the Racialization of Sexual Violence in White American Newspapers, 1870–1900," *Journal of the History of Sexuality* 20, no. 3 (September 2011), 465–97. Based on a sample of issues over three decades, Guy Reel documents significant declines in crime reporting in general, and sexual assault in particular, by 1890, and a near-removal of crime news by 1900. Reel, *National Police Gazette*, 56, 63. Over time, depictions of (alleged) rape declined, and instead images of the resulting lynching took their place, which had a similar effect, because they had become (inaccurately, as Ida B. Wells pointed out) a code for rape. Such images took on mythic proportions alongside a dramatic rise in the number of lynchings, nationally, by the early 1890s.

53. As Estelle Freedman shows, over time "legitimate" rape victims in the press were characterized as younger and more innocent, while adult or experienced women received less credibility. Freedman, "Crimes Which Startle and Horrify," 496–97. See also Estelle Freedman, *Redefining Rape: Sexual Violence in the Era of Suffrage and Segregation* (Cambridge, Mass.: Harvard University Press, 2013).

54. As Elliott Gorn notes, scenarios of resisting women "had a double edge, at once upholding 'female virtue' and exciting male readers with hints of its violation." Elliott Gorn, "The Wicked World: the *National Police Gazette* and Gilded Age America," *Media Studies Journal* 6, no. 1 (Winter 1992): 9. The importance of guns (and gun imagery) in the *Police Gazette* is beyond the scope of this chapter, but it is notable that the multitude of stories valorizing guns coincides with Fox's own business in commercial gun sales. See, for example, his advertisement for mail-order delivery of weapons. *National Police Gazette*, August 2, 1892, 15.

55. "Astounding Audacity" and "A Ravisher's Escape," *National Police Gazette*, May 18, 1878, 7. On the prevalence of text stories of rapes by tramps and desperados, fitting

the idea that rape was caused by strangers invading the home or attacking vulnerable girls in outdoor settings, see Freedman, "Crimes Which Startle and Horrify," 474–77.

56. Frank Luther Mott, *A History of American Magazines, 1850–1865*, vol. 2 (Cambridge, Mass: Belknap, 1967), 331. As David Welky writes, the *Police Gazette* "self-consciously aimed its appeal at native-born, working-class white men" and emphasized traditional power relationships and gender roles. Welky, "We Are the People," 102; Gorn, "Wicked World," 10.

57. Welky, "We Are the People," 110. This made sense for the Belfast-born Fox, who (according to legend) created in his early days in New York a lasting bond with an Irishman named O'Brien, who got him his first job. It is, however, ironic that Fox, an immigrant of few years' standing, created a fiercely anti-immigrant publication, which ignored his own non-native status by catering to a broader, second-generation Irish population. On the apocryphal meeting with "O'Brien," which he may have invented as very good publicity for his expanding audience in the Irish-American community, see Davenport, "Dirt Disher," 26. On *Leslie's* physiognomy of Irish Americans, see Brown, *Beyond the Lines*, 137–143. On the racialized Irish immigrant in mainstream illustration, see Jacobson, *Whiteness of a Different Color*, esp. 52–55.

58. "The Ignorant Vote," *Harper's Weekly*, December 9, 1876, 242. Only at the turn of the twentieth century did the Irish fully assert their "whiteness" in mainstream visual culture, partly in contrast to "swarthy" newcomers from Italy and southeastern Europe, and perhaps more important because of the increasing prevalence of Irish journeymen among the ranks of illustrators and cartoonists. On negative depictions of Irish in nineteenth-century popular culture, see L. Perry Curtis Jr., *Apes and Angels: The Irishman in Victorian Caricature* (Washington, D.C.: Smithsonian Institution Press, 1997); Kerry Soper, "From Swarthy Ape to Sympathetic Everyman and Subversive Trickster: The Development of Irish Caricature in American Comic Strips between 1890 and 1920," *Journal of American Studies* 39 (August 2005): 2, 257–96; Noel Ignatiev, *How the Irish Became White* (New York: Routledge, 2008).

59. Editorial, *National Police Gazette*, November 25, 1882.

60. On the Women's Christian Temperance Union's Department for the Suppression of Impure Literature (later the Department of Purity in Literature), see Parker, *Purifying America*, 56–63. On the growing attention paid by the New York Society for the Suppression of Vice to crime-story weeklies after 1880, and its pursuit of state legislation to suppress, see Beisel, *Imperiled Innocents*, 64–66. On the *Police Gazette's* declining crime coverage over time, see Reel, *National Police Gazette*, 56, 63.

61. Elliott Gorn, *The Manly Art: Bare-Knuckle Prize Fighting in America* (Ithaca, N.Y.: Cornell University Press, 1986), 181. See also Gorn, "Wicked World," 13–15; Reel, *National Police Gazette*, 51–54. On the *Police Gazette* and saloon culture, see Roy Rosenzweig, "The Rise of the Saloon," in *Rethinking Popular Culture: Contemporary Perspectives in Cultural Studies*, ed. Chandra Mukerji and Michael Schudson, 130–38 (Berkeley: University of California Press, 1991); Howard Chudacoff, *The Age of the Bachelor: Creating an American Subculture* (Princeton, N.J.: Princeton University Press, 1999), 193–94; Mott, *History of American Magazines* 2:328–31.

62. On the lasting significance of the *Bennett* decision, see Horowitz, *Rereading Sex*, 433–35; Beisel, *Imperiled Innocents*, 176, 178.

Chapter 2. "Language More Effective than Words"

1. I discuss Comstock's interventions with sporting newspapers like the *Police Gazette*, and consequent racialization of images of sexual assault, in chapter 1.

2. "Wong Chin Foo," *Harper's Weekly*, May 26, 1877, 405. Only two issues of the *Chinese American* remain in archives, published on February 3 and March 31, 1883. They were published in Chinese characters, transcribed and printed using the photolithography technique on yellow paper. Wong changed the name to *Hua Mei Xin Bao* sometime after the first issue (*New Chinese American News*). The *Chinese-American* folded in September 1883, when the staff fled (with the equipment) after being intimidated by Wong's adversaries. Despite its few short months in print, however, the paper "projected Wong into a leadership role in Chinatown." Scott D. Seligman, *The First Chinese American: The Remarkable Life of Wong Chin Foo* (Hong Kong: Hong Kong University Press, 2013), 100.

3. The *Police Gazette* claimed an official circulation of 150,000. Its claim to reach five hundred thousand readers was likely exaggerated, but it was available in many public spaces, circulated among readers (especially boys) who were not inclined take it home, and something of a fixture of male public life. See chapter 1 for more details.

4. See Lipong Zhu, "'A Chinaman's Chance' on the Rocky Mountain Mining Frontier," in *Chinese on the American Frontier*, ed. Arif Dirlik (New York: Rowman and Littlefield, 2001), 232. The wide array of positive Chinese contributions is detailed in other articles in the same volume. See also Arif Dirlik, "Introduction," in *Chinese on the American Frontier*, xxv; A. Dudley Gardner, "Chinese Emigrants in Southwest Wyoming, 1868–1885," 341, 346; Robert R. Swartout, Jr., "Kwangtung to Big Sky: The Chinese in Montana, 1864–1900," 377, in *Chinese on the American Frontier*. On the stereotypes driving anti-Chinese legislation, see Roger Daniels, *Asian America: Chinese and Japanese in the United States Since 1850* (New York: Harper Collins, 1990), 60; Robert G. Lee, *Orientals: Asian Americans in Popular Culture* (Philadelphia: Temple University Press, 1999), 10.

5. Mary Lui's superb analysis of the 1909 "Chinatown Trunk Mystery," for example, minimizes the significance of an opium den image from *Frank Leslie's Illustrated News*, because the text contradicted the inflammatory visual message. Mary Ting Yi Lui, *The Chinatown Trunk Mystery: Murder, Miscegenation, and Other Dangerous Encounters in Turn-of-the-Century New York City* (Princeton, N.J.: Princeton University Press, 2005), 28–30. Similarly, Nayan Shah's innovative deconstruction of the San Francisco opium den as a locus of disease, sexual deviance, and vice minimizes the implications of the opium den rapist trope within the period's contentious political culture. Nayan Shah, *Contagious Divides: Epidemics and Race in San Francisco's Chinatown* (Berkeley: University of California Press, 2001), 94–95, 102. I discuss African American responses to racist sensationalism in chapter 4. By the early twentieth century, the more familiar, feminized stereotype of the Chinese launderer displaced the opium den rapist in popular culture, but traces persisted in the character of what Eugene Wong calls the "sexually

animalistic" Asian male. Eugene Wong, *On Visual Media Racism: Asians in the Motion Pictures* (New York: Arno, 1978). See also Lee, *Orientals*; Thomas Cripps, "The Making of *The Birth of a Race*," in *The Birth of Whiteness: Race and the Emergence of U.S. Cinema*, ed. Daniel Bernardi (New Brunswick, N.J.: Rutgers University Press, 1996); Gina Marchetti, *Romance and the Yellow Peril: Race, Sex, and Discursive Strategies in Hollywood Fiction* (Berkeley: University of California Press, 1993); Donald Kirihara, "Stereotype and Sessue Hayakawa," in Bernardi, *Birth of Whiteness*; Peter X. Feng, "Introduction," in *Screening Asian Americans* (New Brunswick, N.J.: Rutgers University Press, 2002). On the feminization of Chinese men in modern popular culture, see Karen Leong, "'A Distinct and Antagonistic Race': Constructions of Chinese Manhood in the Exclusion Debates, 1869–1878," in *Across the Great Divide: Cultures of Manhood in the American West*, ed. Matthew Basso et al. (New York: Routledge, 2001), 143; Lisa Lowe, *Immigrant Acts: On Asian-American Cultural Politics* (Durham, N.C.: Duke University Press, 1996), 11–12.

6. The British, expanding their exports of Indian opium, pushed opium traffic in China as a source of revenue, despite an official prohibition by the Chinese government. Two Opium Wars resulted in the opening of Chinese ports to foreign trade (including imported Indian opium) and the legalization of opium traffic and use in China. Opium use in China rose dramatically in the 1860s, and once the Burlingame Treaty (1868) removed the emperor's prohibition on emigration, Chinese workers who came to the U.S. to work in the railroads and mines, competing with other low-wage workers in both areas, brought opium with them. David T. Courtright, *Dark Paradise: Opium Addiction in American before 1940* (Cambridge, Mass.: Harvard University Press, 1986), 66–67.

7. Andrew Gyory, *Closing the Gate: Race, Politics and the Chinese Exclusion Act* (Chapel Hill: University of North Carolina Press, 1998), 246, 248; Tomás Almaguer, *Racial Fault Lines: The Historical Origins of White Supremacy in California* (Berkeley: University of California Press, 2008), 179. On the Los Angeles massacre, see William R. Locklear, "The Celestials and the Angels: A Study of the Anti-Chinese Movement in Los Angeles to 1882," *Historical Society of Southern California Quarterly* 42, no. 3 (September 1960): 239–56. On the San Francisco "riots," see W. P. Wilcox, "Anti-Chinese Riots in Washington," *Washington Historical Quarterly* 20, no. 3 (July 1929), reprinted in *Anti-Chinese Violence in North America: An Original Anthology*, ed. Roger Daniels (New York: Arno, 1979), 205. On the Denver "riot," see Roy T. Wortman, "Denver's Anti-Chinese Riot, 1880," in Dirlik, *Chinese on the American Frontier*, 323–36.

8. John Tchen, *New York before Chinatown: Orientalism and the Shaping of American Culture* (Baltimore, Md.: Johns Hopkins University Press, 2001), xxiii. The Page Law severely restricted the migration of Chinese women to American shores, except for wives of dignitaries and merchants. On the 1875 Page Law, see Sucheng Chan, "The Exclusion of Chinese Women, 1870–1943," in *Entry Denied: Exclusion and the Chinese Community in America, 1882–1943*, ed. Sucheng Chan (Philadelphia: Temple University Press, 1991); George Peffer, "Forbidden Families: Immigration Experiences of Chinese Women Under the Page Law, 1875–1882," *Journal of American Ethnic History* 6 (Fall 1986): 28–46. See also Peggy Pascoe, "Gender Systems in Conflict: The Marriages of Mission-Educated Chinese American Women, 1847–1939," in *Unequal Sisters: A Multi-Cultural*

Reader in U.S. Women's History, ed. Ellen Carol DuBois and Vicki L. Ruiz (New York: Routledge, 1990); Judy Yung, *Unbound Feet: A Social History of Chinese Women in San Francisco* (Berkeley: University of California Press, 1995).

9. On the role of racism in anti-Chinese campaigns, see Erica Lee, *At America's Gates: Chinese Immigration during the Exclusion Era, 1882–1943* (Chapel Hill: University of North Carolina Press, 2003), 21; Yen Tzu-Kuei, "Rock Springs Incident," in Dirlik, *Chinese on the American Frontier*, 359. For a survey of anti-Chinese violence, see Sucheng Chan, *Asian Americans: An Interpretive History* (Boston: Twayne, 1991), 48–51; Wunder, "Anti-Chinese Violence in the American West," 212–36; Shih-Shan Henry Tsai, *The Chinese Experience in America* (Bloomington: University of Indiana Press: 1986), 67–72; Craig Storti, *Incident at Bitter Creek: The Chinese Massacre at Rock Springs* (Ames: Iowa State University Press, 1991), 12, 25, 26. See also Wilcox, "Anti-Chinese Riots in Washington," 205; Gyory, *Closing the Gate*, 258. In 1880, California added the "Mongolian" to the "negro" and "mulatto" as ineligible for intermarriage with a white person. On municipal and state restrictions, see Ronald Takaki, *A Different Mirror: A History of Multicultural America* (Boston: Little, Brown, 1993), 204–6. On the "fierce exclusivity" of the 1790 Naturalization Law, see Matthew Jacobson, *Whiteness of a Different Color: European Immigrants and the Alchemy of Race* (Cambridge, Mass: Harvard University Press, 1998), 39; Alexander Saxton, *The Indispensable Enemy: Labor and the Anti-Chinese Movement in California* (Berkeley: University of California Press, 1975), 52–74. Legal intimidation of Chinese workers ranged from queue-cutting ordinances to "cubic-air ordinances" to "laundry laws." Charles J. McClain and Laurene Wu McClain, "The Chinese Struggle for Civil Rights in Nineteenth-Century America: The First Phase, 1850–1870," in *Chinese Immigrants and American Law*, ed. Charles McClain (New York: Garland, 1994), 140–42.

10. Erika Lee, *At America's Gates*, 29. See also Erika Lee, *The Making of Asian America: A History* (New York: Simon and Schuster, 2016).

11. Examples of such *Police Gazette* imagery can be found in "Fatal Fanaticism of a Christianized Chinaman," *Police Gazette*, November 2, 1878, 8; "Wooing the Fickle Goddess," *Police Gazette*, January 11, 1879, 16; "Tony Pastor's Experience with the Heathen Chinee [sic]," *Police Gazette*, August 30, 1879, 13; "A Chinese Planting Picnic," *Police Gazette*, July 24, 1880; "Introducing Dead Cats in Evidence," *Police Gazette*, September 25, 1880, 13; "How a Chinaman Swears," *Police Gazette*, April 30, 1881, 5.

12. "A Rise in China," *Police Gazette*, November 5, 1881, 4; "Anchored by his Pigtail," *Police Gazette*, November 12, 1881, 13. Images of Chinese migrants appeared an average of ten times per year (roughly 1 percent of all images), about half as frequently as images of African Americans, which appeared up to twenty (roughly 2 percent) times per year. On anti-Chinese political cartoons, see Richard Samuel West, *The San Francisco Wasp: An Illustrated History* (Periodicity Press, 2004). The *Wasp* was wary of Kearney but also unapologetically anti-Chinese.

13. "Glimpses of Gotham," *Police Gazette*, March 20, 1880, 15. On the Workingmen's Party claims of sexual danger from Chinese workers, see The Workingmen's Party of California, *The Labor Agitators; or, The Battle for Bread* (San Francisco, 1879). On Kearney and the Workingman's Party, see Dale Knoebel, *America for the Americans: The Nativ-*

ist Movement in the United States (New York: Twayne, 1996), 230. Roy T. Wortman, "Denver's Anti-Chinese Riot, 1880," in Dirlik, *Chinese on the American Frontier*, 323–36; Najim Aarim-Heriot, *Chinese Immigrants, African Americans and Racial Anxiety in the United States, 1848–1882* (Urbana: University of Illinois Press, 2003), 190–91; Yen, "Rock Springs Incident," 359; Almaguer, *Racial Fault Lines*, 179.

14. "The Chinese Must Go," *Police Gazette*, January 18, 1879, 1; editorial under same title, p. 2.

15. "A Moon-Eyed Heathen while Courting an 'Ilish Glal,'" *Police Gazette*, November 6, 1880, 8.

16. "Alle Samee Lika Melikan Man," [All the Same Like an American Man] *Police Gazette*, June 4, 1881, 16. "John Chinaman on a Bust," August 6, 1881, 9; "Labial Legal Tender," *Police Gazette*, March 11, 1882, 9.

17. The practice of opium smoking spread east from San Francisco through the mining towns of Nevada, arriving in New York in the early 1870s. Concerns about opium use focused particularly on women, who some said outnumbered men as addicts 3 to 1. There is evidence that some white women became sexually involved with Chinese men, as prostitutes, lovers, and occasionally as spouses. It is possible that opium was a powerful form of enticement, particularly to prostitutes, many of whom were users. However, many Americans were addicted to opiates before the opium den scare began, typically those that were "eaten" in solid form, or drunk, diluted in water. Opium *smoking* required instruction and thus necessitated the expert assistance of den owners. See David Courtwright, *Dark Paradise: Opium Addiction in America before 1940* (Cambridge, Mass.: Harvard University Press, 1986). On the female addict, see Harvey Green, *The Light of the Home: An Intimate View of the Lives of Women in Victorian America* (New York: Pantheon, 1983). For contemporary views, see Charles W. Earle, "The Opium Habit: A Statistical and Clinical Lecture," *Chicago Medical Review* 2 (1880): 442–46; "The Use and Abuse of Opium," Massachusetts State Board of Health, Third Annual Report (Boston: Wright and Potter, 1872), both reprinted in H. Wayne Morgan, ed., *Yesterday's Addicts: American Society and Drug Abuse* (Norman: University of Oklahoma Press, 1974). See also David Musto, *The American Disease: Origins of Narcotics Control* (New Haven, Conn.: Yale University Press, 1983), 75.

18. "Gabe Foster's Opium Den," *Police Gazette*, April 3, 1880, 7; "Slaves to a Deadly Infatuation," *Police Gazette*, August 20, 1881, 16. On perceptions of opium dens in frontier towns, see (in Dirlik, *Chinese on the American Frontier*): Leisman, "Utah's Chinatowns"; Florence Lister and Robert Lister, "Chinese Sojourners in Territorial Prescott"; Russell Maghaghi, "Virginia City's Chinese Community, 1860–1880." See also Arlen Ray Wilson, "The Rock Springs, Wyoming, Chinese Massacre, 1885" (PhD thesis, University of Wyoming, 1967), 20. Charles Dickens first popularized the opium den in his unfinished novel *Mystery of Edwin Drood* (London: Oxford University Press, 1966), published posthumously in America in 1871. See Barry Milligan, *Pleasures and Pains: Opium and the Orient in Nineteenth-Century British Culture* (Charlottesville: University Press of Virginia, 1995), 85.

19. "Opium Smoking in China," *Harper's Weekly*, September 4, 1880, 565. "Opium

Smoking in New York" and "American Opium Smoking," in *Harper's Weekly*, September 24, 1881, 645.

20. *Red Bluff Sentinel*, February 7, 1880; *Sacramento Daily-Record Union*, February 23, 1880, and April 21, 1881; *Russian River Flag*, April 21, 1881. For many, Chinese prostitutes "embodied syphilis" and other sexually transmitted diseases. Shah, *Contagious Divide*, 93–94, 107–9.

21. Shih-Shan Henry Tsai, *China and the Overseas Chinese in the United States* (Fayetteville: University of Arkansas Press, 1984), 73; Jack Chen, *The Chinese of America* (New York: HarperCollins, 1981), 151; Gyory, *Closing the Gate*, 257.

22. As Mary Ting Lui notes, local and state laws prohibiting opium smoking deliberately targeted the Chinese; opium was widely available in the form of medicines and "tonics" that were not prohibited. Lui, *Chinatown Trunk Murder*. See also, John R. Wunder, "The Chinese and the Courts: Justice Denied?" *Pacific Historical Review* 52 no. 2 (May 1983): 191–211. State laws and fines were mostly ineffectual at curbing opium smoking but did push white users to find their own venues. Courtwright, *Dark Paradise*, 78. Some of these court challenges proved effective. For example, in the case *Yick Wo v. Hopkins* the Supreme Court held that the San Francisco Board of Supervisor's laundry regulations were discriminatory in practice, thus violating the Fourteenth Amendment's "equal protection" clause. Charles J. McClain, *In Search of Equality: The Chinese Struggle against Discrimination in Nineteenth-Century America* (Berkeley: University of California Press, 1994), 115–16. Challenges to segregated schooling, and to the legality of exclusion itself, met with mixed success in court. The Supreme Court validated both in the 1890s with the *Plessy v. Ferguson* decision on "separate but equal" facilities (1896) and the power to exclude as an act of national sovereignty in the *Yue Ting v. the United States* decision (1893). McClain, *In Search of Equality*, 205–11.

23. *New York Herald*, May 10, 11, 12, 1883.

24. *New York World*, May 10, 11, 1883. The *World*'s only striking headline about this story appeared the day before Joseph Pulitzer took over the paper on May 11. Subsequently, the new editor Pulitzer buried the story on page 5 under a less sensational headline, "The Chinese in Mott Street," then abandoned it altogether.

25. The *New York Times* had no love for Irish workers; the editorial suggested facetiously that the Chinese, more industrious and willing to labor for low wages than the Irish, were thus more desirable citizens. *New York Times*, May 13, 1883.

26. "Our Chinamen," *Daily Graphic*, May 3, 1883. The *Daily Graphic*, though nominally a Democratic paper, was edited in this period by Isaac M. Gregory, who also edited the Republican-leaning *Puck* humor magazine. See *Journalism: Its Relation to and Influence upon Political, Social, Professional, Financial, and Commercial Life of the United States of America* (New York Press Club, 1905), 68. The gambling story referenced a court case involving merchant Tom Lee, known as the richest Chinese man in New York City, married to a German woman, and the city's only Chinese deputy sheriff. Accused by his Chinese tenants of demanding protection money from owners of gambling dens, he was indicted and stripped of his position but later acquitted when a witness recanted his testimony. Wong supported Lee, though he later launched his own anti-gambling

investigation. Seligman, *The First Chinese American*, 104. See also Qingsong Zhang, "The Origins of the Chinese Americanization Movement: Wong Chin Foo and the Chinese Equal Rights League," in *Claiming America: Constructing Chinese American Identities in the Exclusion Era*, ed. K. Scott Wong and Sucheng Chan (Philadelphia: Temple University Press, 1998), 48–49.

27. Editorial, *Daily Graphic*, May 11, 1883; "The Chinese Opium Dens," *Daily Graphic*, May 11, 1883.

28. "A Growing Metropolitan Evil" and "Lessons from Opium Smoking," from *Frank Leslie's Illustrated Newspaper*, May 12, 1883, 181.

29. "New York City—The Opium Dens at Pell and Mott Streets" and "The Chinese Opium Dens in New York" (text), in *Frank Leslie's Illustrated Newspaper*, May 19, 1883, 204.

30. "The Mongolian Curse," *Police Gazette*, June 2, 1883, 9; editorial, "The Opium Wars," appears on page 6.

31. *New York Times*, June 1, 1883. Philadelphia den owner Kate Chisom described her own introduction to opium smoking not in a Chinatown den but rather in the opium parlor of a French woman named Mrs. Fanlan. *New York Times*, August 29, 1883.

32. "In the Grip of Fiends," *Police Gazette*, August 9, 1884, 1; editorial under the title "The Curse of Opium" found on page 3 (emphasis added).

33. New York cases in *Sacramento Daily Record-Union*, May 12, 1883 (quote), May 23, 1883; *Cheyenne Weekly Leader*, January 31, 1884 (also in the *Daily Leader*, January 24, 1884); *Daily Alta-California*, July 3, 1885 (Davenport case); "The Revolting Revelations in New York," *Sacramento Daily Record-Union*, October 25, 1890. Boston cases in Editorial, *Laramie Weekly Boomerang*, October 8, 1885 (also in *Daily Boomerang*, October 3, 1885); "Victim of a Chinese Opium Den," *Sacramento Daily Record-Union*, June 10, 1886. Chicago cases in "Chicago 'Pipe Hitters,'" *Sacramento Daily Record-Union*, May 14, 1883; "Enticing Them to Ruin," in *Cheyenne Daily Sun*, December 11, 1884; "Killed by Opium Smoking" [Actress Jennie Woods case] in *Cheyenne Daily Leader*, April 7, 1886. "The Chinese Meetings at the East, *Sacramento Daily Record-Union*, April 8, 1886. Philadelphia case in *Cheyenne Weekly Leader*, June 7, 1883 (also in the *Daily Leader*, June 3, 1883). Baltimore case in "Baltimore's Opium Dens," *Laramie Weekly Boomerang*, December 24, 1885 (also in *Daily Boomerang*, December 23, 1885). Summary in "The Chinese in Eastern Cities," *Los Angeles Daily Herald*, September 21, 1887 (quote). Interior western papers also flagged the West Coast cities for vice: see "Who Are Most Affected," *Cheyenne Daily Sun*, September 16, 1885. Allegations in San Francisco in "Startling Facts: Discoveries of the Supervisors of San Francisco," *Sacramento Daily Record-Union*, July 22, 1885. Some papers also noted local, western cases. Cheyenne, Wyoming, cases in "Hittin' the Pipe," *Cheyenne Democratic Leader*, January 31, 1885; "Cheyenne Opium Dens," *Laramie Weekly Boomerange*, October 28, 1886.

34. Wong quoted in Seligman, *First Chinese American*, 103, 122–23. On Wong's political activities, see Qingsong Zhang, "The Origins of the Chinese Americanization Movement: Wong Chin Foo and the Chinese Equal Rights League," in Wong and Chan, *Claiming America*, 48–9.

35. Zheng Zaoru, July 1884, quoted in Seligman, *First Chinese American*, 121. On

Wong's organizing activities, see Seligman, *First Chinese American*, 120–33. Huie Kin, *Reminiscences of an Early Chinese Minister* (1932), excerpt published in Judy Yung, Gordon H. Chang, and Him Mark Lai, eds., *Chinese American Voices: From the Gold Rush to the Present* (Berkeley: University of California Press, 2006), 57–67. On the Democrats' embrace of the opium den to appeal to working-class men's desire for Chinese exclusion, see Carl Sandmayer, *The Anti-Chinese Movement in California* (Urbana: Illinois University Press, 1939), 74.

36. "The Chinese Picnic," *Police Gazette*, June 20, 1885, 1; editorial, "DO WE?" on page 2 (emphasis in original).

37. "What We Have Come To," "A Wholesale Lynching," *Police Gazette*, July 4, 1885, 4–5; editorial, "A Strange Defense," on page 2.

38. 1885 was the worst year of anti-Chinese violence in the United States. Gyory, *Closing the Gate*, 4n5. According to John R. Wunder, the two-year period of 1885–86 contained nearly half of the recorded violent outbreaks against the Chinese in America over the sixty years between 1850 and 1910. Wunder, "Anti-Chinese Violence in the American West, 1850–1910," in *Law for the Elephant, Law for the Beaver: Essays in the Legal History of the North American West*, ed. John McLaren et al. (Regina, Sask.: Canadian Plains Research Center, 1992), 220–23; Paul Crane and Alfred Larson, "The Chinese Massacre," pt. 1, *Annals of Wyoming*, vol. 12, no. 1 (January 1940), 53–54.

39. On the impact of an earlier strike in 1875 upon the spread of Knights of Labor, see Wilson, "The Rock Springs, Wyoming, Chinese Massacre," 27, 69–70; see also David A. Wolff, *Industrializing the Rockies: Growth, Competition and Turmoil in the Coalfields of Colorado and Wyoming, 1868–1914* (Boulder: University Press of Colorado, 2003), 86–100.

40. By 1885, in Rock Springs, Chinese workers not only outnumbered their European/American counterparts but were also more likely to be employed during hard times. See Timothy Dean Draper, "A Little Kingdom of Mixed Nationalities: Race, Ethnicity, and Class in a Western Urban Community—Rock Springs, Wyoming, 1869–1929" (PhD diss., Northern Illinois University, 2007), 98; Robert B. Rhode, *Booms and Busts on Bitter Creek: A History of Rock Springs, Wyoming* (Boulder, Colo.: Pruett, 1987), 49–50.

41. As Alexander Saxton writes, "The white miners involved seem to have been, like the Chinese, mostly aliens. They were described as Cornish, Welsh, Irish, English, and Scandinavian." Saxton, *Indispensable Enemy*, 203.

42. Detailed accounts of the massacre can be found in Yen, "Rock Springs Incident," 355–65; Wolff, *Industrializing the Rockies*, 101–2; for a map of incidents between 1870 and 1900, see Sucheng Chan, "Introduction," in *Bitter Melon: Stories from the Last Rural Chinese Town in America*, ed. Jeff Gillenkirk and James Motlow (Seattle: University of Washington Press, 1987), 25.

43. The "unsafe for women" grievance was second on the list sent by miners to Union Pacific. Isaac H. Bromley, the Union Pacific agent who summarized the investigation afterward, dismissed the charge as unfounded. Bromley, *Chinese Massacre*, 22, 35 (quote), 38. See also Union Pacific, "The Chinese Riot and Massacre of September 2, 1885," chap. 6 in *History of Union Pacific Coal Mines*, 85–86; Dell Isham, *Rock Springs Massacre, 1885* (Fort Collins, Colo.: Dell Isham, 1969), 22. It is last of seven grievances listed by Rhode, in *Booms and Busts*, 56–57. Other sources do not mention the accusation. Inflammatory

reporting prior to the massacre noted in Zaolan Zhou, *Qing Perceptions of Anti-Chinese Violence in the United States: Case Studies from the American West* (master's thesis, University of Wyoming, 2008), 49. Violence was not the only solution, despite the fact that "white" miners had harbored a long-standing resentment against the Chinese workers, dating back to their role as scabs in the failed 1875 strike, and conditions were harsh. Local organizer John Lewis even took steps to avert it, warning Union Pacific officials in advance that conditions in Rock Springs were reaching a boiling point. Evidence of advance planning can be found in the fact that one witness reported afterward that he had heard a rumor a few days before the massacre that there would be "something doing" in Rock Springs, crediting as his source one of the men who ultimately led the mob. See Union Pacific, "The Chinese Riot and Massacre," 86; Isham, *Rock Springs Massacre* (1885), 22–26; "David G. Thomas' Memories of the Chinese Riot," in Dirlik, *Chinese on the American Frontier*, 349–54.

44. "Hackling the Heathen," *Police Gazette*, September 19, 1885, 9; accompanying text, on page 6, reprinted western wire accounts of the massacre without editorial commentary.

45. "The Massacre of the Chinese at Rock Springs, Wyoming," *Harper's Weekly*, September 26, 1885, 637. The caption alleged that this image was based on a photograph, but it is unlikely that a photograph taken at the scene would capture events so clearly; more likely, the photograph captured the static landscape after the event, and the artist constructed a more compelling, multipart narrative scene.

46. "A Crime against American Womanhood, *Police Gazette*, December 5, 1885, 16; editorial, under the title "An Outrage on American Womanhood," on page 2.

47. "The Chinese Pestilence," *Police Gazette*, December 19, 1885, 8–9. Quotes from editorial, "The Chinese Pestilence," on page 2 (emphasis added).

48. "The Mongol Leper Again," *Police Gazette*, January 1, 1886, 2. See also a report of "little Maggie Westbridge," a thirteen-year old girl sent by her mother to live in a new Brooklyn laundry/den with a Chinese man and another woman, who was removed and placed in foster care. "The Monster Mongolian," *Police Gazette*, June 12, 1886, 6; image, "The Monster Mongol," 8. An example of a lynching appears in the image "Hong Di Had to Die," *Police Gazette*, July 30, 1887, 8; the wire story description, "Lynching a Chinese Murderer," on page 3. For comparison, I discuss African American responses to lynching and creation of anti-lynching iconography in chapter 4.

49. Jean Pfaelzer, *Driven Out: The Forgotten War against Chinese Americans* (New York: Random House, 2007), 180, 182. In Dirlik, *Chinese on the American Frontier*, see Kenneth Owens, "Pierce City Incident, 1885–1886," 259–61; James Karlin, "The Anti-Chinese Outbreaks in Seattle, 1885–1886," 106, 120–29; David Stratton, "The Snake River Massacre of Chinese Miners, 1887," 226. See also James Karlin, "The Anti-Chinese Outbreaks in Tacoma, 1885," *Pacific Northwest Quarterly* 39, no. 2 (April 1948), reprinted in Daniels, *Anti-Chinese Violence in North America*, 279, 283; Draper, "Little Kingdom of Mixed Nationalities," 104–5. Eventually, President Cleveland requested, and Congress approved, $150,000 in reparations for lost property on March 2, 1886. No restitution for loss of lives was requested or granted. See Tsai, *Chinese Experience in America*, 70; Saxton, *Indispensable Enemy*, 203.

50. Wong Chin Foo, "Why Am I a Heathen?," *North American Review* 145, no. 370

(August 1887), and Yan Phou Lee, "Why I Am Not a Heathen: A Rejoinder to Wong Chin Foo," *North American Review* 145, no. 371 (September 1887). Both articles reprinted in Judy Yung, Gordon H. Change, and Him Mark Lai, eds., *Chinese American Voices: From the Gold Rush to the Present* (Berkeley: University of California Press, 2006), 70–78, 79–85. Like other Chinese commentators, Wong dismissed the bitterness of Kearney's anti-Chinese rhetoric, viewing it as proof that the Irish could not compete with the Chinese for industrial work but also recognizing its effectiveness as a political organizing strategy; Lee made a similar argument in 1889. Yan Phou Lee, "The Chinese Must Stay," *North American Review* (April 1889): 477. On Wong's journalistic contributions, see Karl Lo and H. M. Lai, eds., *Chinese Newspapers Published in North America, 1854–1975* (Washington, D.C.: Center for Chinese Research Materials, 1977), 5–6; Hsuan L. Hsu, "Wong Chin Foo's Periodical Writing and Chinese Exclusion," *Genre* 39 (Fall 2006): 83–105. When Denis Kearney arrived in New York and tried (unsuccessfully) to give a rally in July 1883, Wong Chin Foo unsuccessfully challenged him to a public debate; at the time, Wong publicized his challenge and Kearney's decision to decline. He finally debated Kearney in October. Seligman, *First Chinese American*, 114–17, 152–53.

51. "A Barber Shop with an Opium Joint," in Wong Chin Foo, "The Chinese in New York," *Cosmopolitan* 5 (June 1888): 307. "The Chinese of New York" was Wong's "most ambitious ethnographic article," according to Hsuan L. Hsu. Hsu, "Wong Chin Foo's Periodical Writing and Chinese Exclusion," *Genre* 39 (Fall 2006): 83–105.

52. Wong, "Chinese in New York," 297. The Scott Act passed in the House in early September 1888 and was signed into law by president Grover Cleveland on October 1, 1888. Tsai, *Chinese Experience in America*, 73. The U.S. Supreme Court upheld the law in *Chae Chan Ping v. U.S.* on May 13, 1889.

53. "In a Restaurant," in Wong, "Chinese in New York," 302. The article contains a wealth of detail. For example, he explained that it typically cost up to $200 to set up a laundry, and interest rates could be as high as 40 percent. He described the centrality of grocers as sources of capital and communications hubs and specified dishes and seating arrangements in restaurants. Wong, "Chinese in New York," 298, 301, 303, 305.

54. Wong, "Chinese in New York," 299, 302, 304–5, 308, 311. Ironically, initiatives designed to suppress opium use were ineffective; efforts to punish both den keeper and users ignored the latter in deference to the typically wealthy, white clientele. Incidents (such as overdoses) might inspire a crackdown, but generally enforcement was sporadic, municipal and state laws having little effect. National legislation, aimed at curbing imports, did limit opium use among the poor, while upper-class white users shifted to "new and more potent varieties" of opiates, such as heroin and morphine. Courtwright, *Dark Paradise*, 78–86.

55. "Chinatown, New York," in Wong, "Chinese in New York," 299. Why Durkin was chosen for the job is unclear, but perhaps Wong (or the editors of the *Cosmopolitan*) were familiar with his (rather respectful) representations of another nonwhite group: African Americans in the New South. In 1885–87, along with Horace Bradley, he produced images of the New South for American illustrated periodical readers. Durkin's best-known illustrations of the New South in *Harper's Weekly* include "The New Orleans Exposition: Arrivals at the Levee," January 10, 1885; "Carnival at New Orleans," March

7, 1885; "Making the 'Virginia Twist,'" January 29, 1887; "A Voudoo Dance," June 25, 1887; "Scenes of Prison Life in the New South," August 2, 1890. Deborah C. Pollack, *Visual Art and the Urban Evolution of the New South* (Columbia: University of South Carolina Press, 2015), 130–32, 137, 154; Estill Curtis Pennington and James C. Kelly, *The South on Paper: Line, Color and Light* (Spartanburg, S.C.: Robert M. Hicklin Jr., Inc., 1985), p. 38; "Durkin, John," in Peter Hastings Falk, *Who Was Who in American Art* (Madison, Conn.: Soundview, 1985), 177.

56. Senator Joseph Dolph (OR), *Congressional Record*, v. 19, pt. 7, 50th Cong. 1st Session, p. 6570. Senator John Tyler Morgan (AL), *Congressional Record*, v. 19, pt. 7, 50th Cong. 1st Session, p. 6574.

57. Editorial, "Chinese Iniquity," *Police Gazette*, April 23, 1892, 2. Senator Charles Felton (CA), *Congressional Record*, pt. 3, 52nd Congress, 1st Session, p. 3480. On Chinese resistance to exclusion, see Bill Ong Hing, *Making and Remaking Asian American through Immigration Policy, 1850–1990* (Stanford, Calif.: Stanford University Press, 1993); Sandmayer, *Anti-Chinese Movement in California*, 104. See also Wei-Min Wang, "Refusal to Be 'Placed on the Level of Dogs': Geary Act Resistance" (senior thesis, University of Texas, 1996). On the legal challenges sponsored by the Chinese Six Companies, see Christian G. Fritz, "A Nineteenth Century 'Habeas Corpus Mill': The Chinese before the Federal Courts in California," *American Journal of Legal History* 32, 1988; Charles J. McClain and Laurene Wu McClain, "The Chinese Contribution to the Development of American Law," in McClain, *Asian Americans and the Law*, 149. The Supreme Court found exclusion legislation constitutional in the *Yue Ting v. the United States* decision (1893). The Gresham-Yang Treaty of 1894 reaffirmed the provisions of the Geary Act. Tsai, *Chinese Experience in America*, 74–76. Discussion over prohibition of Chinese immigration appears in House Reports #2915, 51st Congress 1st Session, p. 6. For public discussion between Rep. Geary and Robert G. Ingersoll on the ethics of the Geary Act, see "Should the Chinese be Excluded?" *North American Review* 157 (July 1893): 58–67.

58. Jacob Riis, *How the Other Half Lives: Studies among the Tenements of New York* (New York: Scribner's, 1890), 96–99

Chapter 3. "A First-Class Attraction on Any Stage"

1. Sitting Bull quoted by missionary Mary Collins (connected with the Indian Rights Association, or IRA) in early December 1890. Robert M. Utley, *The Lance and the Shield: The Life and Times of Sitting Bull* (New York: Ballantine, 1994), 292. National Indian Defense Association (NIDA) activist Catherine Weldon also tried to convince Sitting Bull to denounce the dance, which she viewed as a "false" religion; she left his camp in frustration in early November. Eileen Pollack, *Woman Walking Ahead: In Search of Catherine Weldon and Sitting Bull* (Albuquerque: University of New Mexico Press, 2002), 121–27; 134–37. On NIDA's efforts to secure tribal land and treaty rights, compared to the IRA's assimilationist approach, see C. Joseph Genetin-Pilawa, *Crooked Paths to Allotment: The Fight over Federal Indian Policy after the Civil War* (Chapel Hill: University of North Carolina Press, 2012). Sitting Bull was not an evangelist for the dance; as Utley notes, he "never danced himself and he never directed the dance." Utley, *Lance and the Shield*, 285.

2. Elmo Scott Watson, "The Last Indian War, 1890–91: A Study in Newspaper Jingoism," *Journalism Quarterly* 20, no. 1 (1943): 205. See also Oliver Knight, *Following the Indian Wars: The Story of Newspaper Correspondents among the Indian Campaigners* (Norman: University of Oklahoma Press, 1993), 311–15; Hugh J. Reilly, *Bound to Have Blood: Frontier Newspapers and the Plains Indian Wars* (Lincoln: University of Nebraska Press, 2010), 113–17. However, Watson and others caution that it is unfair to dismiss all journalists at Pine Ridge as sensationalist. Watson, "Last Indian War," 219; Rani-Henrik Andersson, *The Lakota Ghost Dance of 1890* (Albuquerque: University of New Mexico Press, 2008), 250; Reilly, *Bound to Have Blood*, 125–27. On the political motivations of Democratic papers, who blamed the massacre on the Republican administration, see Rex Allen Smith, *The Moon of Popping Trees* (New York: Reader's Digest Press, 1975), 203. On distortions of the Ghost Dance in illustrated *weekly* magazines, see Karen A. Bearor, "The 'Illustrated American' and the Lakota Ghost Dance," *American Periodicals* 21, no. 2 (2011): 143–63; William Huntzicker, "The 'Sioux Outbreak' in the Illustrated Press," *South Dakota History* 20, no. 4 (Winter 1990): 299–322.

3. Alice Beck Kehoe, *The Ghost Dance: Ethnohistory and Revitalization* (Lincoln: University of Nebraska Press: 2006 (1964)), 30.

4. On the similarities of the Ghost Dance to the Numu's (Northern Paiute) traditional Round Dance see Michael Hitman, *Wovoka and the Ghost Dance* (Lincoln: University of Nebraska Press, 1993), 93–96. On the Ghost Dance as a religious practice see Lee Irwin, *Coming Down from Above: Prophecy, Resistance, and Renewal in Native American Religions* (Norman: University of Oklahoma Press, 2008), 292–99. Arguably, the Lakota Ghost Dance in 1890 was a combination of religious practice and nonviolent protest against the Sioux Act. Gregory E. Smoak, *Ghost Dances and Identity: Prophetic Religion and American Indian Ethnogenesis* (Berkeley: University of California Press, 2006), 167–68.

5. Porcupine's Christian reinterpretation is evident in an interview June 1890 in Irwin, *Coming Down from Above*, 305–7; according to the *San Francisco Examiner*, the interview was conducted by Major Carroll at Camp Creek near the Miles City Agency. "He Saw the Indian Christ," *Examiner*, July 1, 1890. Jeffrey Ostler, *The Plains Sioux and U.S. Colonialism from Lewis and Clark to Wounded Knee* (New York: Cambridge University Press, 2004), 272. Cora DuBois identifies the geographic regions most affected by the earlier dance in California in *The 1870s Ghost Dance* (Berkeley: University of California Press, 2007 [1939]), xiii, xxi. On genocide of California Native Americans see Benjamin Madley, *An American Genocide: The United States and the California Indian Catastrophe, 1846–1873* (New Haven: Yale University Press, 2016). See also Boyd Cothran, *Remembering the Modoc War: Redemptive Violence and the Making of American Innocence* (Chapel Hill: University of North Carolina Press, 2014); Brendan C. Lindsay, *Murder State: California's Native American Genocide, 1846–1873* (Lincoln: University of Nebraska Press, 2012); and Clifford E. Trafzer and Joel R. Hyer, eds., *Exterminate Them: Written Accounts of the Murder, Rape, and Enslavement of Native Americans during the California Gold Rush* (Lansing: Michigan State University Press, 1999).

6. Quote from B. S. Paddock, letter to *Omaha Bee*, November 26, 1890, cited in George Kohlbenschlag, *The Whirlwind Passes: Newspaper Correspondents and the Sioux Indian Disturbances of 1890–1891* (Vermillion: University of South Dakota Press, 1990), 39. For

a timeline of how Kicking Bear and Short Bull brought the dance to the Sioux in the summer and fall of 1890, see Irwin, *Coming Down from Above*, 309–11; Smith, *Moon of Popping Trees*, 94. On allotment as a strategy to simultaneously "civilize" the Indian and open reservations for white settlement that was predicated on the annihilation of Indian cultures, see Trachtenberg, *Shades of Hiawatha: Staging Indians, Making Americans* (New York: Hill and Wang, 2004), 29–33. On the division between "progressive" and "non-progressives" over the Sioux Act and the Ghost Dance, and Little Wound and Big Road's warnings about rations, see Louis S. Warren, *God's Red Son: The Ghost Dance Religion and the Making of Modern America* (New York: Basic, 2017), 212–13, 218–220.

7. "The Sioux Reservations," *New York Herald*, November 24, 1890. The Great Sioux Reservation had been established by the Fort Laramie Treaty in 1868 (further shorn of the Black Hills to the west in 1876). The 1889 Sioux Act opened part of the land (roughly half of the land holdings in the earlier reservation) to settlers and divided the rest into six smaller reservations (Standing Rock, Cheyenne River, Rosebud, Pine Ridge, Upper Brule, and Crow Creek). The Sioux interpreted this as a violation of the Fort Laramie Treaty. The act took effect on February 10, 1890; its impact was all the more devastating because the land allocated for the reservations was arid and "unsuitable for farming." Kehoe, *Ghost Dance*, 16–17.

8. On the Sioux Act and consequent divisions among the Lakota see Utley, *Lance and the Shield*, 268–80. It is likely that the purpose of the "special census" was to justify a permanent cut in treaty-mandated rations. Warren, *God's Red Son*, 34.

9. R. L. Craig, "Fact, Public Opinion and Persuasion: The Rise of the Visual in Journalism and Advertising," in *Picturing the Past: Media, History, and Photography*, ed. Bonnie Brennan and Hano Hardt (Urbana: University of Illinois Press, 1999), 36. Michael L. Carlebach, *The Origins of Photojournalism in America* (Washington, D.C.: Smithsonian Institution Press, 1992), 153–65.

10. "The Ghost Dance" by J. M. Meddaugh, 1891, Beinecke Rare Book and Manuscript Library, Yale University; the photograph was likely taken in late summer 1890 at No Water's camp north of Pine Ridge Agency. "Sitting Bull's Ghost Dance," George W. Scott, 1890, Minnesota Historical Society Library, Negative 36841. Sam Clover, the original photographer, likely sold his visual scoop to photographer George W. Scott, stationed with the army in Fort Yates, some time before December 3. Scott specialized in the sale of Western imagery and Indian portraits as cabinet cards. Richard E. Jensen, R. Eli Paul and John E. Carter, *Eyewitness at Wounded Knee* (Lincoln: University of Nebraska Press, 1991), 7–8. A third photographer attempted to take a photograph of the Ghost Dance at White Clay Creek (on Pine Ridge Reservation) with a portable camera, only to find himself surrounded by angry participants who did not want the dance recorded; they allegedly smashed his camera "to fragments." Story recounted by Keeps-the-Battle to Warren King Moorehead (quoted from the *Philadelphia Press*) in W. Fletcher Johnson, *The Red Record of the Sioux: Life of Sitting Bull and History of the Indian War 1890–1891* (Philadelphia: Edgewood, 1891), 342–45. See also Jensen, Paul, and Carter, *Eyewitness to Wounded Knee*, 7.

11. "The Ghost Dance by the Ogallala Sioux at Pine Ridge Agency," *Harper's Weekly*, December 6, 1890 (probably available around November 29). Photograph of Arapaho

dance, dated 1892–93, reprinted in James Mooney, *The Ghost Dance Religion and the Sioux Outbreak of 1890* (Lincoln: University of Nebraska Press, 1991 [1896]), 925.

12. Allen Forman, "Newspaper Art and Artists," *Quarterly Illustrator* 1, no. 4 (1893), 313. Regular news publication of photographs began with the *New York Tribune* in 1897, though other papers experimented with the process before then. Craig, "Fact, Public Opinion, and Persuasion," 45. Pulitzer introduced six new high-speed "Hoe" presses at the *World* in 1884 and an additional "double Hoe Perfecting press" in March 1885. These could produce up to eighty thousand eight-page copies per hour. George Juergens, *Joseph Pulitzer and the* New York World (Princeton, N.J.: Princeton University Press, 1966), 347–49. Hearst installed two similar presses at the *Examiner* in October 1889, updating a less efficient double-perfecting press purchased in 1888. *Examiner*, October 20, 1889. See also Ben Proctor, *William Randolph Hearst: The Early Years, 1863–1910* (Oxford: Oxford University Press, 1998), 56. As newspaper illustration became more common, *Harper's Weekly* saw it as a positive: "There is no more reason why the reader should not receive accurate information or pleasing or satisfying impressions through the fruits of the engraver's art than there is why he should not be given in legible type the printed matter that is suited to his needs and tastes." "Things Talked Of," *Harper's Weekly*, xxxvii, April 22, 1893, 367. Conservative critic E. L. Godkin disagreed, calling illustrated news a "childish view of the world," evidence of the dumbing down of news. Godkin, "Newspaper Pictures," *The Nation*, April 27, 1893.

13. Hearst, "with instinctive theatrical skill, built up suspense that carried from day to day like a serial thriller. . . . He loved 'created news' that could be spun out from day to day." W. A. Swanberg, *Citizen Hearst: A Biography of William Randolph Hearst* (New York: Bantam, 1971), 56.

14. Pulitzer quote in the *New York World*, February 21, 1884, cited in Juergens, *Joseph Pulitzer*, 94. Pulitzer was personally ambivalent about the images; he attempted on at least one occasion to scale them back—the negative effect on circulation forced him to resume. He prided himself on "accuracy" and "wanted his reporters to infuse their articles with color without sacrificing information." Paul Starr, *The Creation of Media: Political Origins of Modern Communications* (New York: Basic, 2005), 256. See also James McGrath Morris, *Pulitzer: A Life in Politics, Print, and Power* (New York: Harper Perennial, 2011).

15. William Randolph Hearst to Father [n.d. (1885)], printed in full in Ken Whyte, *The Uncrowned King: The Sensational Rise of William Randolph Hearst* (Berkeley, Calif.: Counterpoint, 2009), 27 (emphasis added). On Hearst's introduction of images and other innovations at the *San Francisco Examiner*, many modeled on Pulitzer's *World*, see Proctor, *William Randolph Hearst*, chap. 3; David Nasaw, *The Chief: The Life of William Randolph Hearst* (New York: Mariner, 2001), 69–81; Swanberg, *Citizen Hearst*; Ferdinand Lundberg, *Imperial Hearst: A Social Biography* (New York: Forgotten, 2012 (1936)).

16. Pulitzer relinquished editorial control of the *World* that fall, due to blindness; it is unclear how this may have influenced decisions about visual coverage of the Ghost Dance. *World*, October, 16, 1890. Juergens, *Joseph Pulitzer*, 364. The lack of indexing for the *World* and *Examiner*, and the absence of content tagging for images in the nineteenth-century press more generally, tends to discourage scholarly analysis of daily news il-

lustration. The four papers studied here served discreet urban areas, but all circulated beyond their own regions, seeking national consumers and readers. The *Tribune*, founded in 1847 and run by co-owner Joseph Medill through to his death in 1899 (with a brief eight-year period run by Liberal maverick Horace White), was Republican and pro-Lincoln through the war years. After Medill resumed control in 1874, it continued to be a Republican stalwart press. It began to introduce images to compete with the *Chicago Daily News*. See "Chicago Tribune," *Encyclopedia of Chicago*, http://www.encyclopedia .chicagohistory.org/pages/275.html. The *New York Herald* had led the way with images in the 1840s but nearly eliminated them by 1850, reintroducing them only in 1889. Joshua Brown, *Beyond the Lines: Pictorial Reporting, Everyday Life, and the Crisis of Gilded Age America* (Berkeley: University of California Press, 2002), 14.

17. Rebecca Zurier, *Picturing the City: Urban Vision and the Ashcan School* (University of California Press, 2006), 71–72. On the weeklies as supplements to the daily news, see Brown, *Beyond the Lines*, 32. The one daily to attempt illustrated news coverage in the 1870s and early 1880s was the *New York Daily Graphic*, which I discuss briefly in chapter 1, deployed images rather differently.

18. Indian Affairs agents made several attempts to stop the dancing at the Lower Sioux reservations in fall 1890. Ostler, *Plains Sioux*, 276–78. These attempts led occasionally to forceful resistance, sometimes prompted by aggressive behavior of the Indian Police dispatched to stop the dance. Warren, *God's Red Son*, 247.

19. Headlines in the *San Francisco Examiner* drummed up fears of a general pan-Indian uprising by juxtaposing Ghost Dance news with stories about warlike behavior exhibited by a number of Indian tribes. See "The Indian Messiah," *Examiner*, May 24, 1890; "Troops sfter the Apaches," *Examiner*, June 6, 1890; "Cheyennes on the Warpath," *Examiner*, June 12, 1890; "More Settlers Fleeing," *Examiner*, June 14, 1890; "How They Settled It," *Examiner*, June 15, 1890; "Massacred by the Indians," *Examiner*, June 18, 1890; "Killed by Cheyennes," *Examiner*, September 12, 1890; "Like Demons to the Death," *Examiner*, September 18, 1890.

20. "A Weird Incantation," *San Francisco Examiner*, October 5, 1890. The text of the article summarized and quoted from an annual report by Dr. Washington Matthews for the Smithsonian's Bureau of Ethnography. Apart from the *Examiner's* long interest in the Ghost Dance, the use of this image is difficult to explain, and the *Examiner* offered no rationale for its decision to publish it on this date. The same image appeared in another Ghost Dance article several weeks later in the weekly *Illustrated American's* December 13, 1890, issue (probably available around December 6). The Matthews report had been republished in the *American Archeological and Building News* 28, no. 746 (April 12, 1890). See Bearor, "Illustrated American," 156.

21. Though not generally counted among sensational illustrated dailies of the period, the *Tribune* had introduced news illustrations by early 1889 and echoed many of the visual strategies of the *World* and *Examiner*. "The Tribune's Pictures," *Chicago Tribune*, January 13, 1889. On the paper's continued allegiance to the Republican Party, in spite of the tariff issue, see editorial, Chicago *Tribune*, May 27, 1890.

22. "To Wipe Out the Whites," *Chicago Tribune*, October 28, 1890. The leaked memo was also published in the *Washington Post*, October 28, 1890. Election day was November

4. It's unclear how McLaughlin's report to the Commissioner of Indian Affairs (dated October 17) came to be published in the two papers. The full text of this report is available in Usher L. Burdick, *Last Days of Sitting Bull, Sioux Medicine Chief* (Baltimore, Md.: Wirth, 1941), 89–94. Benjamin Harrison to SW, October 31, 1890, Benjamin Harrison Papers, Library of Congress, reel 29, cited in Ostler, *Plains Sioux*, 292.

23. *New York World*, November 2, 1890. I have been unable to find a photograph of the two men together in civilian clothing or in such a pose. The only dual portraits remain from Sitting Bull's four-month tour with the *Wild West* in 1885 and were taken (in costume) at the Notman Studio in Montreal. *New York World*, November 2, 1890. Hofacker left the *World* in 1891 to join the fledgling *New York Recorder*. Forman, "Newspaper Art and Artists," 323.

24. *New York World*, November 2, 1890.

25. Ibid. On the cultural significance of Buffalo Bill Cody and his *Wild West* show in the 1880s and 1890s see Joy Kasson, *Buffalo Bill's Wild West: Celebrity, Memory, and Popular History* (New York: Hill and Wang, 2000); L. G. Moses, *Wild West Shows and the Images of American Indians, 1883–1933* (Albuquerque: University of New Mexico Press, 1996); Sarah J. Blackstone, *Buckskins, Bullets, and Business: A History of Buffalo Bill's Wild West* (Westport, Conn.: Greenwood, 1986); Louis Pfaller, "'Enemies in '76, Friends in '85': Sitting Bull and Buffalo Bill," *Prologue* 1 (1969); Sam A. Maddra, *Hostiles? The Lakota Ghost Dance and Buffalo Bill's Wild West* (Norman: University of Oklahoma Press, 2006); Louis Warren, *Buffalo Bill's America: William Cody and the Wild West Show* (New York: Vintage, 2006); Roger A. Hall, *Performing the American Frontier, 1870–1906* (Cambridge: Cambridge University Press, 2001), 143. On Cody's emulation of P. T. Barnum in using Indians as an attraction—as Barnum said, "They will draw"—see Linda Frost, *Never One Nation: Freaks, Savages, and Whiteness* (Minneapolis: University of Minnesota Press, 2005), 1. McLaughlin is typically photographed with short hair, a mustache, and a bowler hat. Andersson points out that the 7th Cavalry enlisted upon hearing rumors of Sitting Bull's involvement in the Ghost Dance. Andersson, *Lakota Ghost Dance of 1890*, 199. Smith, *Moon of Popping Trees*, 116 (quote).

26. Sitting Bull's opposition to the Sioux Act detailed in Utley, *Lance and the Shield*, 268–22, 278, 281. Smith, *Moon of Popping Trees*, 112; see also Jeffrey Ostler, *Plains Sioux*, 276–79. On the Ghost Dance as a spiritual endeavor, rather than a war dance, see Kehoe, *Ghost Dance*, 30; Smoak, *Ghost Dances and Identity*, chap. 5; Irwin, *Coming Down from Above*, 299–312. Given the dire conditions among the Sioux, however, it is clear that the dance also represented a form of anti-colonialist resistance, in defiance of prohibitions against ritual dancing. Ostler, *Plains Sioux*, 261–62, 272.

27. Popular histories of the Custer story published in the 1880s went through many printings. These include James Buel, *Heroes of the Plains* (St. Louis: Historical Publishing, 1881, 1882, 1883, 1884, 1889); E. G. Cattermole, *Famous Frontiersmen, Pioneers and Scouts: The Vanguards of American Civilization* (Tarrytown, N.Y.: Abbatt, 1926 version on Hathi Trust, probably unchanged from first 1883 publication; reprinted in 1883, 1884, 1886, 1890); General George Custer, *My Life on the Plains and Horrors of Indian Warfare* (1874; repr. 1883, 1885, 1886; repub. as *Wild Life on the Plains* in 1891); T. M. Newson, *Thrilling Scenes among the Indians, with a Graphic Description of Custer's Last Fight with Sitting Bull*

(New York: Belford and Clark, 1884 [repr. ed.]; repr. in 1888, 1889, 1890); Judson Elliot Walker, *Campaigns of General Custer in the Northwest, and the Final Surrender of Sitting Bull* (New York: Jenkins and Thomas, 1881).

28. Dozens of dime novels in the 1880s featured Buffalo Bill, and several featured Sitting Bull; many referenced Custer's defeat. On dime novels see Christine Bold, *Selling the Wild West Popular Western Fiction, 1860 to 1960* (Bloomington: Indiana University Press, 1987); Bill Brown, *Reading the West: An Anthology of Dime Westerns* (New York: Bedford/St. Martin's, 1997). It was in *Buffalo Bill's Grip; or, Oath-Bound for Custer* (1883; repr. 1885, 1890) that dime novel pioneer Prentiss Ingraham told the story of Cody's duel with Yellow [Hand] and taking the "first scalp for Custer"—a story he revised two decades later with Cody as a survivor of Little Bighorn. Published in *Beadle's Weekly*, January 13–March 10, 1883. Custer was known in these stories as the "soul of chivalry," "brave heart," and noted for his "flowing blond locks." Buffalo Bill Cody emulated many of these characteristics in his fictional and public personae. On Custer's status as heroic martyr see Brian Dippie, *Custer's Last Stand: The Anatomy of an American Myth* (Lincoln: University of Nebraska Press, 1994), 31. See also Robert M. Utley, *Custer and the Great Controversy: The Origin and Development of a Legend* (Los Angeles: Westernlore, 1962).

29. Sitting Bull was "a major symbol of native savagery and resistance," according to John M. Coward in *The Newspaper Indian: Native American Identity in the Press, 1820–1890* (Urbana: University of Illinois Press, 1999), 163. See also Coward, *Indians Illustrated: The Image of Native Americans in the Pictorial Press* (Urbana: University of Illinois Press, 2015), 126; Coward, "Making Sense of Savagery: Native American Cartoons in *The Daily Graphic*," *Visual Communication Quarterly* 19 (October–December 2012): 200–215. Sitting Bull was a talented pictographic artist in his own right. He had recorded his own history as a warrior in images but had by the late 1880s ceased to share these with reporters. See for example Candace Greene, "Verbal Meets Visual: Sitting Bull and the Representation of History," *Ethnohistory* 62, no. 2 (April 2015): 217–40.

30. "The Indian Craze over the New Messiah," *Frank Leslie's Illustrated Newspaper*, November 22, 1890, probably available around November 15. On Russell B. Harrison's editorship of *Leslie's* and the Republican Party's efforts to boost settlement and otherwise influence the South Dakota legislature's vote in December 1890 see Heather Cox Richardson, *Wounded Knee: Party Politics and the Road to an American Massacre* (New York: Basic, 2010), 93.

31. Journalists began arriving with the troops on November 20; until then, most national papers relied on Charles Cressey's inflammatory copy for the *Omaha Bee*. See Kohlbenschlag, *Whirlwind Passes*, 33–35; Utley, *Lance and the Shield*, 285–86.

32. *Chicago Tribune, Herald*, November 17, 1890; *World*, November 18, 1890; *Herald*, November 23, 1890. Ruger's report (dated December 7, 1890) criticized the Department of Interior's oversight, but he did not view the Ghost Dance as a major threat. Harrison's decision to move troops in before Ruger's report was complete was probably a response to internal pressure from the Pine Ridge agent but also to political pressures from Democratic Party and desire to placate South Dakota legislature in advance of its vote for U.S. Senator; publicly he justified the buildup on the grounds that preemptive military action was necessary to protect incoming settlers. Ostler, *Plains Sioux*, 293–95.

33. "Redskins Bloody Work" and "The 'Ghost Dance,'" *Chicago Tribune*, November 20, 1890.

34. "Sitting Bull," *Chicago Tribune*, November 20, 1890. "Sitting Bull of the Custer Massacre," [Photographer unknown], The Denver Public Library, Western History Collection (X-31384). Of all the photographs of Sitting Bull, the provenance of this one is the most elusive. Many photographers have claimed credit for the photo. There are claims that it dated to 1883; however, it seems likely that the hat may be the one Cody reportedly gave to Sitting Bull at the conclusion of the *Wild West* tour in October 1885. According to Ernie LaPointe in his collection of oral histories about his great-grandfather Sitting Bull, this was "a white hat with a monarch butterfly on the front of the headband." Ernie LaPointe, *Sitting Bull: His Life and Legacy* (Salt Lake City: Gibbs Smith, 2009), 88. If so, this photograph was likely taken in fall 1885, either by western photographer D. H. Barry (who was traveling with the show) or by another photographer near Standing Rock, possibly in Pierre or Bismarck. The fact that the image does not appear in any of the histories of Sitting Bull published in the early 1880s supports the idea that it was not taken with others from that period. The 1890 reprint with the etched caption "Sitting Bull of the Custer Massacre" appears to have been reproduced, perhaps for sale to journalists at Pine Ridge, sometime during the Ghost Dance crisis in fall 1890.

35. Short Bull's "sermon" was a sensational invention, but at the time it bolstered the *Tribune*'s support for the military buildup. Allegedly delivered on October 31 at the Red Leaf camp at Pine Ridge, the sermon was published in the Republican-leaning *Chicago Tribune* on November 22, 1890, apparently based on an interview with General Miles, who saw it as grounds for military action. Based on its deviation from known Lakota spiritual practices, Ostler believes that it was likely a "fabrication." Ostler, *Plains Sioux*, 296. Short Bull's actual teachings were peaceful. William S. E. Coleman, *Voices of Wounded Knee* (Lincoln: University of Nebraska Press, 2000), 64–65; Warren, *God's Red Son*, 188.

36. *Herald*, November 24, 1890. Western journalist Charles Wesley Allen, who wrote for the *Chadron Advocate*, recalled that the *Herald* asked him to produce "good graphic story" as soon as there was any sign of engagement with troops. *Chadron Advocate*, November 21, 1891, reprinted in Charles Wesley Allen, *From Fort Laramie to Wounded Knee*, edited and with an introduction by Richard E. Jensen (Lincoln: University of Nebraska Press, 1997), 151.

37. "Crazed by Fanaticism," *Examiner*, November 24, 1890.

38. Reporters alleged wildly inflated numbers of between fifteen thousand and twenty-seven thousand Ghost Dancers, when in fact there were fewer than five thousand men, women and children dancing at its peak. More than seven thousand soldiers were deployed to quell the "outbreak."

39. Cody had only recently returned to the United States, midway through a tour in France, out of necessity, to defend the *Wild West* show from critics who believed it was abusive to its Indian performers. (Cody's record is mixed. The show's survival depended heavily on the popularity of the Show Indians as "authentic" historical figures. A few of these had died on tour, but there is evidence that Cody also believed they should be

allowed to make their own choices about work, particularly when conditions on reservations were equally dangerous.) Miles's request probably stemmed from his success
with other informal negotiations of this kind; Cody's motivations were more complex.
Pfaller, "Enemies in '76, Friends in '85," 30–31. See also Robert M. Utley, *The Last Days of
the Sioux Nation* (New Haven, Conn.: Yale University Press, 1963), 125–26; Utley, *Lance
and the Shield*, 293; Ostler, *Plains Sioux*, 313, 315. On the Secretary of Interior's charges of
mistreatment and Cody's return from France to defend the show's treatment of "Show
Indians" see Moses, *Wild West Shows*, 97–105.

40. Henry Nash Smith calls Cody "the most highly publicized figure in all the history
of the Wild West"—a product of writers' minds and popular demand. Smith, *Virgin
Land*, 103. See also Kasson, *Buffalo Bill's Wild West*, 27. The December appearance at Pine
Ridge of his Show Indians, who attempted to bring in the last of the dancers, furthered
this impression. As L. G. Moses notes, there is irony that the *Wild West* performers,
whose job onstage was to perform Indian savagery and attacks on settlers, were enlisted
as links between the Ghost Dancers and the values of American "civilization." Moses,
Wild West Shows, 97–105.

41. Andersson, *Lakota Ghost Dance*, 193, 201–7, and (on consensus about Sitting Bull's
role) 219, 221, 225. The November 25, 1890, *Omaha Bee* account of the interview is unclear:
it identified No Water and Little Wound as the men interviewed but later quoted Big
Road (supported by whispered comments from Little Wound). Little Wound's views on
land and rations cited in *New York Times* and *Washington Post*, November 30, 1890. Months
later, after the massacre at Wounded Knee, Little Wound expressed his belief that many
newspaper sources (including Indian Police, scouts, and agency staff) had misrepresented
the dance to curry favor with Indian Affairs agents; the Indian Police had "lied a great
deal" about the dance, he said. See Warren, *God's Red Son*, 234, 255 (quote). On Congress's
cut in funding for treaty-mandated rations, see *New York Times*, December 1, 1890.

42. "Off the Fight the Sioux," *Examiner*, December 5, 1890. See also "The Indian War
Cloud," *Examiner*, December 3, 1890. By contrast, the *World* visualized the situation
exclusively in its Sunday coverage, to accompany a quasi-educational material; images
included portraits (Chief Gall, Standing Cow) or a Sunday gallery of fourteen portraits
from the 1870s. "In Sioux Country," November 30, 1890; "The Sioux Nation," *World*,
December 7, 1890. The *Herald* suspended its visual coverage entirely in early December.
The *World* did, however, mock the scramble for photographs in an editorial cartoon, "To
Settle the Indian Troubles—Bring in the Camera Fiends." *World*, November 30, 1890.

43. As historian Jeffrey Ostler writes, "It was not the Lakota ghost dancers who were
becoming hostile or threatening to use force; it was the United States." Ostler, *Plains
Sioux*, 288.

44. The Ghost Dance as war narrative echoed Democrats' use of the Custer "massacre"
in summer of 1876 as political ammunition against the Grant administration and his
Indian peace policy. Brian W. Dippie, *Custer's Last Stand: The Anatomy of an American
Myth* (Lincoln: University of Nebraska Press, 1994), 11.

45. "The Ghastly Ghost Dance," *World*, December 4, 1890. Hearst's editorial on the
undercount of Sioux as another abuse of the administration's census power in "The
Sioux Side of the Story," *San Francisco Examiner*, December 7, 1890. See also images

"Starvation, the Real Article" and "Food for Big Indians," *World*, December 14, 1890. Such imagery contributed by blaming the Sioux's suffering on the inaccurate census, linking it to Democrats' allegations that the Harrison administration had deliberately undercounted Democratic urban voters in the larger national census that year. Richardson, *Wounded Knee*, 236–38.

46. "The Navajo Fire Dance," *Illustrated American*, December 13, 1890; "The Recent Indian Excitement in the Northwest," *Frank Leslie's Illustrated News*, December 13, 1890. Both were likely available from December 6, 1890. Bearor, "Illustrated American," 152–56; William Huntzicker, "Sioux Outbreak," 302–9. On the influence of the captivity narrative on popular perceptions of Native Americans see Robert F. Berkhofer Jr., *The White Man's Indian: Images of the American Indian From Columbus to the Present* (New York: Knopf, 1978), 99.

47. Sickels identifies the artist as Lakota chief Little Big Man. "How Custer Died," *Chicago Tribune*, December 7, 1890. The same images were included in W. Fletcher Johnson's 1891 *Life of Sitting Bull* (pages 114–15) with the same misleading captions, thus entering the more permanent historical record.

48. Quote in Watson, "Last Indian War," 208. On the falseness of the "scare" stories, see Thomas Tibbles in the *Omaha World-Herald*, December 13, 1890. On pressure from editors see Tibbles, *Buckskin and Blanket Days* (1905), cited in Reilly, *Bound to Have Blood*, 118.

49. "Some Real Hair Raisers," *San Francisco Examiner*, December 14, 1890.

50. Ostler, *Plains Sioux*, 315–19. The origin of the word "Stronghold" to describe this naturally screened plateau in the "Bad-Lands" to the northwest of Pine Ridge agency is unclear—perhaps it is not a coincidence that it was the name given to the Lava Beds where the last resistors of the Modoc wars surrendered. On the "Stronghold" in the Modoc war see Madley, *American Genocide*, 342. On Lakota dancers' wariness of the troops see Andersson, *Lakota Ghost Dance of 1890*, 201–9. On Miles's strategy of an "overwhelming" display of force see Ostler, *Plains Sioux*, 300–304; 308–9; Smith, *Moon of Popping Trees*, 119, 124.

51. For a detailed account of Sitting Bull's murder and the conflicting accounts of what happened see Ostler, *Plains Sioux*, 320–23; Utley, *Lance and the Shield*, 295–302; Smith, *Moon of Popping Trees*, 157–60.

52. "[Sitting Bull]," *Chicago Tribune*, December 16, 1890. "Sitting Bull seated full length portrait with pipe and signature," 1884, Item #A2250–0001, [Palmquist and Jurgens, photographers]. State Historical Society of North Dakota. Photographers "sought to portray the passing race before it was too late and so their pictures frequently depicted the subjects before their cameras according to traditional themes." Berkhofer, *White Man's Indian*, 101.

53. "Sitting Bull," *New York World*, December 16, 1890. "Sitting Bull studio portrait with one feather," 1884–1886, Item #1952–7444, [David F. Barry]. State Historical Society of North Dakota. Only the *Herald* declined to find a new image; instead it recycled its "Sitting Bull of the Custer Massacre" image from the month before. *New York Herald*, December 16, 1890.

54. *San Francisco Examiner*, December 17, 1890; copied from the *Illustrated Ameri-*

can, December 13, 1890. "Sitting Bull," 1885, II-83091, Wm. Notman and Son, McCord Museum, Montreal. On the famous photograph of Sitting Bull and Buffalo Bill, see Kasson, *Buffalo Bill's Wild West*, 177–81.

55. "Sitting Bull and His Family," *New York Herald*, December 17, 1890. "Sitting Bull Family Portrait," 1882, Item #A2952, [Photographer Unknown], State Historical Society of North Dakota.

56. "Five Types of American Civilization," *New York World*, December 21, 1890. "Buffalo Bill and His Troupe," 1885, II-94132, Wm. Notman and Son, McCord Museum, Montreal. For a fascinating discussion of the distorting power of captions in news photographs, see Carol Quirke, "Reframing Chicago's Memorial Day Massacre, May 30, 1937," *American Quarterly* 60, no. 1 (March 2008): 129–57.

57. "The Indian Police," *San Francisco Examiner*, December 18, 1890. On the paper's advertising milestone, see "The Foremost Paper," *San Francisco Examiner*, December 22, 1890. By early 1891 the *Examiner* boasted a "sworn circulation" of fifty-seven thousand copies per day, and 15,681 inches of advertising, surpassing its competitors, the *San Francisco Call* and the *San Francisco Chronicle*. *San Francisco Examiner*, January 4, 1891.

58. Military leadership suspended plans to dispatch a cavalry unit to the Stronghold (scheduled for December 16) following Sitting Bull's killing, an event that "had a critical impact" and temporarily halted negotiations. Reilly, *Bound to Have Blood*, 119.

59. See Andersson, *Lakota Ghost Dance of 1890*, 228–32.

60. San Francisco *Examiner*, December 30, 1890.

61. Ostler concludes that "of all those who shaped the events that led to the massacre, Miles had the largest hand." Ostler, *Plains Sioux*, 329–48, 354 (quote). Ostler says 170 to 200 were women and children out of approximately 300 members of Big Foot's people: most were killed while fleeing or butchered or executed far from the site. (Seven of fifty-one injured Sioux would later die of their wounds; twenty-five soldiers died, with an additional fifty-nine wounded, mostly in their own friendly fire). Robert Wooster, *Nelson A. Miles and the Twilight of the Frontier Army* (Lincoln: University of Nebraska Press, 1993), 183–87. See also Smith, *Moon of Popping Trees*, 179–200.

62. See, for example, the *New York Herald*, December 31, 1890. Andersson, *Lakota Ghost Dance of 1890*, 240–45.

63. The *World's* Indian Scout reproduced in cruder form a Remington drawing of the same name that had been published on the cover of *Harper's Weekly* on December 27, 1890 (probably available on about December 20). *World*, January 11, 1891.

64. *San Francisco Examiner*, January 2, 7, 10, 13 and 14, 1891. Hearst's role in determining these images was unclear, as he was in fact in Washington, D.C., at the bedside of his father, who was dying. If this report was accurate, Emma Sickels's intervention as a negotiator with Little Wound, which may have resulted in the final appearance of the remaining Stronghold bands, has been lost to the record, perhaps obscured by the military focus of most histories of the crisis and the massacre at Wounded Knee.

65. *San Francisco Examiner*, January 12, 13, 1891. (Beyond the selection shown, multiple other images appeared in these and the January 8, January 9, and the image-heavy Sunday, January 11, issues of the *Examiner*). The new Ghost Dance image appeared in *Frank Leslie's Illustrated Newspaper* on January 10, 1891 (probably available around January

3). For example, both a Jack the Ripper article and a Whitecap story appeared in the *Examiner's* February 14, 1891, issue.

66. See Huntzicker, "Sioux Outbreak," 314–22.

67. On the commercial power of photographs and other paraphernalia following Wounded Knee, see Christina Klein, "'Everything of Interest in the Late Pine Ridge War Are Held for Us for Sale': Popular Culture and Wounded Knee," *Western Historical Quarterly* 25, no. 1 (Spring 1994): 45–68.

68. Most of the Fort Sheridan prisoners were released from their contracts in April 1892; Kicking Bear and Short Bull were released in October 1892. Many re-joined the *Wild West* for the 1893 Columbian Exhibition performances. Moses, *Wild West Shows*, 106–28. See also Maddra, *Hostiles?*, 86, 110.

69. "Bright Eyes Lectures," *World*, January 19, 1891.

Chapter 4. "A Song without Words"

1. "A Song without Words," Indianapolis *Freeman*, November 2, 1895. This chapter adapts an earlier article, "'A Song without Words:' Lynching Imagery in the 1890s Black Press," in *Journal of African American History* 97, no. 3 (Summer 2012): 240–69.

2. On the evolution of anti-lynching photography, see Leigh Raiford, *Imprisoned in a Luminous Gaze: Photography and the African American Freedom Struggle* (Chapel Hill: University of North Carolina Press, 2011). See also Dora Apel, *Imagery of Lynching: Black Men, White Women, and the Mob* (New Brunswick, N.J.: Rutgers University Press, 2004); Kenneth Gonzales-Day, *Lynching in the West: 1850–1935* (Durham, N.C.: Duke University Press, 2006); Shawn Michelle Smith, "The Evolution of Lynching Photographs," in *Lynching Photographs*, ed. Dora Apel and Shawn Michelle Smith (Berkeley: University of California Press, 2007); Amy Wood, *Lynching and Spectacle: Witnessing Racial Violence in America, 1890–1940* (Chapel Hill: University of North Carolina Press, 2009).

3. On the origins of blues, see Adam Gussow, *Seems Like Murder Here: Southern Violence and the Blues Tradition* (Chicago: University of Chicago Press, 2002).

4. As Garland Martin Taylor suggests, Lewis's "core" visual strategy was the positive depiction of what he saw as "representative" figures; he estimates that Lewis produced 175 images during his tenure at the *Freeman*. See Garland Martin Taylor, "Out of Jest: The Art of Henry Jackson Lewis," *Critical Inquiry* 40, no. 3 (2014): 202. See also Marvin D. Jeter and Mark Cervenka, "H. J. Lewis, Free Man and *Freeman* Artist," *Common Place* 7, no. 3 (April 2007), http://www.common-place-archives.org/vol-07/no-03/jeter -cervenka. On Lewis's earlier work for illustrated weeklies, see Patrick S. Washburn, *The African American Newspaper: Voice of Freedom* (Evanston, Ill.: Northwestern University Press, 2007), 70.

5. On Moses Tucker's satirical cartoons, see Andreá Williams, "Cultivating Black Visuality: The Controversy over Cartoons in the Indianapolis *Freeman*," *American Periodicals* 25, no. 2 (2015): 124–38. On the *Freeman*, see Aleen J. Ratzlaff, "Illustrated African American Journalism: Political Cartooning in the *Indianapolis Freeman*," in *Seeking a Voice: Images of Race and Gender in the 19th Century Press*, ed. David B. Sachsbaum, S. Kitrell Rushing, and Roy Morris Jr. (West Lafayette, Ind.: Purdue University Press, 2009), 131–40; Jeter and Cervenka, "H. J. Lewis." A self-styled political independent, Cooper believed

that the black community put too much faith in the Republican Party to defend their interests. Henry Suggs, *The Black Press in the Middle-West: 1865–1995* (Westport, Conn.: Greenwood, 1996), 56. Cooper supported Democratic candidate Grover Cleveland in the 1888 election and warned Republicans that they would find the victorious Republican Benjamin Harrison disappointing. See "Colored Republicans Jubilant," *Freeman*, November 16, 1888; "The Race Problem," *Freeman*, February 2, 1889; "Time and Prejudice," *Freeman*, March 2, 1889; "The Race Problem," *Freeman*, March 30, 1889.

6. Unless explicitly noted, all newspapers cited in this chapter were produced by African Americans editors and journalists. This chapter examines a broad sample of the period's black press, more than twenty such newspapers, from a range of political perspectives and geographic locations, from years 1889 to 1900. According to I. Garland Penn, there were 206 African American journals in 1893; far fewer now exist in archives. See J. Garland Penn, "The Progress of the Afro-American since Emancipation," in Wells et al., eds., *The Reason Why the Colored American Is Not in the World's Columbian Exhibition*, in Trudier Harris, ed., *Selected Works of Ida B. Wells-Barnett* (New York: Oxford University Press, 1991), 92–116.

7. On the evolution of the black press, see Armistead Pride, *A History of the Black Press* (Washington, D.C.: Howard University Press, 1997); Martin Dann, *The Black Press 1827–1890: The Quest for National Identity* (New York: Putnam's, 1971); David Domke, "The Black Press in the 'Nadir' of African Americans," *Journalism History* 20, no. 3/4 (Autumn 1994); Emma Lou Thornbrough, "American Negro Newspapers, 1880–1914," *Business History Review* 40, no. 4 (Winter 1966): 467–90; Frederick G. Detweiler, *The Negro Press in the United States* (College Park, Md.: McGrath, 1922, 1968); Henry Suggs, ed., *The Black Press of the South* (Westport, Conn.: Greenwood, 1983). (I use the phrase "black press" to remain consistent with decades of scholarship).

8. "Editorial," *A.M.E. Church Review*, July 1892. On the special role of African-American newspapers, see Wells, "The Requirements of Southern Journalism," *A.M.E. Zion Quarterly*, January 1893; Mrs. W. L. Marshall, "The Future of the Afro-American Press," *Trumpet*, reprinted in *Parsons Blade*, September 23, 1893.

9. Portraits of Frederick Douglass abounded: see, for example, "Honorable Frederick Douglass," *Parsons Blade*, December 23, 1893. Samples of religious iconography can be found in *A.M.E. Church Review*, July 1890; "A.M.E. Conference," *St. Paul Appeal*, May 21, 1892; *Detroit Plaindealer*, July 4, 1890; and "Portraits of A.M.E. Bishops Meeting at General Conference in Philadelphia," *St. Paul Appeal*, June 4, 1892. Educational stories appear in "Tuskegee Conference," *Detroit Plaindealer*, March 4, 1892; images of Booker T. Washington, Rev. R. J. [Henry], Secretary Mosi; Mr. M. T. Dillon; Teachers in "Afro-Americans' Work," *St. Paul Appeal*, March 12, 1892; Hamptons Institute, "Hope of Two Nations," *St. Paul Appeal*, June 18, 1892; "Tuskegee College," *St. Paul Appeal*, September 10, 1892; "Taking Advantage of Our Disadvantages," *A.M.E. Church Review*, January 1, 1894.

10. Jackson received wide coverage, including "Great Inducements Offered for a Match between Jackson and Sullivan," *Detroit Plaindealer*, December 6, 1889; "Pete Jackson Cleans Out the Gang," *Cleveland Gazette*, June 21, 1890; "Sporting News," *Detroit*

Notes to Chapter 4

239

Plaindealer, May 6, 1892; "Champion Jackson," *Cleveland Gazette*, November 5, 1892. On Jackson's tour as Uncle Tom, see "Jackson, As Uncle Tom," *Parsons Blade*, February 11, 1893. Coverage of George Dixon includes "Dixon, Victor," *Cleveland Gazette*, November 1, 1890; "A World's Champion," *Detroit Plaindealer*, July 1, 1892; quote regarding Dixon in Editorial *Cleveland Gazette*, September 10, 1892.

11. See, for examples, "Naval Officer Patty," *Cleveland Gazette*, August 31, 1889; "Officers of the Virginia Building, Loan and Trust Company," *Cleveland Gazette*, March 19, 1892; "Republican National Convention," *St. Paul Appeal*, June 11, 1892; Albert Mack, of "Colored Y.M.C.A.," *Wisconsin Afro-American and Northwest Recorder*, October 29, 1892; "Paul Laurence Dunbar," *Cleveland Gazette*, January 7, 1893; "Phillis Wheatley," *St. Paul Appeal*, July 16, 1892.

12. Women's columns appeared in "For the Ladies," *Detroit Plaindealer*, October 3, 1890; "In Woman's Behalf," *Huntsville Gazette*, December 5, 1891; "Woman's World," *St. Paul Appeal*, September 3, 1892; "Our Women," *Parsons Blade*, September 16, 1893, April 14, 1894; "Afro American Women," *Baltimore Afro-American*, August 3, 1895; "Women's Column," *Baltimore Afro-American*, February 25, 1896. Singers include "Madam Marie Selika," *Cleveland Gazette*, August 8, 1891; Mary I. Webb of Cincinnati, "Our Ideal Vocalist," *Cleveland Gazette*, June 27, 1891. See also "A Talented Teacher," *Cleveland Gazette*, August 15, 1891; Mary Champ Campbell—poet, *Cleveland Gazette*, September 5, 1891; "Our Book List," *A.M.E. Church Review*, April 1, 1893; "Miss Margaret Black," *Baltimore Afro-American*, June 20, 1896.

13. Editorial, *Parsons Blade*, January 28, 1893; see also "Encampment Notes," *Detroit Plaindealer*, August 7, 1891; "Their Grand March," *Parsons Blade*, September 24, 1892; "G.A.R.," *Parsons Blade*, October 1, 1892.

14. Mitchell made his paper a success, introducing an electric press in 1890, but supplemented the paper's income with earnings as a printer and stationer, and perhaps support from the Republican Party. Christopher Waldrep, *African Americans Confront Lynching: Strategies of Resistance from the Civil War to the Civil Rights Era* (Rowman and Littlefield, 2009), 27–28.

15. Editorial, *Detroit Plaindealer*, September 27, 1889; "A Worthy Journal," *Parson's Blade*, October 1, 1892.

16. Quotes from "A Few Friendly Words," *Northwest Recorder*, November 19, 1892; "Cooper Analyzed," *Leavenworth (Kan.) Advocate*, January 31, 1891. Cooper saw cartoons as a pedagogical tool that would develop readers' critical visual skills. As Andreá Williams writes, "Cooper made the bold, but unpopular claim that, when created by and for African American viewers in a black periodical, black caricatures served a self-reflexive, didactic function rather than the denigrating one in white media." Williams, "Cultivating Black Visuality, 124.

17. "The Hercules of Today," *Freeman*, March 22, 1890. Image republished as "Still in Line," *Freeman*, January 5, 1895, and "A Patient and Long Sufferer," *Freeman*, August 28, 1897.

18. "Some Daily or Rather Nightly Occurances in the South," *Freeman*, September 21, 1889.

19. "Ethiopia to Uncle Sam," *Freeman*, September 21, 1889. Ethiopia was incorporated into the Freeman's masthead from December 21, 1889, with the words "And Ethiopia shall stretch forth her hand." She also appeared in a cartoon lamenting Northern prejudice in "Extremes of Caucasian Hatred," *Freeman*, November 7, 1891.

20. "A Neck Tie Party Was Held," *Police Gazette*, August 30, 1890. On the mythology of the black rapist, see Trudier Harris, *Exorcizing Blackness: Historical and Literary Lynching and Burning Rituals* (Bloomington: Indiana University Press, 1984); Robyn Wiegman, *American Anatomies: Theorizing Race and Gender* (Durham, N.C.: Duke University Press, 1995), 95–96; Martha Hodes, *White Women, Black Men: Illicit Sex in the Nineteenth Century* (New Haven, Conn.: Yale University Press, 1997); Nell Irvin Painter, "Race, Gender, and Class in *The Mind of the South:* Cash's Maps of Sexuality and Power," in *W. J. Cash and the Minds of the South*, ed. Paul Escott (Baton Rouge: Louisiana State University Press, 1992). On the persistence of the rapist mythos, see Grace Hale, *Making Whiteness: The Culture of Segregation in the South, 1890–1940* (New York: Pantheon, 1998); Gail Bederman, *Manliness and Civilization: A Cultural History of Gender and Race in the United States, 1880–1917* (Chicago: University of Chicago Press, 1995); Angela Y. Davis, "Rape, Racism, and the Myth of the Black Rapist," in Davis, *Women, Race, and Class* (New York: Random House, 1981); Glenda Elizabeth Gilmore, *Gender and Jim Crow: Women and the Politics of White Supremacy in North Carolina, 1896–1920* (Chapel Hill: University of North Caroline Press, 1996); Sandra Gunning, *Race, Rape, and Lynching: The Red Record of American Literature, 1890–1912* (Oxford: Oxford University Press, 1996); Jacquelyn Dowd Hall, "The Mind That Burns in Each Body: Women, Rape, and Racial Violence," in *The Politics of Sexuality*, ed. Ann Snitow, Christine Stansell, and Sharon Thompson (New York: Monthly Review, 1983). On the *Police Gazette*'s depiction of rape by white "deviants," see Estelle Freedman, "'Crimes Which Startle and Horrify . . .': Gender, Age, and the Racialization of Sexual Violence in White American Newspapers, 1870–1900," *Journal of the History of Sexuality* 20, no. 3 (2011): 465–97. On the erasure of white rape of African American women, see Leslie Dunlap, "The Reform of Rape Law and the Problem of the White Man: Age of Consent Campaigns in the South, 1885–1910," in *Sex, Love, Race: Crossing Boundaries in North American History*, ed. Martha Hodes (New York: NYU Press, 1999); Mia Bay, *The White Image in the Black Mind: African-American Ideas about White People, 1830–1925* (New York: Oxford University Press, 2000); Catherine Clinton, "With a Whip in His Hand: Rape, Memory and African American Women," in *History and Memory in African-American Culture*, ed. Genevieve Fabre and Robert O'Meally (New York: Oxford University Press, 1994); Patricia Morton, *Disfigured Images: The Historical Assault on Afro-American Women* (Westport, Conn.: Greenwood Press, 1991).

21. "The Southern Outrages," *Freeman*, January 18, 1890.

22. Smith had founded the *Gazette* in 1882, a year after graduating from high school, and under his guidance it became one of the more militant African American newspapers. See Summer E. Stevens and Owen V. Johnson, "From Black Politics to Black Community: Harry C. Smith and the Cleveland *Gazette*," *Journalism Quarterly* 67, no. 4 (Winter 1990): 1090–102. Domke includes the *Gazette* in his list of "militant" newspapers. Domke, "The Black Press in the 'Nadir.'" Emma Thornbrough calls it the "hardiest example of Negro journalism." Thornbrough, "American Negro Newspapers," 471.

23. "Our National Cemetery," *Freeman*, September 27, 1890. See also "The Southern Outrages," *Freeman*, January 18, 1890; "Of Race Interest," *Cleveland Gazette*, January 4, 1890. For coverage of President Harrison, see "President Harrison and the Negro Vote," *Freeman*, April 6, 1889; "The Political Pharisees," *Freeman*, April 27, 1889; "The Colored Brother's Lament," *Freeman*, June 15, 1889; "The Freeman's Political Horoscope," *Freeman*, August 3, 1889; "Bait for 1892," *Freeman*, November 16, 1889; "Fishing for Colored Suckers," *Freeman*, October 24, 1891.

24. Lewis died of pneumonia in April 1891, survived by a wife and seven children. Taylor, "Out of Jest," 199. Tucker was fired and committed to an insane asylum in April 1892. Williams, "Cultivating Black Visuality," 138n32. Both artists' work continued to appear in the *Freeman* through the 1890s.

25. On the president's silence, see "The Future of the Race," *A.M.E. Church Review*, October 1890; editorials, *Plaindealer*, April 3, 17, 1891; "Is the White South Civilized?" *A.M.E. Zion Quarterly*, July 1891; "The Mafia Dead," *Freeman*, March 21, 1891; quote from "Daily Occurrence," *Progress* (Omaha, Neb.), reprinted in *Coffeyville Afro-American Advocate*, March 18, 1892. It is not coincidental that the lynching was organized by the White League, as Matthew Jacobson notes, or that mainstream newspapers praised the mob's actions. It remains unclear whether the Italian men or the Mafia more generally had been involved in Hennessey's murder or had merely provided convenient scapegoats. Matthew Jacobson, *Whiteness of a Different Color: European Immigrants and the Alchemy of Race* (Cambridge, Mass.: Harvard University Press, 1998), 56–61. Quote from editorial, *Detroit Plaindealer*, April 3, 1891. The *Plaindealer* walked back its support for the Italians a few weeks later, responding to criticism that they were supporting the Mafia (a newly adopted epithet the press used to disparage Italian-American immigrants generally) but maintained that the mass lynching had revealed Louisianians' "utter contempt of law [which] should be shown up in its true light." Editorial, *Plaindealer*, April 17, 1891.

26. Ida B. Wells, "Lynch Law in the South," Speech at Tremont Temple, Boston, February 13, 1893, in Mildred Thompson, *Ida B. Wells-Barnett: An Exploratory Study of an American Black Woman, 1893–1930* (Brooklyn, N.Y.: Carlson, 1990), 171–87. Mia Bay, *To Tell the Truth Freely: The Life of Ida B. Wells* (New York: Hill and Wang, 2009); Paula Giddings, *Ida, a Sword among Lions: Ida B. Wells and the Campaign against Lynching* (New York: Amistad, 2008); Patricia Schechter, *Ida B. Wells-Barnett and American Reform, 1880–1930* (Chapel Hill: University of North Carolina Press, 2001). See also Carol Stabile, *White Victims, Black Villains: Gender, Race and Crime News in U.S. Culture* (New York: Routledge, 2006).

27. "The Memphis Massacre," and editorial, *Huntsville Gazette*, March 12, April 2, 1892; "Our Civilization's Shame," *Cleveland Gazette*, April 2, 1892. Editorial, *Detroit Plaindealer* (hereafter *Plaindealer*), March 18, 1892; "A Day of Fasting," *Plaindealer*, May 6, 1892. Opposition to Wells in Reverend B. A. Imes, *Memphis Appeal-Avalanche*, June 30, 1892, in Thompson, *Idea B. Wells-Barnett*, 36. Digests of lynchings appeared in "The Bloody Record," *Plaindealer*, March 4, 1892; May 6, 1892, and other issues; "Outrage Column," *Wisconsin Afro-American and Northwest Recorder*, August 13, 1892; "The American Pastime," *Plaindealer*, January 13, 1893; "The Record of Shame," *Plaindealer*, February 3, 1893; "This Week's Lynching Record," *Coffeyville Afro-American*, July 29, 1892; "A Bloody

Record of Crime," *Parsons Blade* (hereafter *Blade*), September 30, 1893. For more details about *Parsons Blade*, see Teresa C. Klassen and Owen V. Johnson, "Sharpening of the *Blade*: Black Consciousness in Kansas," in *Journalism Quarterly* 63, no. 2 (Summer 1986): 298–304.

28. Wells, "Lynch Law in All Its Phases," in Thompson, *Ida B. Wells-Barnett*, 171; "Lynch Law," *A.M.E. Church Review*, April 1892; editorial, *Cleveland Gazette*, May 28, 1892; editorial, *Coffeyville Afro-American Advocate*, July 29, 1892.

29. "Still Asleep," *Freeman*, May 14, 1892. The Douglass quotation is a slight revision of his exact words: "If the southern outrages on the colored race continue, the Negro will become a chemist. Other men besides anarchists can be goaded into the throwing and making of bombs." *Cleveland Gazette*, May 28, 1892, cited in Giddings, *A Sword among Lions*, 220–21. *Chattanooga Times* reprinted in "Fred. Douglass on Mob Law," *Huntsville Gazette*, May 21, 1892; "Southern Outrages," *Plaindealer*, May 27, 1892; editorial, *Cleveland Gazette*, May 7, 1892. Quote from "Reaping the Whirlwind," *Plaindealer*, July 15, 1892.

30. Barnett quote from "Daily Occurrence," *Omaha Progress*, reprinted in *Coffeyville Afro-American Advocate*, March 18, 1892. "The Race Rises Up," *Richmond Planet*, July 27, 1889; "They Are Indignant," *Cleveland Gazette*, September 12, 1891; editorial, *Plaindealer*, January 1, 1892; "Fleeing for Their Lives," *Cleveland Gazette*, March 26, 1892; "Indignation Meeting," *Cleveland Gazette*, April 2, 1892; "Refused to Sing 'America,'" *Cleveland Gazette*, April 2, 1892; editorial, *Plaindealer*, April 29, 1892; "A Mass Meeting," *Cleveland Gazette*, May 7, 1892; "Broke a Limb," *Cleveland Gazette*, May 7, 1892; editorial, *Huntsville Gazette*, May 28, 1892; "Awful!!!," *Cleveland Gazette*, May 7, 1892; editorial, *Coffeyville Afro-American Advocate*, July 1, 1892; "Union Is Strength," *Plaindealer*, July 15, 1892; "They Denounce," *Cleveland Gazette*, August 27, 1892; "A Brutal Outrage," *Cleveland Gazette*, October 1, 1892; "Miss Wells Indorsed [*sic*]," *Cleveland Gazette*, August 4, 1894. Secret meetings documented in editorials, *A.M.E. Zion Quarterly*, April 1893; *Kansas City Star*, reprinted as "Colored People Indignant," *Blade*, July 1, 1893. On the May 31 protests, see "A Day of Fasting," *Plaindealer*, May 6, 1892; "To the Colored People of the United States," *Huntsville Gazette*, April 30, 1892; "Cincinnati Department," *Plaindealer*, May 13, 1892; "Let Us Fast and Pray," *Plaindealer*, May 13, 1892; "A Day of Prayer," *Cleveland Gazette*, May 14, 1892. *Cleveland Herald*, reprinted as "Southern Fiendish for the Negro," *Coffeyville Afro-American Advocate*, May 20, 1892; "Fasting and Prayer," *St. Paul Appeal*, May 28, 1892; "Fittingly Observed," *Cleveland Gazette*, June 4, 1892; "A Plea for the Negro" *A.M.E. Church Review*, July 1892. While this does not represent what Lewis Baldwin calls "liberation" activism, it does reveal the depths of anger and loss. Baldwin, "Historical Reflections," in *The New Day Begun: Afro-American Churches and Civil Culture in Post–Civil Rights America*, ed. R. Drew Smith, (Durham, N.C.: Duke University Press, 2003, 29. See also Wilmore, *Black Religion and Black Radicalism: An Interpretation of the Religious History of African Americans* (New York: Orbis, 1998), 163–74.

31. James E. Bricus, Letter to Editor, *Coffeyville Afro-American Advocate*, March 25, 1892; also "Mobs Make Mistake," *Coffeyville Afro-American Advocate*, June 17, 1892; "The Reign of Judge Lynch," *Huntsville Gazette*, August 6, 1892; "At Their Dirty Work Again," *Blade*, September 24, 1892; "It Will Not Settle Itself," *Blade*, December 24, 1892.

32. "Our Republic,"*Plaindealer*, June 3, 1892. See also *St. Paul Appeal*, June 4, 1892. On the Fourteenth Amendment argument, see Waldrep, *African Americans Confront Lynching*.

33. "Land of the Free," *San Francisco Elevator*, June 18, 1892.

34. "Some Day," *Freeman*, June 25, 1892; image reappears as "A Slave Still," *Freeman*, August 4, 1894, and "Let Us Note the Signs of the Times," *Freeman*, June 29, 1895.

35. "Elopes with a Creole," *Cleveland Gazette*, June 21, 1890; "He Loved a Colored Girl," *Cleveland Gazette*, July 11, 1891; "A White Girl," *Cleveland Gazette*, July 18, 1891; "A Mixed Marriage," *Cleveland Gazette*, October 31, 1891; "Because He Had a Colored Wife," *Cleveland Gazette*, December 26, 1891; "White Women Fight Over an Afro-American," *Cleveland Gazette*, February 20, 1892; "An Elopement," *Cleveland Gazette*, March 5, 1892; "Mixed Marriages," *Gazette*, April 9, 1892. On false rape accusations, see *American Citizen*, reprinted in *Coffeyville Afro-American Advocate*, March 11, 1892; "She Confessed," *Cleveland Gazette*, April 2, 1892.

36. *American Citizen*, reprinted in *Coffeyville Afro-American Advocate*, March 11, 1892; "She Confessed," *Cleveland Gazette*, April 2, 1892.

37. "'You Black Brute,'" *Huntsville Gazette*, January 9, 1892; "Horrible but True," *Cleveland Gazette*, January 16, 1892; editorial, *Cleveland Gazette*, January 23, 1892; "A White Brute's Awful Crime," *Langston City Herald*, July 16, 1892; "Another White Rapist," *Langston City Herald*, August 13, 1892; D. Augustus Straker, "Address," *A.M.E. Church Review*, October 1892; "Defending the Race," *Chicago Conservator*, clipped in *Blade*, February 4, 1893; "Speak Out against Mob Law," *Huntsville Gazette*, February 18, 1893. On rape of African American women, see "A Brutal Outrage," *Cleveland Gazette*, October 1, 1892; "Three Colored Women Outraged by White Ruffians," *Wisconsin Afro-American and Northwest Recorder*, March 1893; "A Mob Lynches," *Cleveland Gazette*, May 4, 1895. On rape of black women during slavery, see Francis Long, "Race Antagonism," *A.M.E. Church Review*, January 1889; editorial, *Plaindealer*, November 7, 1891; "A Dastardly Outrage," *N.O. Ferret*, reprinted in *Cleveland Gazette*, January 7, 1893; "Dastardly Outrage," *Blade*, January 14, 1893; letter from T. W. Ganaway, "The Smith Tragedy," *Blade*, April 8, 1893.

38. The Accused Men," *Cleveland Gazette*, October 1, 1892. See also editorial, *Plaindealer*, March 3, 1893; "Colored National Convention Called," *Blade*, September 30, 1893. "Brutal Outrage," *Mirror*, n.d., reprinted in *Langston City Herald*, October 15, 1892.

39. George L. Knox took over from Edward E. Cooper as publisher in June 1892. Cooper remained on staff at least for a time as the paper's business manager; W. Allison Sweeney also remained as editor. The new publisher immediately declared the paper's Republican leanings and its commitment to reelect President Harrison. *Freeman*, June 18, 25, 1892. Knox, a friend of Harrison's, turned the paper into "a Harrison mouthpiece." Suggs, *Black Press in the Middle-West*, 57.

40. Editorials and "Southern Outrages" in the *Cleveland Gazette*, May 21, May 28, and June 4, 1892; "Is the Afro-American League a Failure?," *A.M.E. Church Review*, July 1892; "The President and the Negro," *Blade*, October 1, 1892. Some papers blamed African American Democrats for Grover Cleveland's victory; see "The Unkindest Cut of All," *Blade*, December 24, 1892. On postelection violence, see editorial, *Plaindealer*,

January 6, 1893. "The Great Southern Exodus," *Freeman*, November 5, 1892. The image had also appeared on April 13, 1889.

41. Hale, *Making Whiteness*, 207.

42. Editorial, *Plaindealer*, March 3, 1893. Similar arguments echoed throughout the black press. See for example "Conditions in the South," *A.M.E. Church Review*, January 1894; Straker, "Lynch Law," *A.M.E. Church Review*, October 1894; Douglass, "Lessons of the Hour," *A.M.E. Church Review*, October 1894; See also Wells, "Lynch Law in All Its Phases," 184. The *Plaindealer* remained in print from 1883 to 1893. While working as messenger for the *Detroit Post* in the early 1880s, Pelham edited and wrote articles for an amateur newspaper called the *Venture*. In 1883 he and his elder brother, Robert Pelham Jr., along with William H. Anderson, Walter H. Stowers, and (later) Byron G. Redmond, founded the *Detroit Plaindealer* to promote African American economic interests and political rights. Pelham went on to hold a number of appointed government positions and was known as one of the most influential African American leaders in Detroit. Sugg, *Black Press in the Middle-West*, 136. See also David Katzman, *Before the Ghetto: Black Detroit in the Nineteenth Century* (Urbana: University of Illinois Press, 1975); Herb Boyd, *Black Detroit: A People's History of Self-Determination* (New York: Amistad, 2017).

43. "Thirty Years of Progress," *Plaindealer*, March 3, 1893. The artist for this image (signed "T. Fleming") is unknown.

44. "Free (?) America" *Northwest Recorder*, March, 1893.

45. Editorial, *Blade*, January 28, 1893; Rev. Mr. J. P. King., "Can This Be True?," *Northwest Recorder*, March 1893; editorial, *Blade*, February 18, 1893; editorial, *Plaindealer*, February 24, 1893. Ida B. Wells, *The Red Record: Tabulated Statistics and Alleged Causes of Lynching in the United States* (1895), reprinted in *On Lynchings: Ida B. Wells-Barnett*, ed. Patricia Hill Collins (New York: Humanities, 2002), 76–77. The *Blade* disappeared in 1897 after it broke from the Republican Party in support of the People's Party in 1896. Klasson et al., "Sharpening the *Blade*," 299–304. Suggs, *Black Press in the Middle-West* 115–16.

46. Jesse C. Duke, "How to Combine Our Efforts," *A.M.E. Zion Quarterly*, January 1894 (emphasis added). Wells in "Lynch Law," in *The Reason Why*, in Harris, ed., *Selected Works*, 74–92, images 88–89, 91.

47. "Horrible!" *Cleveland Gazette*, April 7, 1894. "The Louisiana Lynchings," *Blade*, September 30, 1893; "Horrible Lynching Affair," *Blade*, November 25, 1893.

48. Editorial, "Conditions in the South," *A.M.E. Church Review*, January 1894.

49. Straker, "Lynch Law in the South," *A.M.E. Church Review*, October 1894; Douglass, "Lessons of the Hour," *A.M.E. Church Review*, October 1894. See also Wells, "Lynch Law in All Its Phases," in Thompson, *Ida B. Wells-Barnett*, 184.

50. Douglass, "Lessons of the Hour," *A.M.E. Church Review*, October 1894; Straker, "Address," *A.M.E. Church Review*, October 1892.

51. "Lynchings in '94," *Richmond Planet*, January 19, 1895.

52. Quoted in "Editorial / Frederick Douglass," *A.M.E. Church Review*, April 1, 1895.

53. "How to Stop Lynching," *Woman's Era*, May 1, 1894. "Apologists for Lynching," *Woman's Era*, June 1, 1894. It is unclear whether Ruffin or her daughter Ridley wrote

the pieces in question. Rodger Streitmatter suggests that the *Woman's Era* was in print as early as 1890, based on her letters. See his "Josephine St. Pierre Ruffin: Pioneering African American Newspaper Publisher," *A Living of Words: American Women in Print Culture*, ed. Susan Albertine (Knoxville: University of Tennessee Press, 1995), 49–52.

54. "A Lynching Scene," *Planet*, June 23, 1894. "You shudder at the picture. OF COURSE YOU DO!" [1891], Broadsides and Ephemera Collection, Duke University Library Digital Collections, https://repository.duke.edu/dc/broadsides/bdsva103748. On Mitchell, see Ann Field Alexander, *Race Man: The Rise and Fall of Fighting Editor, John Mitchell Jr.*, (Charlottesville: University Press of Virginia, 2002). Mitchell had begun his career as the Richmond correspondent for the *New York Freeman* until he took over the editorship of the *Richmond Planet* in 1884, building a name for himself as a fiery and uncompromising journalist and public man. Like Duke and Wells, Mitchell had braved mob retaliation in defending an African American man from a rape charge. Journalism historian J. Garland Penn called Mitchell a "bold and fearless writer almost to a fault," whose "forte as an editor [was] to battle against outrages perpetrated upon his people in the South." Penn, *The African American Press and Its Editors* (Springfield, Mass: Willey, 1891). Elected to the Richmond City Council in 1888, he remained the *Planet's* editor and a leader in the community through the 1890s. He died penniless in 1929. See also Suggs, *Black Press in the Middle-West*; Thornbrough, "American Negro Newspapers."

55. "Notice!" *Freeman*, August 11, 1894. Image also appeared as "Protection for the Negro," *Freeman*, June 1, 1889; "Things Have Not Changed, *Freeman*, January 12, 1895; "Scenes from the Southland," *Freeman*, June 13, 1896.

56. "Not a Word in Defense of the Negro," *Blade*, December 9, 1893. Straker, "Lynch Law," *A.M.E. Church Review*, October 1894.

57. "A Retrospective View," *Freeman*, November 3, 1894.

58. "Prays for His Persecutors," *Richmond Planet*, January 19, 1895. Wells, *Red Record*, 90, 104–5.

59. "Ohio Refused to Deliver Him," *Planet*, January 26, 1895.

60. "McKinley in 1896," *Cleveland Gazette*, January 27, 1894; see also "That Lynching" and "That Riot," in *Cleveland Gazette*, December 12, 1894.

61. "Firing at Long Range," *Planet*, February 2, 1895; "White Men to the Rescue," *Planet*, February 23, 1895.

62. "Silenced the Witnesses," *Planet*, March 16, 1895.

63. Suzanne Lebsock, *A Murder in Virginia: Southern Justice on Trial* (New York: Norton, 2003); Alexander, *Race Man*, 59.

64. Wells reemerged to speak out against atrocities such as the Wilmington massacre in 1898 and the Sam Hose lynching in 1899. See Giddings, *Sword among Lions*, 364; Bay, *To Tell the Truth Freely*, 223. Kevern Verney, *The Art of the Possible: Booker T. Washington and Black Leadership in the United States, 1881–1925* (New York: Routledge, 2001), 22–23; Christopher Waldrep, *The Many Faces of Judge Lynch: Extralegal Violence and Punishment in America* (New York: Palgrave, 2002), 124.

65. *Christian Advocate* [n.d.], reprinted in "Mob Law," *Baltimore Afro-American*, December 14, 1895.

66. Editorial, *Cleveland Gazette*, May 30, 1896; "The 'Jim Crow' Case," *Freeman*, May 23, 1896. On the value of Harlan's minority opinion see, for example, "That Decision," *Cleveland Gazette*, May 30, 1896; quote from *Omaha Enterprise*, May 30, 1896.

67. "McKinley and Ohio's Anti-Lynching Law," *Cleveland Gazette*, May 30, 1896; "Hanna Talks," *Cleveland Gazette*, October 3, 1896; "We Can Trust Him," *Cleveland Gazette* from September 12, 1896, through election day. "The Political Mule of '96," *Freeman*, September 12, 1896 (a similar cartoon had appeared as "Don't Monkey with a Mule," August 29, 1891); "Remaining in the Republican Party," *Cleveland Gazette* August 22, 1896.

68. "Why Not Rejoice?" *Wilmington [Record]* reprinted in *Raleigh Gazette*, November 21, 1896. See also Richard B. Sherman, *The Republican Party and Black America: From McKinley to Hoover, 1896–1933* (Charlottesville: University Press of Virginia, 1973); Michael Perman, *Struggle for Mastery: Disfranchisement in the South, 1888–1908* (Chapel Hill: University of North Carolina Press, 2001); William D. Harpine, *From the Front Porch to the Front Page: McKinley and Bryan in the 1896 Presidential Campaign* (College Station: Texas A&M University Press, 2005). "Booker T. Washington, A.M." and "Prof. Washington's Visit," *Planet*, November 21, 1896.

69. "The Reign of Lawlessness," *Planet*, February 27, 1897, and thereafter.

70. "Fair Ohio in Disgrace," *Freeman*, June 12, 1897; "An Ohio Mob," *Freeman*, June 12, 1897; "Not Guilty," *Cleveland Gazette*, October 23, 1897. "Not Guilty," *Planet*, July 17, 1897. Editorial, *Freeman*, August 28, 1897; "Infernal Brutes," *Cleveland Gazette*, February 26, 1898; "A Patient and Long Sufferer," *Freeman*, August 28, 1897; Ida B. Wells Calls on President McKinley," *Cleveland Gazette*, April 9, 1898.

71. Rape hysteria grew in July 1898, an effective racial wedge to destroy the Fusionist (Populist/Republican) alliance; cartoon vampires and thugs kept up a steady "drumbeat of race-baiting." Michael Honey, "Class, Race, and Power," in *Democracy Betrayed: The Wilmington Race Riot of 1898 and Its Legacy*, ed. David S. Cecelsky and Timothy B. Tyson (Chapel Hill: University of North Carolina Press, 1998), 172–73. According to Laura Edwards, "what happened in Wilmington became an affirmation of white supremacy not just in that one city, but in the South and in the nation as a whole." Edwards, "Captives of Wilmington," in Cecelsky and Tyson, *Democracy Betrayed*, 115. Richard Yarborough describes the 1898 campaign in the lead-up to the massacre in Wilmington as "one of the most extensive, unrelentingly racist propaganda campaigns in this country's history." Yarborough, "Violence, Manhood, and Black Heroism," in Cecelsky and Tyson, *Democracy Betrayed*, 227. As Glenda Gilmore says, "The federal government's failure to act in the aftermath of the Wilmington racial massacre became a pattern it followed for another fifty years." Gilmore, "The Flight of the Incubus," in Cecelsky and Tyson, *Democracy Betrayed*, 87. See also Lee Ann Whites, "Love, Hate, Rape, Lynching," in Cecelsky and Tyson, *Democracy Betrayed*.

72. Editorial, *Freeman*, November 19, 1898; "Editor Manly," *Freeman*, November 26, 1898; "The Wilmington Riots," *Freeman*, December 3, 1898; "Major's Melange," *Freeman*, December 3, 1898; "The Nation's Shame," *Cleveland Gazette*, November 19, 1898, "Reduce Their Representation, *Cleveland Gazette*, November 28, 1898; "McKinley's Speech," *Cleveland Gazette*, February 25, 1899.

73. On the 1898 election, see "We Are Not So Easily Buncoed," *Freeman*, October

29, 1898; "Oh! Justice Thou Has Fled to Brutish Beasts," *Freeman*, November 5, 1898. "The Republican Tidal Wave," *Planet*, November 12, 1898. On the rape mythos in the 1898 campaign and Wilmington riot, see Gilmore, *Gender and Jim Crow*, 87–88. On negative responses to McKinley, see"McKinley's Name," *Cleveland Gazette*, June 3, 1899; "Fortune Scores McKinley," *Cleveland Gazette*, June 17, 1899; "The Sam Hose Lynching," *Cleveland Gazette*, June 17, 1899]. On the situation in the Philippines, see "The Slaughter in the Philippines," *Cleveland Gazette*, June 24, 1899; "Refusing to Enlist," *Cleveland Gazette*, July 18, 1899. On Mitchell's critique McKinley's "reconciliation" drive and the Philippines campaign, see Willard B. Gatewood, *Black Americans and the White Man's Burden, 1898–1903* (Urbana: University of Illinois Press, 1975). See further critique of President McKinley in "McKinley Scored" and "Under His Nose," *Cleveland Gazette*, August 26, 1899; "President Wm. McKinley" and "Burned at the Stake," *Planet*, October 28, 1899; "Col. Roosevelt," *Cleveland Gazette*, October 27, 1900; "Republican Principles v. Republican Administration," *Cleveland Gazette*, November 3, 1900; "Our Nation's Chief," *Freeman*, November 10, 1900. Only the *Freeman* vocally lamented McKinley's assassination in 1901: "Assassination," *Freeman*, September 21, 1901.

74. Lynching illustrations during World War I include "The Dawn of a New Day," *Planet*, June 23, 1917; "Wake Up Uncle or You Are Going to Fall," *Baltimore Afro-American*, August 8, 1919; "—And Take These with You," *Chicago Defender*, January 10, 1920, all in William Jordon, *Black Newspapers and America's War for Democracy, 1914–1920* (Chapel Hill: University of North Carolina Press, 2001), 99, 136, 154.

Chapter 5. "Wanted to Save Her Honor"

1. On advertisers' growing recognition of the importance of women as news consumers, see Michael Schudson, *Discovering the News: A Social History of American Newspapers* (New York: Basic, 1978), 100.

2. I use her correct name, Barbella, except when quoting primary sources from the period. As Idanna Pucci points out, apart from erasing Barbella's real history, the naming error probably contributed to the characterization of Barberi as a "hot-blooded" Italian woman: it evoked the words "barbaric" and "barber" (calling to mind the razor used to kill Cataldo), both reinforcing the association with violence. See Idanna Pucci, *The Trials of Maria Barbella: The True Story of a Nineteenth-Century Crime of Passion* (New York: Vintage, 1997).

3. For a detailed account of the case, see Pucci, *Trials of Maria Barbella*. As Estelle Freedman notes, "seduction" was often a code word for rape in the late nineteenth century. Estelle Freedman, *Redefining Rape: Sexual Violence in the Era of Suffrage and Segregation* (Cambridge, Mass.: Harvard University Press, 2013), 42–43.

4. For a detailed history of the *Recorder's* brief career as a New York daily, see Lorna Watson, "The *New York Recorder* as a Woman's Newspaper, 1891–1894" (master's thesis, University of Wisconsin, 1939). On James B. Duke and the creation of the American Tobacco Company merger in 1890, see John K. Winkler, *Tobacco Tycoon: The Story of James Buchanan Duke* (New York: Random House, 1942), chap. 5; John Wilbur Jenkins, *James B. Duke, Master Builder: The Story of Tobacco, Development of Southern and Canadian Water, and the Creation of a University* New York: Doran, 1927), 91–94.

5. *New York World*, April 27, 1895. *New York Recorder*, April 27, 1895.

6. On the resurgence of women's political organizations in the 1890s, see Eleanor Flexnor, *Century of Struggle: The Woman's Rights Movement in the United States* (Cambridge, Mass: Belknap, 1975), chap. 13; in Marjorie Spruill Wheeler, ed., *One Woman, One Vote: Rediscovering the Woman Suffrage Movement* (Troutdale, Ore.: New Sage, 1995), see Sara Hunter Graham, "The Suffrage Renaissance" (157–78), Rosalyn Terborg-Penn, "African American Women and the Struggle for the Vote" (135–56), and Wanda Hendriks, "Ida B. Wells-Barnett and the Alpha Suffrage Club of Chicago" 263–76.; Lumsden, *Rampant Women: Suffragists and the Right of Assembly* (Knoxville: University of Tennessee Press, 1997), chap. 1. On the creation of the National American Woman's Suffrage Association (NAWSA) in 1890, see Ellen Carol DuBois, *Woman Suffrage and Women's Rights* (New York: New York University Press, 1998), 170–71. See also Nancy Cott, *The Grounding of Modern Feminism* (New Haven, Conn.: Yale University Press, 1989); Anne Firor Scott, *Natural Allies: Women's Organizations in American History* (Urbana: University of Illinois Press, 1992).

7. On Italians' racial status in the 1890s'United States, see Matthew Jacobson, *Whiteness of a Different Color: European Immigrants and the Alchemy of Race* (Cambridge, Mass.: Harvard University Press, 1998), 60, 62 (quote); Peter Vellon, *A Great Conspiracy against Our Race: Italian Immigrant Newspapers and the Construction of Whiteness in the Early Twentieth Century* (New York: New York University Press, 2014), 2; Stefano Luconi, "Black Dagoes? Italian Immigrants' Racial Status in the United States: An Ecological View," in *Journal of Transatlantic Studies 14*, no. 2 (2016): 188–99. Thomas Guglielmo, *White on Arrival: Italians, Race, Color, and Power in Chicago, 1890–1945* (New York: Oxford University Press, 2003), 22–23 (quote). See also David Roediger, *Working toward Whiteness: How America's Immigrants Became White; The Strange Journey from Ellis Island to the Suburbs* (New York: Basic, 2006), 51. On stereotypes of Southern Italians, see John Dickie, "Stereotypes of the Italian South," and Gabriella Gribaudi, "Images of the South" in Robert Lumley and Jonathan Morris, eds., *The New History of the Italian South: The Mezzogiorno Revisited* (Exeter: University of Exeter Press, 1997).

8. On Anglo-American fears of Mediterranean women's passions, see Donna Gabaccia and Franca Iacovetta, preface to *Women, Gender, and Transnational Lives: Italian Workers of the World* (Toronto: University of Toronto Press, 2002), 31. On Italian immigrant women's labor activism, see Jennifer Guglielmo, "Italian Women's Proletarian Feminism in the New York City Garment Trades," in Gabaccia and Iacovetta, *Women, Gender, and Transnational Lives*, 248–50. On Italian immigrant women's power within families, see Donna Gabaccia, *From the Other Side: Women, Gender, and Immigrant Life in the U.S., 1820–1990* (Bloomington: Indiana University Press, 1995), 16. Roughly five million Italian peasants arrived between 1890 and 1910, some as a means to maintain a traditional lifestyle at home—or more often in revolt against a landlord at home. Elizabeth Ewen, *Immigrant Women in the Land of Dollars: Life and Culture in the Lower East Side, 1890–1925* (New York: Monthly Review, 1995), 50–51.

9. *New York World*, April 27, 1895, 11. *New York Recorder*, April 27, 1895. In 1893 the *New York World*'s circulation averaged four hundred thousand copies per issue. John D. Stevens, *Sensationalism and the New York Press* (New York: Columbia Univ. Press, 1991), 73.

10. Hendrik Hartog, *Man and Wife in America: A History* (Cambridge, Mass.: Harvard University Press, 2002), 218, 224, 227, 230, 237. Robert Ireland, "Frenzied and Fallen Females: Women and Sexual Dishonor in the Nineteenth Century U.S.," *Journal of Women's History* 3, no. 3 (Winter 1992): 97, 100 (see also 112n3 on restriction to husband alone). On the *Sickles* case, see Allen D. Spiegel and Peter B. Suskind, "Uncontrollable Frenzy and a Unique Temporary Insanity Plea," *Journal of Community Health* 25, no. 2 (April 2000): 157–79. Historians view the Barbella case as a study in the "fight for social justice on behalf of a powerless Italian immigrant woman" and as an example of the significance of medical testimony in cases of extreme emotional disturbance. See Elizabeth Giovanna Messina, "Women and Capital Punishment: The Trials of Maria Barbella," 60, and Lawrence Fleischer, "Maria Barbella: The Unwritten Law and the Code of Honor in Gilded Age America," 68, in *In Our Own Voices: Multidisciplinary Perspectives on Italian and Italian American Women*, ed. Elizabeth G. Messina (Boca Raton, Fla.: Bordighera, 2003).

11. See, for example, Victoria Nourse, "Passion's Progress: Modern Law Reform and the Provocation Defense," *Yale Law Review*, March 1997, 1358–62, quote p. 1364. See also Carolyn Ramsey, "Provoking Change: Comparative Insights on Feminist Homicide Law Reform," *Journal of Criminal Law and Criminology*, Winter 2010; Martha R. Mahoney, *Exit: Power and the Idea of Leaving in Love, Work, and the Confirmation Hearings*, 65 S. CAL. L. REV. 1283, 1283 (1992).

12. "A Message in Blood," *Police Gazette*, June 15, 1883, 12 (text, p. 2). "He Wrote in Blood," *Pittsburgh Post*, May 24, 1889, 1. Similar cases include "Shocking Wife Murder," *Police Gazette*, April 10, 1880, 11; "Awful Wife Murder," *Police Gazette*, September 2, 1882, 12.

13. "Killed Her Husband," *Police Gazette*, November 25, 1893, 6. The Associated Press source for this story reported the provocation more clearly still; Minor "was accused by his wife of deserting her for another woman." *Sacramento Record-Union*, November 7, 1893.

14. *Police Gazette*, January 13, 1894, 6 (emphasis added). Yusta's attorneys eventually claimed that she acted in self-defense, but the judge would not allow witnesses to testify to that effect. Because of Yusta's youthfulness, however, the trial generated a great deal of interest and support, and she was ultimately found guilty of manslaughter in the second degree, with a four-year sentence. See *Omaha Daily Bee*, March 1, 2, 3, 4, 7, 13, 1894; see also *New Ulm (Minn.) Review*, March 7, 1894; *St. Paul Daily Globe*, March 13, 1894. Charges of accessory to murder against Debelloy were later dropped. *Omaha Daily Bee*, March 9, 1894. The *Police Gazette* did not revisit the case after its initial coverage, however.

15. "Clubbed by a Wronged Wife," *Police Gazette*, October 14, 1893, 7.

16. "Knife for an Unfaithful Husband," *Police Gazette*, January 9, 1897, 3.

17. "She Was Untrue," *Police Gazette*, February 1, 1896, 12 (text, p. 6).

18. The paper was far less likely to understand female violence against husbands as 'hot blooded,' even in similar circumstances; hot blood was largely a male excuse, in print and in law. See Hartog, *Man and Wife in America*; Nourse, "Passion's Progress"; Caroline A. Forell and Donna M. Matthews, *A Law of Her Own: The Reasonable Woman*

as a Measure of Man (New York: NYU Press, 2000), xviii, xx. Carolyn Ramsey's recent article challenges that view, arguing that a more complicated gender politics was at work. Carolyn Ramsey, "Intimate Homicides: Gender and Crime Control, 1880–1920," *University of Colorado Law Review*, Winter 2006. "Died for Her Honor," *Police Gazette*, October 28, 1893, 12 (text p. 3); "Wild With Jealousy," *Police Gazette*, March 23, 1895, 9 (text, p. 7).

19. Linda Gordon, *Heroes of Their Own Lives: The Politics and History of Family Violence, Boston, 1880–1960* (Urbana: University of Illinois Press, 2002), 288.

20. "Legal Redress for Assaulted Wives," *Woman's Journal*, January 18, 1879, 20. See also Elizabeth Pleck, *Domestic Tyranny: The Making of American Social Policy against Family Violence from Colonial Times to the Present* (Urbana: University of Illinois Press, 1999), 102. "A Cure for Wife Beating," *Woman's Journal*, April 8, 1882, 105; "Wife-Beating in Pennsylvania," *Woman's Journal*, September 25, 1886, 311.

21. "Women and the Police," *Woman's Journal*, February 1, 1879, 36; "A Wife Murderer," *Woman's Journal*, April 12, 1884, 118. As Estelle Freedman shows, women made similar arguments about the power of the vote to redefine rape. Freedman, *Redefining Rape*, 57–59.

22. "Slayers of Women," *Woman's Tribune*, September 5, 1891, 1.

23. Editorial, *Farmer's Wife*, July 1892, 5.

24. "The Education in Brutality," *Advocate of Peace*, October 1892, 155; "Education in Brutality," (quote) *Advocate of Peace*, April 1893, 82–83. As Judith Walkowitz demonstrated, English feminists in the 1890s deplored the Jack the Ripper stories, for example, because they "invested male domination with a powerful mystique." Judith Walkowitz, *City of Dreadful Delight: Narratives of Sexual Danger in Late-Victorian London* (Chicago: University of Chicago Press, 1992), 220, 222. On the WCTU's campaign against the *Police Gazette*, see Alison Parker, *Purifying America: Women, Cultural Reform and Pro-censorship Activism, 1873–1933* (Illinois University Press, 1997), 56, 220–21. On the WCTU's critique of alcohol and violence, see Ruth Bordin, *Women and Temperance: A Quest for Power and Liberty, 1873–1900* (Philadelphia: Temple University Press, 1981), 162; Gordon, *Heroes*, 254. Like the WCTU, pacifists viewed prizefighting as an "education in brutality." On the paternalism of anti-obscenity activists in the 1890s who sought to shield women from dangerous influences, see Lee Ann Wheeler, *Against Obscenity: Reform and the Politics of Womanhood in America, 1873–1935* (Baltimore, Md.: Johns Hopkins University Press, 2004), 13, 21. On the notion that images celebrating "boys brigades" fostered the militaristic climate leading the to Spanish-American war, see "The Crime of Sensational Journalism," *Advocate of Peace* 60, no. 1 (April 1898), 79.

25. Quoted in Parker, *Purifying America*, 64–65. The *Union Signal* published only one story about Barbella's case. *Union Signal*, August 8, 1895.

26. Gordon, *Heroes*, 254 (quote), 255, 257. Ellen Carol DuBois and Linda Gordon, "Seeking Ecstasy in the Battlefield: Pleasure and Danger in Nineteenth Century Feminist Thought," in Carol Vance, ed., *Pleasure and Danger: Exploring Female Sexuality* (Boston: Routledge and Kegan Paul, 1984), 139, 140, 143. Norma Basch, *Framing American Divorce: From the Revolutionary Generation to the Victorians* (Berkeley: University of

California Press, 1999). See also Pleck, *Domestic Tyranny*; A. James Hammerton, *Cruelty and Companionship: Conflict in Nineteenth-Century Married Life* (New York: Routledge, 1992), 50, 67. Citing a study by F. H. Wines in 1888, the *Atlanta Constitution* claimed that crimes of passion tended to be committed by "foreigners" (except Canadians, Scots, and English)—as opposed to crimes of "interest" among native-born Americans. "Is Crime on the Increase?" *Atlanta Constitution*, October 12, 1888, 4. In 1889, as a national debate simmered over the establishment of a uniform (more conservative) divorce law, Elizabeth Cady Stanton argued that any such legislation under consideration would be invalid in the absence of woman's vote, as she had no voice in the terms. "Woman is in a transition period from slavery to freedom and she will not accept the conditions of married life that she has heretofore meekly endured." Stanton, "Divorce versus Domestic Warfare," *Arena* 1 (1889): 561. See also Lynn Carol Halem, *Divorce Reform: Changing Legal and Social Perspectives* (New York: Free Press, 1980), 47–9; Lawrence M. Friedman, *Private Lives: Family, Individual, and the Law* (Cambridge, Mass.: Harvard University Press, 2005), 34, 42.

27. "Are Women Protected?" *Woman's Journal*, February 28, 1891, 68 (emphasis added).

28. Editorial, *Woman's Tribune*, March 28, 1891, 1.

29. Lucy Stone, "Setting Fire to His Wife," *Woman's Journal*, February 6, 1892, 46, and "Protection of Wives," *Woman's Journal*, April 9, 1892, 118.

30. "A Shameful Verdict," *Woman's Journal*, November 5, 1892 (emphasis added).

31. "A Murderer of Women," *Woman's Journal*, March 15, 1890, 84.

32. "Topeka Police Court," *Farmer's Wife*, September 1893, 4. "Raving Mad," clipped from the *Butler (Mo.) Union*, in the *Kansas Sunflower*, October and November 1893, 6.

33. Due to gaps in archival collections of the *Police Gazette* for key dates in 1895–96, direct comparison of the paper's coverage of Barbella's arrest and trials with that of the illustrated dailies is not possible.

34. As the *Journalist* elaborated in 1893, "A subscriber to a paper who has had a daily sensation dished up to him every morning resents it if that paper should fall short in its supply." "Indecent Journalism," *Journalist*, August 5, 1893. Quoted in Stevens, *Sensationalism*, 77–78.

35. *New York World*, July 12, 16, 1895; *New York Recorder*, July 12, 16, 1895 (quote July 13). Rebecca Salome Foster, a widow, attended many women imprisoned in the Tombs. The judge in the case was identified as Recorder John F. Goff. Pucci, *Trials of Maria Barbella*, 41.

36. *New York World*, July 17, 1895. The *New York Herald's* focus on her physiognomy similarly lost the opportunity to secure women readers. Elizabeth Giovanna Messina argues that Barbella may in fact have been suffering "from unrecognized symptoms of PTSD." See Messina, "Women and Capital Punishment," 60.

37. *New York Recorder*, July 17, 1895.

38. Ibid. As Lawrence Fleischer argues, "Maria's attempt to advance the defense of honor through her court-appointed lawyer—with no women jurors and no jurors with non-Anglo names—was a formidable task given that she carried the victim's razor and killed him in front of many witnesses." Lawrence Fleischer, "Maria Barbella: The

Unwritten Law and the Code of Honor in Gilded Age New York," in Messina, *In Our Own Voices*, 68.

39. Amos H. Evans, lawyer, quoted in *New York Recorder*, July 18, 1895.

40. *New York World*, July 18, 1895.

41. *New York Recorder*, July 19, 1895.

42. *New York World*, July 19, 20, 1895.

43. *New York Recorder*, July 20, 1895 (emphasis added).

44. Mention of petitions in the *New York Tribune*, July 23 and 25, and August 2 and 24, 1895, and in the *New York Herald*, July 24 and 28, 1895; mass meetings and fundraisers in *New York Times*, August 8, 1895, and *New York Herald*, July 21 and 25, 1895, and *New York Tribune*, July 25 and August 2, 1895. Maria's most loyal supporter was the well-connected Contessa di Brazza Savorgnan, an American-born society woman with strong connections in New York who traveled from Italy specifically to meet Barbella. Another supporter was Father Ferretti of the Church of the Transfiguration. Pucci, *Trials of Maria Barbella*.

45. Dixi [possibly a pseudonym for Di Brazza], *Business Journal*, July 1895; Hanna K. Korany letter in *New York World*, July 19, 1895.

46. Blake letter to *New York World*, July 19, 1895; Stanton statement in *New York World*, July 20, 1895; E. B. Chatfield letter to *New York Tribune*, July 21, 1895 (emphasis added).

47. Grannis and Loew, letters to the *New York World*, July 19, 1895.

48. "A Judicial Murder," *Woman's Journal*, August 3, 1895. On "gallows chivalry," see Annulla Linders and Alana Van Gundy-Yoder, "Gall, Gallantry, and the Gallows: Capital Punishment and the Social Construction of Gender, 1840–1920," in *Gender and Society* 22, no. 3 (June 2008): 324–48.

49. *Woman's Tribune*, August 17, 1895; *Union Signal*, August 8, 1895. Ironically, the *Woman's Journal* now bolstered its support for Barbella by publishing newspaper clippings that supported the heat-of-passion defense for men. *New Orleans Times-Democrat; St. Louis Globe-Democrat;* and *Seymour (Ind.) Republican*, all published in the *Woman's Journal*, August 24, 1895.

50. Dixi, *Business Journal*, July 1895; Stanton, *New York World*, July 20, 1895; Helen Miles, "If Women Had Tried Her," *New York Herald*, July 21, 1895; Anthony, *New York Herald*, July 28, 1895; *Union Signal*, August 8, 1895.

51. Freedman, *Redefining Rape*, 128–29. From the outset, the *Recorder*'s headlines depicted Barbella as a "child/woman," July 17, 1895; "A Judicial Murder," *Woman's Journal*, August 3, 1895; Blackwell editorial, *Woman's Journal*, August 10, 1895. Maria's alleged youth gave momentum to the movement toward age-of-consent legislation, as many argued that her "seduction" would constitute statutory rape in states other than New York. ADA John McIntyre accused activists of deliberately misrepresenting her age to exaggerate the seduction story and "to shield her and arouse public sympathy." *Woman's Tribune*, August 17, 1895 (quote). See also *Woman's Journal*, August 24, 1895. The *New York Tribune* blamed confusion about her age for the "sympathy run mad." *New York Tribune*, August 16, 1895.

52. Stone had died two years earlier. Blackwell quotes from *Woman's Journal*, August 3

and 10, 1895; Henry B. Blackwell to Sarah Lawrence, August 10, 1895, Blackwell Family Papers, folder 135, box 9, Schlesinger Library.

53. Attorney Clara Foltz, one of the first women to practice law in the United States, used the Barbella case in support of her quest of public-defender legislation. See Barbara Allen Babcock, "Inventing the Public Defender," *American Criminal Law Review* 43, no. 4 (Fall 2006): 1267–315.

54. *New York Tribune*, April 22, 1896. For a detailed discussion of Judge O'Brien's reasoning, see Fleischer, "Maria Barbella," 73–4.

55. *New York World*, April 22, 1896.

56. Watson, "*New York Recorder*."

57. I discuss Hearst's early years at the *San Francisco Examiner* in chapter 3.

58. Hearst bought the *Morning Journal* from John D. McLean, who purchased it only months earlier for $1 million from Albert Pulitzer and had paid at least $360,000 for improvements. Hearst chose it over other possibilities (the *Recorder* and the *Times*) because it had a higher circulation. He brought in his best talent from the *San Francisco Examiner* to run it and then began to siphon off the *World*'s staff. See Judith Robinson, *The Hearsts: An American Dynasty* (Newark, Del: University of Delaware Press, 1991), 255; David Nasaw, *The Chief: The Life of William Randolph Hearst* (Boston: Houghton Mifflin, 2000), 96–100. He attempted to buy the *Recorder* from James Duke as early as 1891. Ben Procter, *William Randolph Hearst, the Early Years: 1863–1910* (New York: Oxford University Press, 1998), 34. Low costs in white wood-pulp paper allowed Hearst to undercut the *World* at 1 cent per sixteen-page copy; that October (1895), the *World* sought new "octuplet" press for twelve-, fourteen-, and sixteen-page editions. Ted Curtis Smythe, *The Gilded Age Press: 1865–1900* (Westport, Conn.: Praeger, 2003), 139–40. Hearst changed the name of the paper to the *Journal* after its relaunch in November 1895 and then changed it again to the *New York Journal* in July 1896. An evening edition, the *New York Evening Journal*, ran from June 1897 through 1909, while the morning paper, now named the *New York Journal and Advertiser*, continued to serve a different audience through 1901, when it was again renamed as the *New York Journal and American*.

59. Hearst had learned from his experience with the *Examiner* that he could drive out competition because he could afford to lose money, and he spent freely on more pages, contests, ads, novelties, and the like. By November 1896, just as the Barbella retrial was opening, his efforts paid off in a robust circulation of 150,000 copies a day on average, just thirty-five thousand behind the *World*. The *World*'s efforts to respond to the new paper—cutting its own price per issue to one cent—did nothing to regain lost circulation. Stevens, *Sensationalism*, 85–89. In 1897 Hearst created the *Evening Journal* to compete with Pulitzer's *Evening World*. The *Recorder* soon folded. Smythe, *Gilded Age Press*, 175, citing Editor, "The New York Situation," in *Newspaper Maker* 4 (October 15, 1896): 6. The final date of publication for the *Recorder* is unknown; according to Don C. Seitz, *Joseph Pulitzer—His Life and Letters* (New York: Simon and Schuster, 1924), pp. 186–7, the *Recorder* "perished a fortnight before the defeat of Bryan in 1896." Cited in Watson, "*New York Recorder*," 85. The last issue of the *Recorder* in archival/microfilm collections is September 6, 1896.

60. Pulitzer's hesitancy to back Democratic presidential candidate Williams Jennings Bryan (because of his advocacy of "free silver" coinage) also cost him Democratic readers. Stevens, *Sensationalism*, 87. Smythe, *Gilded Age Press*, 181–82. See also Morris, *Pulitzer*, 322; W. A. Swanberg, *Pulitzer* (New York: Scribner's, 1967), 206–7.

61. *New York Journal*, November 17 and 20 (quote and image), 1896.

62. "Says Evidence Was Ignored" and "Epilepsy to Be Maria's Defense," *New York Journal*, November 20, 21, 1896.

63. *New York World*, November 21 and 29 (image), 1896.

64. *New York Evening World*, November 27, 1896.

65. *New York Journal*, November 17, 20, 21, 23 (image), 26, 27, 28, 1896. More mainstream coverage of the second trial can be found in the *New York Daily Tribune*, November 26, 1896; *New York Times*, November 21, 24, 26, 1896, and December 5 and 8, 1896.

66. "Cosas de America," *Echo D'Italia*, November 19, 1896, 3. "L'Assoluzione di Maria Barbera," *Echo D'Italia*, December 17, 1896, 3. I am grateful to Maria Scutari for her translation of these articles. The *World* has long enjoyed a reputation of treating immigrants respectfully, but this was not the case for its coverage of Italian or Chinese immigrants.

67. *New York Journal and Advertiser*, November 28, 1896.

68. *New York Evening World*, December 9, 1896.

69. Lillie Devereux Blake, "Our New York Letter," *Woman's Journal*, December 19, 1896.

70. The expanded provocation defense had real consequences for women, of both a progressive and regressive nature. Under the Model Penal Code, now adopted by many states, sentence reductions from murder to manslaughter in cases where the provocation was rejection, separation, or divorce rely heavily on the killer's perception of an existing or continuing relationship. Because the majority of intimate homicide cases involve a male perpetrator and female victim, the law has effectively preserved male perception of right to control or dominate women, even in the absence of or after the termination of an existing relationship. Nourse, "Passion's Progress," 1364.

Epilogue

1. "A 'New Journalist's' Plan," *New York Times*, February 7, 1897. "All the News That's Fit to Print" began to appear on the masthead after February 10, 1897. Ochs had displayed the phrase in electric lights in Madison Square since he assumed control of the paper in August 1896, offering a prize to any reader who could come up with a better slogan. See *New York Times*, October 27, 1896. The paper ultimately kept Ochs's slogan, which began to appear in the paper's self-promotions in early February 1897. Ochs removed weekday images shortly after his arrival at the paper in 1896, implying that he deemed them "unfit to print." Rebecca Zurier, *Picturing the City: Urban Vision and the Ashcan School* (Berkeley: University of California Press, 2006), 74. I discuss details on the Barbella case in chapter 5. On the boycott campaign and the origins of the term "yellow journalism" in early 1897, see W. Joseph Campbell, *Yellow Journalism: Puncturing the Myths, Defining the Legacies* (Westport, Conn.: Praeger, 2001), 25–41, or Campbell,

The Year That Defined American Journalism: 1897 and the Clash of Paradigms (New York: Routledge, 2013), 25–27. I discuss the strip-search drawing, and reaction, in more detail in the Introduction.

2. Quote from then-New York City Police Commissioner Theodore Roosevelt. "Foes to New Journalism," *New York Times*, March 30, 1897.

3. The *World* also took credit for the solution to the "headless torso" case, but it was the *Journal's* prize money that elicited a response to the critical clue. John D. Stevens, *Sensationalism and the New York Press* (New York: Columbia University Press, 1991), 92–94. Campbell notes that Hearst's "journalism of action" borrowed heavily from the 1880s work of William T. Stead (who approved of the *Journal's* style). Campbell, *Year that Defined American Journalism*, 81, 83–84. On Stead's muckraking as an early form of sensationalism, see Gretchen Soderlund, *Sex Trafficking, Scandal, and the Transformation of Journalism, 1885–1917* (Chicago: University of Chicago Press, 2013), 24–66. On the Montreal case in 1884, see George Juergens, *Joseph Pulitzer and the New York World* (Princeton, N.J.: Princeton University Press, 1966)], 95. For a detailed analysis of Leslie's "swill milk" campaign, see Jennifer E. Moore, "'Ours Has Been No Pleasing Task': Sensationalism in *Frank Leslie's* Campaign against Swill Milk," in Sachsman and Bulla, *Sensationalism*. See also Joshua Brown, *Beyond the Lines: Pictorial Reporting, Everyday Life, and the Crisis of Gilded Age America* (Berkeley: University of California Press, 2002), 27–28.

4. Augustin Cosio had been imprisoned in a small house with his daughters Evangelina and her sister by the Spanish authorities on the Isle of Pines (now known as the Isle of Youth) in the summer of 1896 for his role in the Cuban struggle for independence from Spain. When Evangelina appealed to the new Spanish governor, Colonel José Berriz, for her father's freedom, she alleged that he attempted to insult (in other words, sexually assault) her, so she enlisted her friends, who briefly held him captive. (This may have been deliberate strategy to capture him, foiled when his troops intervened to rescue him.) She was charged with attempted murder and rebellion. See Carol Wilcox, "Cuba's 'Hot Little Rebel' and Spain's 'Criminal Fugitive': The Prison Escape of Evangelina Cisneros in 1897," in Bulla and Sachsman, *Sensationalism*, 155–70; Kristin L. Hoganson, *Fighting for American Manhood: How Gender Politics Provoked the Spanish-American and Philippine-American Wars* (New Haven, Conn.: Yale University Press, 2000), 58–61; Campbell, *Year That Defined American Journalism*, 161–94. For a popular take on the story, see Wilbur Cross, "The Perils of Evangelina" *American Heritage* 19, no. 2 (1968).

5. Calling themselves the Junta, they sought to influence U.S. views of the Cuban independence struggle as a chivalric battle for civilization over brutal Spanish oppression. The Partido Revolucionario Cubano (Cuban Revolutionary Party, PRC) under José Martí's leadership blended pro-imperial, revolutionary, and popular Cuban national movements, but after Martí's death in 1895 the PRC in New York was dominated by a white, educated elite that took a hierarchical approach to government and lobbied hard for U.S. intervention. Guerra, *The Myth of José Martí: Conflicting Nationalisms in Early Twentieth-Century Cuba* (Chapel Hill: University of North Carolina Press, 2005), 50, 81. See also George W. Auxier, "Propaganda Activities of the Cuban Junta in Precipitating the Spanish-American War, 1895–1898," *Hispanic American Historical Review 19*, no. 3

(August 1939): 286–305; Mark Peceny, *Democracy at the Point of Bayonets* (University Park: Pennsylvania State University Press, 1999), 56–60; Bonnie M. Miller, *From Liberation to Conquest: The Visual and Popular Cultures of the Spanish-American War* (Amherst: University of Massachusetts Press, 2011), 7. On the reading of sensational accounts of Cuban atrocities into the Congressional Record, see Marcus M. Wilkerson, *Public Opinion and the Spanish-American War* (New York: Russell and Russell, 1967 [1932]), 54–61. He discusses the newspaper campaign in support of belligerency in chap. 5, 62–82.

6. On strategic and economic motivations inspiring pro-intervention groups, see Peceny, *Democracy at the Point of Bayonets*, 54–55. On the enthusiasm of Protestant missionaries, see Stuart Creighton Miller, *Benevolent Assimilation: The American Conquest of the Philippines, 1899–1903* (New Haven, Conn.: Yale University Press, 1982), 18. On the insistence that a martial response was necessary to restore U.S. manliness, see Hoganson, *Fighting for American Manhood*, 45–54. On reports of deplorable conditions and deaths in the Spanish-controlled *reconcentración* camps, see John L. Offner, *The Unwanted War: The Diplomacy between the United States and Spain over Cuba, 1895–1898* (Chapel Hill: University of North Carolina Press, 1992), 112–13.

7. Ben Procter, *William Randolph Hearst: The Early Years, 1863–1910* (New York: Oxford University Press, 1998), 105–11; Wilcox, "Cuba's 'Hot Little Rebel'"; Campbell, *Year That Defined American Journalism*. On the framing of the tale as a romance, with Cosio as a model woman, see Hoganson, *Fighting for American Manhood*, 56–61; Miller, *From Liberation to Conquest*, 17. See also Amy Kaplan, "Romancing the Empire: The Embodiment of American masculinity in the popular historical novel of the 1890s," *American Literary History 2*, no. 4 (Winter 1990): 660, 666, 675; Matthew Jacobson, *Special Sorrows: The Diasporic Imagination of Irish, Polish, and Jewish Immigrants in the United States* (Cambridge, Mass.: Harvard University Press, 1995), 161–62. Marcus Wilkerson calls it "perhaps one of the most notable instances of newspaper aggressiveness in history." Wilkerson, *Public Opinion and the Spanish-American War*, 87. Details of the story can be found in "The Cuban Girl Martyr," in Charles H. Brown, *The Correspondents' War: Journalists and the Spanish-American War* (New York: Scribner's, 1967), 93–102.

8. *New York Journal and Advertiser*, October 10 (image) and October 24, 1897. Spanish newspapers not surprisingly railed against this example of yellow journalism and U.S. support for the rebels, while Cuban insurgent newspapers in New York saw Cosio as "a symbol of the rebels' fiery patriotism." Wilcox, "Cuba's 'Hot Little Rebel,'" 157–58. The *New York World* eventually competed for coverage, and even anti-sensational dailies such as the *New York Times* and the conservative Democratic *Sun* joined the campaign for Cosio's freedom. W.A. Swanberg, *Pulitzer* (New York: Scribner's, 1967), 232–33.

9. As Hoganson notes, framing the Cosio story (and a letter from Spanish Ambassador to the United States Enrique Depuy De Lôme, which maligned President McKinley) in terms of national honor made it more difficult for opponents of war and empire to counter. Hoganson, *Fighting for American Manhood*, 84. Ted Curtis Smythe credits the campaign as being one in which "the *Journal* created its own heroine." Ted Curtis Smythe, *The Gilded Age Press: 1865–1900* (Westport, Conn.: Praeger, 2003), 96, 188–91. See also Joseph E. Wisan, *The Cuban Crisis as Reflected in the New York Press* (New York: Octagon, 1965), 329–32.

10. *New York Journal*, February 17 (image), 1898, and February 20, 1898. *New York World*, February 17, 1898, and February 20, 1898. A few days later, the *Journal* amended its interpretation with a simple, giant-font headline, "Torpedo Hole in the Maine"; the *World* published the "First Actual Photographs from the Wreck," which showed the destroyed ship nearly submerged in Havana harbor. As Bonnie M. Miller shows, the *World*'s image of the *Maine* being struck by a torpedo was recycled (with adaptations) from an image a year earlier showing the ship fighting a gale. Miller, *From Liberation to Conquest*, 58, 64.

11. The *New York Tribune* had recently distinguished itself as the first metropolitan daily to reproduce halftone photographs in a high-speed rotary press. In its January 21, 1897, issue, the *Tribune* had successfully reproduced a simple photograph of New York Republican party boss, Thomas Platt. It was a significant innovation, though as a small step up from illustrated portraits (based on photographs), it was unlikely to attract new readers. On the technological invention that made the *Tribune*'s breakthrough possible, see Campbell, *Year That Defined American Journalism*, 21. See also Frank Luther Mott, *American Journalism, A History, 1690–1960* (New York: Macmillan, 1962), 501–2; Gregory Borchard, Stephen Bates, and Lawrence J. Mullen, "Publishing Violence as Art and News: Sensational Prints and Pictures in the 19th-Century Press," in Sachsman, *Sensationalism*, 57–58.

12. *New York Tribune*, February 18, 1898.

13. *Chicago Tribune*, February 18, 1898 (emphasis added). During the *Maine* episode the *New York Journal*'s circulation more than doubled, from 420,000 to more than a million copies, while the *World* rose from 711,000 to greater than a million. Miller, *From Liberation to Conquest*, 68. High circulation did not necessarily translate directly into profits, however, because of the expenses for the special correspondents, artists (such as Remington), and travel, among other things. Campbell, *Yellow Journalism*, 116. Stevens, *Sensationalism*, 97.

14. The *Journal* claimed political neutrality but leaned Democratic and was highly critical of McKinley's caution. Its assertion that a mine had caused the explosion was borne out some weeks later by an official report by the court of inquiry. A 1976 report identified an internal explosion, caused by gases, instead; this result was in turn disputed in a 1998 report. Bonnie Miller discusses the debate over the causes of the *Maine*'s destruction, including the conflicting conclusions of the 1974 and 1998 reports, in *From Liberation to Conquest*, 72. See also Smythe, *Gilded Age Press*, 189. The *Maine* explosion led directly to the passage of Congress's war resolution in April 1898. Lewis L. Gould, *The Spanish-American War and President McKinley* (Lawrence: University Press of Kansas, 1982), 50–51.

15. Richard Hofstadter notes the "rising tide of jingoism" as a factor leading to war in *The Paranoid Style in American Politics* (New York: Vintage, 2008 [1964]), 150. The *Journal*'s political cartoons relentlessly attacked the McKinley administration for refusing to fight. Spencer, *Yellow Journalism*, 221–23. However, emphasizing the power of the "yellow press" to push the nation into war risks overlooking other contributing factors. As Campbell notes, the two papers "may have mirrored but they assuredly did not cause the irreconcilable differences between the U.S. and Spain over Cuba." Campbell,

Yellow Journalism, 116–21. Stevens suggests politicians, not papers, created war fever with a combination of imperial designs and sympathy for the Cuban rebels. Stevens, *Sensationalism*, 98.

16. Details of press coverage of the war can be found in Meredith W. and David M. Berg, "The Rhetoric of War Preparation: The New York Press in 1898," *Journalism Quarterly* 45 (Winter 1968): 653–60. See also Brown, *The Correspondents' War*, 80–82; George Bronson Rea, *Facts and Fakes about Cuba: A Review of the Various Stories Circulated in the United States Concerning the Present Insurrection* (New York: Munro's, 1897), 229–32. J. M. Hamilton et al. argue that it was a combination of "yellow" and conservative newspapers that created an "enabling environment" for war. See J. M. Hamilton et al., "An Enabling Environment: A Reconsideration of the Press and the Spanish-American War," *Journalism History* 7, no. 1 (February 2006): 78–93.

17. On the political implications, and on the upcoming 1898 election, see Miller, *Benevolent Assimilation*, 21–23; Gould, *Spanish-American War*, 32–33.

18. Louis A. Perez Jr. notes that fear of Cuban rebels' success likely pushed the U.S. to intervene: "Intervention was as much against the expanding Cuban claim of sovereignty as the declining Spanish claim." Perez, *The War of 1898: The United States and Cuba in History and Historiography* (Chapel Hill: University of North Carolina Press, 1998), 70, 79. On stereotypes of Filipinos and their changing representations as the war progressed, see Hoganson, *Fighting for American Manhood*, 134–38; Miller, *From Liberation to Conquest*, 38–40; Sevando D. Halili Jr., *Iconography of the New Empire: Race and Gender Images and the American Colonization of the Philippines* (Quezon City: University of the Philippines Press, 2006), 43–80; Miller, *Benevolent Assimilation*, 58–59, 88–92. On depictions of heroic U.S. soldiers and weak antiwar activists, see Hoganson, *Fighting for American Manhood*, 11, 62. For a discussion of newspapers' silence on atrocities committed by U.S. soldiers in the Philippines, see Richard E. Welch, *Response to Imperialism: The United States and the Philippine-American War, 1899–1902* (Chapel Hill: University of North Carolina Press, 1978), 134. On the racial hierarchy that justified forceful occupation, see Michael H. Hunt, *Ideology and U.S. Foreign Policy* (New Haven, Conn.: Yale University Press, 1987), 52. African Americans were torn between enthusiasm for the war and revulsion at its inherent racism. See William B. Gatewood, *Black Americans and the White Man's Burden, 1898–1903* (Urbana: University of Illinois Press, 1975), 278–79; George P. Marks, ed., *The Black Press: Views American Imperialism (1898–1900)* (New York: Arno, 1971), 100–171. On the U.S. determination to forestall revolutionary governments in Cuba and the Philippines, see Peceny, *Democracy at the Point of Bayonets*, 50. On U.S. propaganda to counter reports of atrocities in the Philippines, see Miller, *Benevolent Assimilation*, 58–59.

19. Kevin G. Barnhurst and John Nerone, *The Form of News* (New York: Guildford, 2001), 135, 137, 138.

20. The *New York Tribune* was not the first daily to publish a halftone image reproduction of a photograph: the *Herald* had included an illustrated supplement with halftones (again, produced on a slower flat-bed rather than rotary press) in 1893, and the *Journal* included a halftone of a "pretty girl" in 1896, also in a specially produced supplement. The *Tribune* was, however, the first to do so on a rotary, high-speed press. The *Chicago*

Tribune soon followed the *New York Tribune*'s lead, on March 21, 1897. By 1900, halftones were in common use, though some publishers resisted due to older equipment, conservative aversion to the use of images, or continued faith in the power of interpretive illustration. Robert Taft, *Photography and the American Scene: A Social History, 1839–1889* (New York: Dover, 1938), 446–50.

21. See, for example, Dora Apel and Shawn Michelle Smith, *Lynching Photographs* (Berkeley: University of California Press, 2007); Linda Lumsden, *Rampant Women: Suffragists and the Right of Assembly* (Knoxville: University of Tennessee Press, 1997).

Index

Page numbers in *italics* refer to figures.

AMANDA FRISKEN is a professor of American Studies at SUNY College at Old Westbury. She is the author of *Victoria Woodhull's Sexual Revolution: Political Theater and the Popular Press in Nineteenth Century America.*

The History of Communication

The University of Illinois Press
is a founding member of the
Association of University Presses.

———————————————

University of Illinois Press
1325 South Oak Street
Champaign, IL 61820-6903
www.press.uillinois.edu